Autumn Glory

AUTUMN GLORY

Baseball's First World Series

LOUIS P. MASUR

HILL AND WANG

A division of Farrar, Straus and Giroux

New York

Hill and Wang

A division of Farrar, Straus and Giroux

19 Union Square West, New York 10003

Copyright © 2003 by Louis P. Masur

All rights reserved

Distributed in Canada by Douglas & McIntyre Ltd.

Printed in the United States of America

Published in 2003 by Hill and Wang

First paperback edition, 2004

The Library of Congress has cataloged the hardcover edition as follows:

Masur, Louis P.

   Autumn glory : baseball's first World Series / Louis P. Masur.— 1st ed.

      p.   cm.

   Includes bibliographical references and index.

   ISBN 0-8090-2763-1 (hard : alk. paper)

   1. World Series (Baseball) (1903).   2. Boston Red Sox (Baseball team)—History—20th

century.   3. Pittsburgh Pirates (Baseball team)—History—20th century.   I. Title.

GV878.4 .M37 2003

796.357'646—dc21

2002032891

Paperback ISBN-10: 0-8090-1636-2

Paperback ISBN-13: 978-0-8090-1636-5

Designed by Abby Kagan

www.fsgbooks.com

3   5   7   9   10   8   6   4   2

FOR DAVE, MARK, AND RA

I got to see the bigger point of baseball, that it can give us back ourselves. We're a crowd animal, a highly gregarious, communicative species, but the culture and the age and all the fear that fills our days have put almost everyone into little boxes, each of us all alone. But baseball, if we love it, gives us back our place in the crowd. It restores us.

—Anne Lamott, *Bird by Bird*

So there is glory for all the contestants, and supreme satisfaction for all base ball lovers.

—*Sporting Life*, October 1903

CONTENTS

Autumn Glory

"THE MOST PERFECT THING IN AMERICA"

HE WANTED TO HOLD THE BALL IN HIS HAND. He walked slowly, but not just because of age. Pitchers always had a deliberate way about them. In his playing days he stole a few bases, but foot speed wasn't his gift. What he remembered well, what he could never forget, was the hard feel of the ball in his right hand and the sound it made as it sped toward the plate. How he loved to throw. Out after out, inning after inning, game after game, year after year. The pitches mounted, but his arm stayed strong through twenty-two seasons in the major leagues. He pitched into his forties. He had memories of General Grant, and now General Eisenhower was President. So much had changed, but the game had remained the same. ✳

Cy Young came to Yankee Stadium on September 30, 1953, to throw out the ceremonial opening pitch of that year's Fall Classic, commemorating the golden anniversary of the first World Series, played in 1903. He was eighty-six years old. Bill Dinneen, who had been his teammate on the Boston Americans then, stood to his left. Seated to his right was Fred Clarke, the manager and left

fielder of the opposition Pittsburgh Pirates, one of the finest teams
at the turn of the century. Tommy Leach, the third baseman on
that team, was also in attendance. He recalled the first World Series as "the wildest World Series ever played." Honus Wagner, star
shortstop on the Pirates, was invited, but he was too ill to travel
from his home in Carnegie, Pennsylvania. Two years later, Young
would make a pilgrimage to Pittsburgh to see Wagner and participate in the unveiling of a statue of him outside of Forbes Field.
Within months of that visit, both men would be gone.

Seeing the immense crowd and feeling the excitement in the
air, Young, Dinneen, Clarke, and Leach could have smiled know-
ingly, for the celebratory scene was eerily like the one fifty years
earlier when it had all begun. In the fall of 1953, fans were filling
Yankee Stadium to capacity; in the fall of 1903, the crowd at the
Huntington Avenue Base Ball Grounds in Boston overflowed
onto the field. In the fall of 1953, talented players—Mantle, Berra,
Reynolds, Snider, Robinson, Erskine—amazed the fans with their
ability; in the fall of 1903, players every bit as good—Young,
Dinneen, Collins, Wagner, Clarke, Phillippe—thrilled crowds of
thousands. For a long week in both years, interest in world events
yielded to baseball.

Baseball as a game was no different in 1953 than it had been in
1903. And it is essentially no different today. The pitcher stands 60
feet 6 inches away from home plate. Ninety feet separate one base
from another. It is a perfect distance. So many times the runner is
safe or out by a matter of inches. The field is green and the
grounds are vast. It seems like too much space for only nine players to cover. The game comes down to the ball: throwing it, hitting it, catching it. How simple it has always seemed, but it never
has been. Thousands of fans crowd the stadium. They follow the
home team's every move, feeling brighter with a victory and dim-
mer with a loss. A journey from April through October leads either to a world's championship or to nowhere, hopes realized or
expectations dashed. Winter is for dreaming.

So it has been since 1903, when the National League and

American League ended two years of warfare and the champions of each league faced off in October for the World Championship Series. Baseball as we know it dates from that 1903 season. To be sure, there are differences of degree in the game. The equipment is better. The players are stronger. Some rules have been varied. But Cy Young could walk to the mound tomorrow and throw blazing strikes. Honus Wagner could smash a double into the gap, or fire from deep in the hole to nab a runner by a step. And just like every other player in the last hundred years, they would play all season for the chance to compete in October. But at the start of the 1903 season they did not know what awaited at the end— and now, because of that season and what their teams did, everyone knows.

The story of the first World Series is the story of the birth of baseball as a modern game, as an American ritual. The day after the Yankees lost the Series in 2001, in the last inning of the seventh game, a middle-aged man declared that the trauma he had suffered as a child, watching his Brooklyn Dodgers lose repeatedly to their rivals from the Bronx, had at last been alleviated. Such is the place of the Series in the life of every baseball fan. On October 30, 2001, in Game Three of that same Series, played at Yankee Stadium in the midst of a national crisis, the President of the United States strode to the mound and threw a strike for the ceremonial first pitch, and millions of Americans breathed more easily. Such is the place of the Series in the life of the nation.

Just a few years after the first World Series in 1903, a writer remarked that "when thirty thousand people in a single city shut up shop and forsake their work and everything else to watch the final struggle between the leaders at the season's end, it is small wonder." Rather, it would be remarkable if people acted any other way. Autumn had quickly become World Series time, and the postseason championship games had come to stand for "the very quintessence and consummation of the Most Perfect Thing in America"—baseball.

GAME ONE, THURSDAY, OCTOBER 1

THE CROWD IN BOSTON GATHERED EARLY. The city's streets were choked with "good natured fans, laughing, chatting, happy in the opportunity to see the clash of champions." Although the game was not scheduled to begin until 3 p.m., by noon thousands had filled the Huntington Avenue Base Ball Grounds. The reserve grandstand seats had already sold out, and fans clamored for general admission tickets. But there would be no 25-cent tickets available for this game. Grandstand seats cost $1.00 and the bleachers 50 cents. A souvenir scorecard set fans back another dime. Some folks groused at being priced out of the ballpark, but many more were content to pay extra to witness history in the making.

"The day was made a holiday," reported one out-of-town newspaper. "The usually placid Hub was stirred to its conservative foundations by the enthusiasm of its own big army of fans and the influx of thousands of visiting rooters, who were even more exuberant than the home people. Every train coming into the big Union Station was loaded with excited individuals who appeared to look upon the occasion as the one big event of their lives."

Fans jammed the streetcars that took them to the baseball grounds. The men wore jackets, ties, and hats (bowlers or tam o'shanters). The women ("baseball enthusiasm knows no sex") dressed in smart tops and long skirts. The day was warm and clear, a lovely Indian summer afternoon "that appealed to everyone to get out of doors for the mere pleasure of living," and people left their topcoats at home. What looked like an indistinguishable mass of "human freight" pressed toward the ticket booths. A few dozen policemen did their best to keep the throng moving along. Well before game time, the bleachers on both the first- and third-base sides of the field were packed. So too the pavilion area toward left field. The only patches of empty seats were in the reserve grandstand sections, where patrons felt no need to rush. With all the seats sold, officials ran a rope across the deepest part of the outfield and allowed the crowd to flow onto the grass behind it. And on the terrace surrounding the grounds, fans were packed a dozen deep. They climbed as well onto the outfield fences and roosted wherever they could find a spot to squeeze in. To those sitting in the stands, it looked as if these fans would fall, but they "stuck like leeches to their vantage posts and were happy in the ability to see the diamond." Side by side across the grounds stood "professional men and grocery clerks, ministers and college professors . . . all bound together by one great, all-absorbing love for the national game."

Built in 1901, on the property where the traveling circus and Wild West shows had pitched their tents when they passed through town, the Huntington Avenue Grounds proved immediately successful. Boston had a National League team that played at the South End Grounds, located on the other side of the New York, New Haven, and Hartford railroad tracks, but fans took to the ball being played by the newly established American League, and almost 300,000 people had come out that first year to support Boston's American League team. The Huntington Avenue Grounds were typical of the wooden parks of the era. The ballpark had been built quickly, sporting a single level of grandstand

and bleacher seats on each side of the diamond and featuring a cavernous outfield that measured 530 feet to center field.

A little before 2 p.m., the groundskeepers sprayed the diamond with water and the Boston Americans jogged out for batting practice. "Boston" was spelled out across their white jerseys. They wore blue socks and white caps with a blue band around the base. The fans shouted out the players' names as they came on the field. Player-manager Jimmy Collins, considered by many the best third baseman in the game, led his squad. He had jumped from Boston's National League team to the newly created American League franchise in 1901, and several players, as well as many fans, followed him across the tracks. Chick Stahl, the center fielder, and Buck Freeman, the right fielder, moved crosstown the same year. Freeman hit for power in an age when the home run had not yet become the barometer of highest achievement in the game; his 25 blasts in 1899 would stand as a record until Babe Ruth hit 29 home runs in 1919. In 1902, Bill Dinneen, a promising young right-handed pitcher, also jumped from Boston's National League franchise to its American League counterpart, where he rejoined his former teammates.

Most of the Boston Americans had some National League pedigree. Only Hobe Ferris, the second baseman, and Patsy Dougherty, the left fielder, had started their careers with the Americans. Fred Parent, the diminutive shortstop, had played two games in 1899 with St. Louis in the National League before catching on with the new Boston franchise in 1901. First baseman Candy LaChance, who got his nickname because he preferred peppermints over chewing tobacco, had played seven years in the National League and jumped to Boston in 1902. Lou Criger, who had established himself as a first-rate defensive catcher, had played three years with Cleveland and two with St. Louis before coming to the Americans in 1901.

One pitcher, in particular, appreciated having Criger behind the plate during their five years together in the Midwest—Cy Young. The two had come east together. Young had been in professional baseball since 1890. Thirty-four years old when he joined Boston, he showed immediately what he could do in the new league by winning 33 games in his first season. At six feet two inches and more than 200 pounds, Young was a paragon of the sturdy country boy, a farmer and rail-splitter from Tuscawaras County, Ohio. He stayed in shape all winter by working on his farm "doing chores that not only were good for my legs, but for my arm and back. Swinging an axe hardens the hands and builds up the shoulders and back." As a result of his off-season regimen, Young claimed to have needed only a dozen pitches to warm up for a ball game. The day before the championship series with Pittsburgh began, Collins told his star pitcher that he would open the first game. "All right, I will try to be there," Young replied.

Young was the last of the Americans to enter the field, and the entire crowd stood to cheer him. Many of the rooters waved

American flags. The team was one to admire. That season the players had demonstrated that they could play as a unit. Boston had won 91 games and lost only 47. They had shut out the opposition 20 times and won 19 games by only one run. They played particularly well at home, going 48–22, and their ride to the pennant had been fairly smooth; the second-place Philadelphia A's finished a distant 14½ games behind. With his quiet manner and steady work ethic, Collins conveyed confidence. Asked to predict who would win the series, he modestly answered, "We will pick up a few games."

The Pittsburgh baseball club had arrived in Boston the previous afternoon. They entered a metropolis of nearly 600,000 people, but the city was not what it had been fifty years earlier. Although Boston retained its nickname the Hub, and was sometimes called the City of Culture in recognition of its tradition of universities and museums, cities such as New York and Chicago had thrived by staying in tune with the industrial times. Boston had not. The city was still trying to rebuild from a devastating fire in 1872, which destroyed sixty-five acres of valuable property in the center of the business district. The Whig/Republican Protestants who had led the city for most of the nineteenth century now found that Democratic Irish-Catholics held sway. Politics and culture divided Boston; the success of Collins's team in 1903 was that it helped to unify the populace and restore the city to national relevance.

The Boston Americans faced a formidable team in the Pittsburgh Pirates, who had just won their third consecutive National League pennant. During the season, they had won 91 games and lost only 49 times. They shut out the opposition 16 times, and were shut out only 4 times all season. This was a clutch team with veteran leadership: they were 23–10 in one-run games, and they won 18 times in their final at-bat. Remarkably, they had as good a record on the road as at home. The Pirates had endured illness, injury, and even fisticuffs; they were intimidated by nothing.

On their way to Boston, the Pirates had stopped in Buffalo to

PITTSBURG BASE BALL CLUB.

PENNANT WINNERS 1901-1902-1903.

play the Eastern League Bisons in an exhibition game which they had won easily, 9–1. Getting off the train at the Back Bay station, the Pittsburgh players took carriages to the Hotel Vendome, a sprawling building constructed in French Renaissance style and the first public building in Boston with electric lights. Fans of the Americans crowded the lobby, looking to gamble on the series and seeking to provoke the opposition.

"We're going to give you and the Pirates a licking you'll never forget," yelled one fan.

"Who with? With that old man Cy Young?" answered star shortstop Honus Wagner.

Fred Clarke sought to protect his players from the tumult and to take their minds off baseball. He organized a card game and then led a group of players, including Wagner, to Soldiers' Field in Cambridge, where they watched a college football game between Harvard and Bowdoin (Harvard won, 24–0). In the evening, some Pirates went to the theater. Their manager, Fred Clarke, spoke with certainty about his team: "I never went into a game yet that I did not expect to win."

On game day, the Pirates entered the grounds sporting dark blue-black caps with the letter "P" in front, blue-and-gold-striped socks, and plain off-white wool jerseys with royal blue collars. The players passed the Boston bench without saying a word. They stretched and then took infield practice for fifteen minutes—and even the Boston partisans cheered wildly at the display they put on.

Pitcher Sam Leever hit the ball toward second. Wagner, a marvel at short, stabbed it up the middle and, with his glove hand, flipped the ball to second baseman Claude Ritchey, covering the bag. Ritchey whirled and fired to Kitty Bransfield at first, who then pivoted and sent the sphere home to catcher Ed Phelps. Without moving his feet, Phelps threw down to third baseman Tommy Leach, who scooped the ball with his glove and, as he jumped, shifted it to his throwing hand and fired it back across the diamond to first base. "A great wave of applause swept over the crowd," noted a Pittsburgh reporter, who editorialized that "a gang which could do this could surely play some ball, and right then and there Boston patrons and Boston players began to pray for rain."

"The great series for the championship of the world between the champions of the National League and the American League is now on," declared *Sporting Life*. "Ready to Battle for the World's Championship," announced the headline of the *Boston Globe*'s morning edition on October 1, 1903. "The eyes of the baseball world are on this city today," reported the *Pittsburg Leader*, "for this afternoon will open about the most important and widely interesting series in the history of the national game." Eighteen telegraph wires had been installed at the grounds to carry news of the game as it unfolded to nearly fifty newspapers around the country. In some cities, baseball fans would gather outside the newspaper offices and await inning-by-inning results.

"The whole country is watching with great interest the world's championship contest between Boston and Pittsburg," proclaimed the *Sporting News*. (Between 1890 and 1911, the "h" in "Pittsburgh" had been dropped by the United States Board of Geographic Names.) "Base ball stands alone in the hearts of the American people," continued the paper, and never before in history had so many people been interested in the game.

Fans had hoped for this all along. The rival leagues had been at war for two years, and now, in the first season of peace, superiority would be established on the playing field. A postseason championship series would give meaning to the drama of the year. It would offer conclusion and closure. For a fortnight in October, two teams would compete in a series of games, a World's Series. The only time that seemed to matter was the two hours between three and five in the afternoon. The other parts of the day were spent analyzing and anticipating. Travel days were the hardest on the fans because they allowed too much time to think. Come October, "every American and his wife [would be] living in a base ball world." This was in effect the first October. It was the first time baseball consumed everything else around it. It would do so again, and again, and again.

Despite the pleas of fans and journalists, no official plan to play a postseason championship series had been reached until the second week of September, when Barney Dreyfuss, president and owner of the Pittsburgh Athletic Company, and Henry Killilea, first-year owner of the Boston American League Ball Club, finally signed an agreement. The series would be five out of nine, with the first three games played in Boston (October 1, 2, and 3), the next four in Pittsburgh (October 5, 6, 7, and 8), and the final two games back in Boston (October 10 and 12). Only players who were on the team as of September 1 would be eligible to play.

After some squabbling, the owners had agreed that Hank O'Day of the National League and Thomas Connolly of the American League would serve as umpires. O'Day had been a big-league pitcher before becoming an umpire in 1894. He managed the Cincinnati Reds in 1912 and the Chicago Cubs in 1914 before returning as an umpire. By the end of his umpiring career in 1927, he had worked ten World Series. Connolly, who was born in Manchester, England, and learned the game as a teenager in Natick, Massachusetts, umpired the first American League game in 1901. By the time he retired from field duty to become chief umpire in 1931, he had worked eight World Series. He had also showed himself unafraid to toss any unruly player from a regular season game, including Babe Ruth, whom Connolly tossed in the third inning of a game in 1922 after the slugger had already hit a home run but in his second time at bat argued a strike call.

After Dreyfuss and Killilea made the plans final, the World Series almost came undone, for suddenly the Boston players refused to participate. Unlike the Pirates, whose contracts ran to October 15, the Boston players had contracts that expired on September 30. They refused to play in the series on the terms Killilea was offering: a fifty-fifty split between owner and players. Outraged that the players would try to dictate terms to him, Killilea wired Jimmy Collins on September 24 that the series was off.

The manager was distraught. He condemned the owner for asking for half of the receipts, especially after a season in which his team had won more than 90 games and packed the home grounds whenever they played. "The players wanted to give him one-half provided that he pay their salaries for two more weeks," said Collins. Otherwise, they felt they were entitled to a higher share. But Killilea declined. "It is too bad that the Boston public, which has given us such loyal support, cannot see us play for the world's championship. There is not one chance in a hundred of the games being played," declared Collins.

As word spread of the cancellation, fans reacted with regret and disgust. They tended to side with the players rather than the owner, for it was the players with whom they identified and to whom they gave their loyalty. The situation highlighted the problem with "syndicate ball and foreign owners," as the press put it. Killilea was a prominent midwest attorney whose ownership of

The World Series agreement signed by Barney Dreyfuss
and Henry Killilea on September 16, 1903

the club was one of many investments. "Does any one suppose," wondered one writer, "that had he but resided in the town where his money was invested in baseball and where he could be in daily touch with his players that they would have revolted and washed their soiled linen in public?"

Some journalists, however, roasted the American League champions. The *Boston Post* pointed out that Killilea paid higher salaries than any other owner in the league, that in several exhibition games he had given his players the full receipts, and that he never docked a player's pay for illness or injury. He even paid Charley Farrell his season's salary after the catcher broke his leg one week into the season. The Pittsburgh press accused the Americans of dodging the Pirates and observed that "if there is anything that the public objects to it is the 'hold-up' game in sports." The *Sporting News* concluded that "the demand of the players . . . was unreasonable and showed a spirit of greed which will go a long way toward disillusioning the public, which thinks the players' sole dreams all season long are of victories and pennants instead of eagles and ducats."

The Pirates' owner, Barney Dreyfuss, fumed. He had ordered posters advertising the series and had retained the services of umpire O'Day, whose contract called for him to be paid whether or not the games were played. And Dreyfuss had already turned down numerous other requests for postseason contests. The three-time National League champions were a big drawing card anywhere they played, and he wanted games in October to add to the team's coffers. His club, he protested, "had already spent too much money to stand idly by and see the series which the ball people of the country have clamored for called off by a bunch of disgruntled ball players." Furthermore, he had John McGraw of the New York Giants, the National League's second-place team, lurking in the background. The tenacious McGraw, who despised the upstart American League, now offered to play the Pirates in a postseason National League series. But Dreyfuss wanted an interleague series, and he insisted that the Americans "meet us or else hand to us the championship belt and proclaim us champions of the world."

Ban Johnson, founder and president of the American League, put pressure on Killilea to accommodate the players. Johnson felt that the prestige of his league depended on playing the National League pennant winners. Jimmy Collins made one last effort to revive the series and had the team's business manager telephone Killilea at his home in Milwaukee. After a half-hour conversation, the absentee owner offered new terms, and Collins immediately accepted them on behalf of the Boston players. The terms were described as liberal, but they were not disclosed. One report had it that the new split had 75 percent going to the players. Collins and the team were happy to agree, not only because they realized that, whatever the amount, a good payday was in store for them, but also because managers and players from other cities had been accusing them of being afraid to face the formidable Pirates. "What scores of telegrams and 10-page letters failed to do," mused a writer, "the telephone accomplished."

The one-day cancellation gave only momentary pause to the wagers being placed on the series. Baseball is a betting game, and America is a gambling culture. "Fortunes Bet on Games," screamed the headlines. Tens of thousands were bet each day: Sport Sullivan, a well-known gambler, wagered $2,500 that Boston would win. Charley Waldron, owner of the Palace Theater, bet $1,400 on the same outcome. Frank M'Quiston, a Pittsburgh reporter who represented a syndicate of bettors, arrived with $15,000 looking to back the Pirates. He had little trouble placing the bets. One Pittsburgh fan gave first baseman Kitty Bransfield $1,000 and instructed him to get the best odds possible but to place the money no matter what. With the series opening in Boston, and Cy Young on the mound, the prevailing odds had the Americans a 5–4 favorite. But the odds changed during the series with each game and with the shifting locales. Some gamblers preferred betting on more exotic propositions: one Pittsburgh rooter bet $100 against $1,000 that Boston would not win a single game. The Pirate players were just as confident as the fans. As early as mid-August, Pittsburgh's reserve catcher Harry Smith was willing to stake $500 against $250. "If the clubs ever meet," reported the *Sporting News*, "there is scarcely a Pittsburg player who will not have money on the result."

Part of the appeal of betting on baseball was the belief that the game could not be fixed. "Baseball is too open a game to be crooked," observers remarked. A player could make an error on purpose, but everyone would know. And there was too much money at stake just from winning the series (and betting on themselves) for players to be tempted to throw the contest. The games "will be for blood and they will all be won or lost on their merits." It was common knowledge that ballplayers loved to gamble: cards, dice, the poolroom, the ponies. But Joe Tinker, a Chicago Cubs shortstop, proclaimed that fixing or throwing ball games was impossible because it required the collusion of a number of players. "To fake in a base ball game," he said, "everyone on both teams must be in on the deal. This makes it impossible to fix matters. Some often say that the pitchers are bought. Now what does this amount to? Every team has at least four pitchers, and if one was really bought how long would he be allowed to stay in the box if the opposing team was bumping him. . . . A slab artist can not do much in the way of throwing games." There had been cases of throwing games, or "hippodroming" as it was called, back in the 1860s and 1870s. But at the turn of the century it seemed that baseball now stood on a professional, organized foundation, and no one believed it was possible to fix a series.

The major concern of gamblers and fans going into the series was the relative condition of the teams. Both clubs had their advocates. Boston supporters thought that their pitchers Cy Young, Bill Dinneen, and Tom Hughes far outmatched Pittsburgh's Deacon Phillippe, Sam Leever, and Bill Kennedy. Pirate adherents dismissed Young and Dinneen as being more lucky than skillful, and they trumpeted their catcher Eddie Phelps as a superior stickman to his weak-hitting counterpart Lou Criger. While Boston bettors conceded the talents of Pittsburgh outfielders Fred Clarke (he covered so much ground reporters described him as "ubiquitous"), Ginger Beaumont, and Jimmy Sebring, they stressed that Buck Freeman had more than 100 RBIs and Patsy Dougherty had led the league with 195 hits.

As for the infield, commentators viewed Boston's right side, with Candy LaChance at first and Hobe Ferris at second, as inferior to Pittsburgh's Kitty Bransfield and Claude Ritchey. On the left side, Boston's Jimmy Collins ("the king of third basemen") outclassed Pittsburgh's Tommy Leach. As for shortstop, there could be no disagreement: Boston's Freddy Parent was adequate, whereas Pittsburgh's Honus Wagner was "the best ball player in the world." In the end, the teams looked well matched. The Pirates, perhaps weaker on the mound and behind the plate, "are so strong in the infield and outfield, at the bat and on the bases that . . . they are pretty near the ideal team." But Boston "goes into every game with confidence . . . , they play impressively and they do win games."

Part of the betting and rooting momentum in favor of Boston resulted from the ways the two teams had ended the regular season. Although Collins's team, having already clinched the pennant, played careless ball in the last week (they lost 4 out of their final 8 games), overall they closed out their campaign in winning style, winning 19 out of 27 games. But Clarke's men stumbled in September, losing 6 out of their last 7 and winning only 14 out of 26 games. The problem was injury. Deacon Phillippe and Sam Leever, both of whom had won more than 20 games, had sore arms. Ed Doheny, Pittsburgh's left-handed ace, had taken a leave from the team after displaying erratic behavior. Infielders Tommy Leach and Claude Ritchey both had hand and leg injuries. Worst of all, Honus Wagner was trying to recover from a badly strained leg sustained during the first game of a Labor Day doubleheader when he was chasing the Cubs' Joe Tinker and felt something pop. The shortstop could not put his foot to the ground without pain. But despite strained ligaments, he returned to the lineup on

September 12. The "bruised and maimed" shortstop refused to rest, saying that "idleness would kill him." But he still felt hobbled.

The Pirates, however, would not use injury as an excuse. Everyone was a little nicked or bruised after playing ball for six months. Now was the time to focus on competing; the hurting would come later. Tommy Leach, sporting a bandaged hand as he stepped off the train in Boston, spoke for most players when he said that he had played before with even worse afflictions. "A little thing like a swollen finger would not keep me out of the game," he declared.

Cy Young knew all about durability. Already a veteran of fourteen years of major-league experience, the thirty-six-year-old belied his surname. During the season, he had become the winningest pitcher in baseball history with 361 victories, and he led the American League with 28 wins. He was "always in the best of condition," an admirer observed: "The years have rolled by without making any perceptible difference in Young's pitching. . . . His terrific speed shows no diminishing and his cool, calculating brains continue to pull him out of many tight holes." Boston fans pinned their hopes for a championship on the star's performance. "I will do my best," Young said, "and that is all any man can do."

As the bell from the South Church tower struck three, Young strolled to the mound and the Americans took the field. All around, the crowd buzzed with excitement. Massed behind the Americans' bench were the Royal Rooters, a group of zealous fans who followed the team's every move. They had first become organized in the 1890s as supporters of Boston's National League team and its Irish star Mike "King" Kelly. But they migrated along with some of their favorite players to the American League. As an added incentive, it cost only half of the 50-cent National League ticket price to attend a game at Huntington Avenue. One of the leaders of the boisterous Rooters was Michael T. McGreevey, a devoted baseball fan who named his saloon Third Base because it was the last place one stopped before going home. His nickname was "Nuf Ced," since that was how he ended every argument. McGreevey was so entrenched in Boston baseball that on the souvenir card sold at the grounds that day his face, in an advertisement for his saloon, looms above pictures of Collins and Clarke.

The Pirates also had their supporters. Barney Dreyfuss purchased a block of seats for his friends, and about 100 Pittsburgh fans made the trip to Boston for the games. Among them was the president of the Franklin Savings and Trust Company, who drove to Massachusetts from Washington, D.C., in an automobile, still a novel contraption. The Pittsburgh delegation of fans, who arrived together and wore badges decorated with the team's colors, took their seats and "cheered for their favorite buccaneers long and loud." This led the Royal Rooters and other Boston fans to answer back. "Distant Bunker Hill monument fairly shivered and looked down in amazement at the demonstration," thought one observer.

Young stood on the mound and rolled the ball in his hand. The ball had been made by craftsmen and machines in a process that took about half an hour. Its center consisted of a Para rubber nugget an inch in thickness. Woolen yarn was wound around the rubber. Next, the ball was dipped into liquid cement and then wound with several inches of white and blue three-ply yarn. After again being dipped in cement, the ball was covered with two figure-eight pieces of tanned horsehide. These were first fastened with brass staples and then sewn before the ball was rolled by both hand and machine to make the stitches even. The finished baseball weighed about 5¼ ounces and stretched 9¼ inches in circumference. National League balls carried the name of A. G. Spalding and Brothers and had stitches of black and red thread. American League balls were produced by A. J. Reach Company and had blue and red stitching. A ball cost about $1.25; at that price, teams were stingy about putting new ones in play.

In time, the ball would change. After 1910, cork rather than rubber filled the center, and as a result, the ball became livelier.

Later in the decade, new sources for yarn, and machines that wound it tighter, seemed to make the ball jump farther. After 1920, when home runs and averages soared, the dead ball that had characterized the first two decades of twentieth-century baseball took on pejorative connotations. But the players who performed during that era did not know what the future would bring. Only after the fact did players who saw the lively ball recall the ball of their own time as "pretty dead." "You had to wallop it to make it go," remembered Honus Wagner, who nonetheless was skeptical about just how different it was from the lively ball. It didn't matter to him what ball was used as long as when he hit it no one caught it. "I like my base hits," he said using the present tense more than twenty-five years after retiring as a player. "On days when I got two, I wanted three or four. That's one way ball players are always alike."

Cy Young was ready to pitch. He watched as the batter, Pittsburgh's center fielder, Ginger Beaumont, came to the plate. Beaumont had led the National League in hits with 209 and runs scored with 137. When he reached base, the Pirates often knocked him home. Now, grinning at the pitcher, Beaumont dug in. Home-plate umpire Connolly put his mask on and yelled "Play!" Young took a deep breath, reared back, and fired the first pitch of the World Series.

After taking the pitch for a strike, Beaumont worked the count to 3–2. He hit the next pitch toward center field, but Chick Stahl made a running catch. The crowd cheered. Left fielder Fred Clarke came up to bat. He was still considered something of a boy-manager, having taken over the Louisville Colonels in the National League in 1897, when he was only twenty-four years old. Clarke was born in Des Moines, Iowa, and played in the city league there before trying to become a professional ballplayer. He placed an ad in the *Sporting News* and heard from a club in Hastings, Nebraska, that offered him $40 a month. From there, he played on teams in Missouri and Alabama in the Southern League. He nearly left baseball in 1893, when he tried to get a claim on land opened up in Oklahoma, but he didn't arrive there quickly enough. The following year, Clarke found himself playing for Louisville in the National League.

Clarke was coming off a difficult season full of illness and injury. He had even suffered a beating at the hands of a player on

The crowd at Huntington Avenue Base Ball Grounds
MCGREEVEY COLLECTION, BOSTON PUBLIC LIBRARY

the rival New York Giants. Despite all that, he had finished second in the National League in batting with a .351 average, and he led the league in doubles. The lefty batter swung hard at Young's offering and fouled the ball to Lou Criger, the Boston catcher. Two down, and the crowd's cheers grew louder.

Up stepped third baseman Tommy Leach. "Wee" Tommy stood barely five feet six inches and weighed only 150 pounds, but he had speed and surprising power. His forearms bulged like a sailor's; "he's little, but mighty," said one reporter. In 1902, he led the National League in home runs with 6. Leach crouched low at the plate and smashed a flat fastball to right field, where it reached the fans massed behind the ropes and was ruled a triple. Even during the regular season, fans at well-attended games were allowed onto the field, and balls hit beyond the ropes into the crowd went for a ground-rule triple. Throughout the series at the Huntington Grounds, those fans who congregated behind the

outfield ropes would be a factor, though in this first game observers agreed that "the hits which went into the crowd all would
have counted for at least three bases, irrespective of the ropes."

With Leach leading off third, Honus Wagner strode to the
plate. Showing their admiration, the Boston fans cheered him. It
was hard not to study him closely. He looked so awkward, with
his huge hands (like "hams," they said) and bowed legs (like
"parentheses"), and yet "he could run like a scared rabbit." Wagner had won the National League batting title in 1903 with a .355
average and had led with 54 extra-base hits. He had also knocked
in 101 RBIs. He could intimidate any pitcher, even the steadfast
Cy Young. Years later, Wagner would tell the story of a young St.
Louis pitcher who was throwing hard and had the Pirates mysti-
fied. Wagner let two fastballs go by for strikes. On the next pitch,
Wagner reached out, caught the ball bare-handed, and threw it
back to the mound. "Changeup, huh?" he sneered. The umpire
called the hitter out, but the pitcher became so unnerved that he
walked the next five batters.

Wagner slouched and leaned forward from the right side of
home plate. Some said he looked like a gorilla with a bat. He
choked up slightly and kept his hands a few inches apart from
each other. His bat extended 35 inches and weighed about 42
ounces. To get a piece of wood that big around in time to hit a
fastball, a player had to have strong arms and quick wrists, and
Wagner did. He drove a liner over the shortstop's head into left
field, scoring Leach for the first run of the game. He then stole
second, as Criger made a poor throw to second baseman Hobe
Ferris. Pittsburgh first baseman Kitty Bransfield stepped in and hit
a weak grounder to second, where Ferris, perhaps preoccupied
with the steal, bobbled the ball: Kitty was just safe at first, while
Wagner advanced to third. With Claude Ritchey now at bat,
Bransfield tried to steal second and Criger threw wildly into center field. Wagner scored and Bransfield went to third. Ritchey
then walked and stole second.

The game was only minutes old, but it had already reached a

critical juncture: two runs in and two runners in scoring position, all with two outs. Young needed to bear down or the game might be lost for Boston in the first inning. Right fielder Jimmy Sebring came to bat. Only twenty-one years old, he had just completed his first full season in the major leagues. Sebring batted from the left side and he poked the ball to the opposite field, scoring two more runs for the Pirates. The next batter, catcher Ed Phelps, struck out, but the agony continued for Boston when Criger missed catching the third strike, allowing Phelps to reach first base safely. The inning finally ended when the Pittsburgh pitcher, Deacon Phillippe, struck out. The Pirates were leading 4–0, and Boston had yet to bat.

Seldom are games won in the top of the first inning, though. The Americans needed only to answer back with a run or two of their own to shake their opening jitters. It would be Deacon Phillippe's job to stop them. Charles Louis Phillippe was born in Virginia (his father was a captain in the Confederate Army), but he learned the game in South Dakota, where he played semipro ball. He played two years of minor-league ball for the Minnesota Millers before being signed in 1899 to pitch for the Louisville Colonels in the National League. A devout Lutheran, Phillippe initially refused to pitch on Sundays. As a result, he earned the nickname "Deacon," a sobriquet frequently given to players who avoided the drinking and gambling that often went along with the life of a ballplayer, especially on the road. Phillippe pitched well as a twenty-seven-year-old rookie; remarkably, in only his seventh game, he threw a no-hitter against the New York Giants. In 1900, he was part of the group of players, including Honus Wagner, Fred Clarke, Tommy Leach, and Claude Ritchey, that the Colonels' president, Barney Dreyfuss, brought along with him from Louisville when he purchased a substantial interest in the Pittsburgh Pirates. Phillippe won 22 and 20 games in 1901 and 1902, seasons dominated by the Pirates, but he toiled at times in the shadows of his teammates Jack Chesbro and Jesse Tannehill. When Chesbro and Tannehill abandoned the Pirates for the American

League after 1902, Phillippe stood alone as the ace of the staff. He responded by winning 25 games in 1903, but now the man the papers sometimes billed as "the great Phillippi" met the most severe challenge of his career.

Phillippe first faced left fielder Patsy Dougherty, a lefty batter who had hit .331 during the season, and struck him out on three pitches. That brought manager and third baseman Jimmy Collins to the plate. Born in Niagara Falls, New York, in 1870, Collins had gone to St. Joseph's College and worked for the Lackawanna Railroad before becoming a professional ballplayer in 1893 with Buffalo, in the Eastern League. He signed with National League Boston in 1895, played briefly that year with Louisville, and then returned to Boston until he jumped crosstown, in 1901. Phillippe's pitches baffled Collins, who also struck out. Phillippe was throwing a "wide out curve" that had the Americans "stretching their necks and shoulders . . . in a vain effort to connect."

With two out, center fielder Chick Stahl managed to flick a curve ball weakly into left field for a hit. That brought up a left-handed batter, Buck Freeman. The Boston right fielder had led the American League with 13 home runs and 104 RBIs. The crowd hoped for a long ball now, but Freeman ended the inning with a fly ball to right.

In the top of the second inning, with one out, Fred Clarke made a mental error when he smashed a ball to left and, thinking it had rolled beyond the ropes for a ground-rule triple, slowed down and was thrown out at second by Patsy Dougherty. Leach flied out to right to end the inning. As the Pittsburgh manager jogged out to left field between innings, Phillippe told him not to worry: "I've got my fast pitch going all right, and I guess we can hold them." The pitcher was true to his word. In the bottom of the inning he struck out the side of Fred Parent, Candy LaChance, and Hobe Ferris. The Boston fans, who throughout the games at Huntington Grounds showed superb sportsmanship, applauded the opposing team's pitcher as he trotted off the field.

The Pirates tacked on a run in the third inning after Kitty

Bransfield tripled on a ball that went through Freeman's legs in right field, and with two outs, Jimmy Sebring singled him home. Boston again went down in order. And in the fourth inning, the Pirates added another run when Tommy Leach singled with one out, scoring Beaumont, who had reached on an error by second baseman Ferris and had advanced into scoring position on Clarke's single to left. The score stood at 6–0, with Wagner and Bransfield due up. Some fans implored Collins to remove Cy Young from the game. "Take him out! Take him out," they cried. But Collins ignored their pleas, and Young rewarded his faith by retiring the next two batters.

The Pirates had shown their offensive prowess from the start, and now, in the bottom of the fourth, they began to display their defensive ability. Collins led off the inning for Boston. After lashing a ball just foul he hit "a vicious liner" to left field. The ball was six inches off the ground when Fred Clarke made a diving catch, one of several spectacular defensive plays he would make during this game. Then Stahl flied deep to center field, but Beaumont got back to the ropes and leaped to make the catch. With two down, however, Boston finally threatened. Freeman smashed the ball toward first base and reached safely when all Bransfield could do was knock it down. Parent hit a ground ball to Leach, but the third baseman made a wild throw to first, and suddenly there were Boston runners on second and third. Two runs would get the Americans back in the game. The fans buzzed with expectation. But first baseman Candy LaChance grounded weakly back to Phillippe, and the threat was erased.

The fifth and sixth innings went quickly. Then came "the eventful seventh." In the top of the inning, Claude Ritchey grounded out to short. Jimmy Sebring hit the ball over Freeman's head in right field. Thinking it would surely go past the ropes and into the crowd, Freeman started walking to retrieve it. Sebring never slowed as he rounded the bases, and when the ball came to a stop ten feet short of the ropes, he was trying for home. Stahl ran over from center field, recovered the ball, and threw to Ferris, who fired to Criger at the plate, but not in time. Jimmy Sebring had hit the first home run in the World Series.

In the bottom of the seventh inning, with Boston behind 7–0, its luck seemed to turn. Freeman led off with a triple, hitting the fence in right. "Pandemonium reigned" throughout the crowd. "The sadness and silence of six long innings was lifted like a veil, and the horns and rattles that had not been heard from in more than an hour started their uproar afresh." On a count of two balls and one strike, Fred Parent tripled to the ropes in left, and Freeman scored Boston's first World Series run. The crowd had reason to believe that Phillippe, who up to that point had struck out seven batters and relinquished only two hits, was finally tiring. When LaChance came to bat, with the fans screaming "Line it out!" he flied deep to Clarke, who made another outstanding catch, going back on the ball in left field. Parent tagged up and scored easily, making the score 7–2. Phillippe then hit Ferris in the ribs when his slow curve failed to break over the plate.

The pitcher was coming undone. The fans' "enthusiasm was intense." Criger stepped in with a chance to redeem himself for his errors in the first inning and two groundouts at bat. But the catcher "hit the atmosphere" three times and sat down. Young, who had batted over .300 during the season, struck out on three pitches to end the rally.

The top of the order for Pittsburgh started the eighth inning, but neither Beaumont nor Clarke reached base safely. With two out, Leach tripled for the second time in the game, and Wagner walked. This gave the Pirates speed on the bases, and they attempted a double steal, but Leach was tagged out at the plate when Ferris fired the ball back home to Criger. This exciting play did nothing for the Americans at the plate. Phillippe quickly retired the opposition in the bottom of the eighth inning.

Pittsburgh went down in order to open the ninth, and that left Boston one last chance to rally. When Buck Freeman reached first on a rare error by Wagner, the crowd started to buzz. Parent smashed a sizzling drive to left. Two on, none out. LaChance flied out. Ferris then singled the ball up the middle, and Freeman scored Boston's third run. One out, two men on. There was still a chance to make a game of it, though the bottom of the order was due up. Collins decided to have Jack O'Brien pinch-hit for Criger, the weakest hitter on the team. But O'Brien himself was a bench player who had filled in during the season at several different positions and had hit an anemic .210. After fouling off a few pitches, he struck out.

With two outs, Charley Farrell came up to bat for Young. Farrell was a veteran who had begun the year as the starting catcher but was only now returning to action after his broken leg in April. He had a "reputation for hitting the ball to the right place at the right time." He swung at the first pitch and smashed it just foul down the left-field line. He took the second pitch for strike two. On the third pitch, Farrell sent the ball bounding up the middle, but Phillippe strained and grabbed it. As the "game but crippled" catcher tried to run, the pitcher threw to first for the final out of the game. Pittsburgh had won the first game of the World Series by a score of 7–3.

The crowd of more than 16,000 shuffled out through the gates. "We will beat them tomorrow," the Boston fans said, their trust in their team undiminished. But the signs were not promising. Conveniently forgetting errors committed by Criger and Ferris, one Boston writer thought that there were "few 'ifs' to offer as the cause of Boston's downfall. No dumb plays threw away golden chances, and there was no single play on which the game turned." Young's pitches looked as good as ever, although he uncharacteristically walked three batters. "All his old-time speed was there," reporters noted, "and so were those bewildering curves that so often tried the eyesight and temper of the heaviest batsmen in the national game." But the Pirates could flat-out hit. "I want another chance at them," said Young. "I think I can turn the tables."

It was hard to fathom the nervousness of the Boston players or to explain their bad case of "stage fright" in what turned out to

have been "that fatal first inning." Perhaps they were too con-
scious of the celebrities sitting in the first row above each bench:
Ban Johnson and Harry Pulliam, the league presidents; the former
governor of Massachusetts Murray Crane; State Senator "Big
Mike" Sullivan; assorted mayors and Democratic politicians from
all over the state; and the famous boxer James J. Corbett, who had
ended the career of the bare-knuckle champion, John L. Sullivan,
a decade earlier when he knocked him out after twenty-one
rounds. "Everybody seemed to be at the game," observed one
correspondent, whose assignment was to mix with the crowd.

Also sitting close to the field was Marian Lawrence Peabody,
who was taking in her first game ever. Peabody was the great-
granddaughter of Amos Lawrence, an affluent Boston merchant
and philanthropist, and her father was an Episcopal bishop in
Cambridge. Born in 1875, Peabody had been raised among the
social elite of Boston, and her life was filled with debutante balls
and European tours; she would marry her cousin Harold Peabody
in 1906. On her return to Brattle Street from the ballpark, she
opened her diary and gushed about the afternoon. "It was the
greatest fun!" she exclaimed. From her elite perspective the crowd
was "tough but awfully good-natured." As her group left the
grounds in the large barouche they had chartered, Peabody became self-conscious, for though in some ways she enjoyed driving
off "through the crowd like a party of aldermen," for example after a concert at Symphony Hall, this crowd did not cotton to so-
cialites, especially not after a loss, and she heard "much remark"
and what she characterized as "good-natured comment." "It was
very embarrassing. We none of us knew where to look & sat &
giggled helplessly."

During the game, from her location near the field, Peabody
observed the fans and the ballplayers. "You felt so chummy &
friendly with the players. Everyone seemed to know them so
well," she said. Young was the men's favorite, but Wagner was
hers: "He was a wonderful athlete & looked like a common Greek
God if such a thing is possible & he talked the most expressive &

fascinating slang & champed his square jaws all the time chewing away."

Peabody soon forgot about baseball, though perhaps not Wagner, and she left town for a weekend in Marblehead. The everyday fans, however, could not so readily get the Pirates off their minds. Pittsburgh had "played a game that could scarcely be outclassed." Their fielding was a revelation to Boston fans and reporters alike. Clarke and Beaumont both made brilliant catches in the outfield. The infielders "covered acres of territory and cut off many a seeming base hit." And Leach, "the little invalid," gave the lie to reports of his hand injury by smashing "Cy's curves to all sections of the field." Leach had 4 hits in 5 times at bat and hit the ball until "Cy Young screamed for police or nightfall."

In the end, all credit went to Phillippe, who "inning after inning stood before the heaviest hitters on the Boston team and pitched a game that the locals simply could not fathom." He struck out 10 batters and walked none. "The English language seems light and frivolous," waxed a Pittsburgh reporter, when it comes to "the task of describing the pitching of Deacon Phil."

Frank M'Quiston, the *Pittsburgh Dispatch* correspondent whose playful prose was notable for its sardonic tone, relished the outcome and could not resist taking a swipe at New England elitism. "A colony of frogs in a nearby swamp," he mused, "where every frog, in order to gain space to swim must show that at least two of his ancestors had been eaten by the pilgrim fathers on the Mayflower . . . climbed on their different leaves and began to tune. It seemed that all said, 'Phil! Phil! Phil!' " So much for the providential destiny of the city on a hill, and so much for the snobbery of Puritan descendants who condescended to the smoky, working-class city of the Alleghenies. "The Boston people," M'Quiston crowed, "are tonight wondering how they lived so long without seeing a real team play ball. They saw Pittsburg today."

Thanks to the telegraph, fans in Pittsburgh also had a chance to follow the game. According to the *Dispatch*, "nearly all the men and a great many women in the downtown district thought of nothing but baseball." They assembled in front of the newspaper buildings and anticipated scoring updates as if awaiting the results of a presidential election. Desire for news of the game crossed all social boundaries. Outside the offices of the *Pittsburg Post*, common interest in the game "made all classes of citizens akin, and the banker did not hesitate to ask of the street gamin" what the bulletin revealed. "Women, too, took an unusual interest in the event," reported the *Post*, and in the streetcars and department stores they stopped to ask, "what's the score?"

The defeat of the Boston Americans cost their supporters thousands of dollars, and in the restaurants and hotels around town people wondered if the Americans had lost the game on purpose. In response, Jimmy Collins commented, "We were licked and there is little to say." The weather had been perfect, the crowd orderly, the umpiring unimpeachable, the game clean. "Everything was lovely except the result," remarked a Boston rooter. He had a full day to wait before the series would resume.

THE FIRST GAME

PITTSBURG.	AB.	R.	B.	P.	A.	E.
Beaumont, cf.....	5	1	0	3	0	0
Clarke, lf.........	5	0	2	4	0	0
Leach, 3b.........	5	1	4	0	1	1
Wagner, ss........	3	1	1	1	2	1
Bransfield, 1b.....	5	2	1	7	0	0
Ritchey, 2b.......	4	1	0	1	2	0
Sebring, rf........	5	1	3	1	0	0
Phelps, c	4	0	1	10	0	0
Phillippe, p.......	4	0	0	0	2	0
Total..........	40	7	12	27	7	2

BOSTON.	AB.	R.	B.	P.	A.	E.
Dougherty, lf.....	4	0	0	1	1	0
Collins, 3b........	4	0	0	2	3	0
Stahl, cf..........	4	0	1	2	0	0
Freeman, rf......	4	2	2	2	0	0
Parent, ss.........	4	1	2	4	4	0
La Chance, 1b.....	4	0	0	8	0	0
Ferris, 2b.........	3	0	1	2	4	2
Criger, c	3	0	0	6	1	2
Young, p..........	3	0	0	0	1	0
*O'Brien..........	1	0	0	0	0	0
†Farrell..........	1	0	0	0	0	0
Total..........	35	3	6	27	14	4

*Batted for Criger in ninth. †Batted for Young in ninth.

Pittsburg	4	0	1	1	0	0	1	0	0—7
Boston	0	0	0	0	0	2	0	1	1—3

Earned runs—Boston 2, Pittsburg 3. Three-base hits—Freeman, Parent, Leach 2, Bransfield. Home run—Sebring. First on balls—Off Young 3. Struck out—By Young 5, Phillippe 10. Passed ball—Criger. Time—1.55. Umpires—O'Day and Connolly. Atendance—16,242.

The box score appeared simultaneously with baseball, and the two have evolved together. While the categories represented in it have changed over time, the idea of a statistical recapitulation that summarizes individual performance is inseparable from baseball itself. The box scores included here are from *Reach's Official American League Base Ball Guide for 1904*. The categories are at-bats (AB.), runs (R.), base hits (B.), putouts (P.), assists (A.), and errors (E.). The sacrifice fly counted as an at-bat until 1908. Thus, LaChance had 4 official at-bats despite twice hitting fly balls that scored the runner from third base. As in modern scoring, walks (referred to as "first on balls" below the line score) did not count as at-bats. Thus, Wagner had walked twice and was credited with 3 official at-bats. Most notably missing here is the statistic for runs batted in (RBIs), which first appeared in the 1880s but was not adopted officially until 1920. Also, there is no separate pitcher's line; earned run average (ERA) would emerge as an official statistic only in 1912 and 1913 in the respective leagues

WAR

IN JANUARY 1903, baseball fans awaited news from the west. At the St. Nicholas hotel in Cincinnati, representatives from the warring National and American leagues met to discuss terms for peace. The city was an apt choice for the gathering. In 1869, the Red Stockings had fielded a team of paid athletes in one of the first games ever played by a fully professional baseball club. They went on to win 130 contests without a loss and helped inaugurate the shift from amateur to professional ball. Beyond the historical link, two of the key delegates to the meeting had personal ties to the city. August Garry Herrmann had recently become part owner of the Reds and, as a relative newcomer to baseball, he carried no personal grudges with him into the negotiations. And Ban Johnson, the burly founder of the American League, had begun his career as a sportswriter and editor for Cincinnati's *Commercial-Gazette*. Admirers called Johnson the Theodore Roosevelt of baseball, and not only because he weighed nearly three hundred pounds and loved to hunt. He relished competition and within two years he had made his league into the fitter of the two. But

Herrmann also had his admirers, and by the conclusion of the meeting he would be heralded as the Moses of baseball.

The names of Roosevelt and Moses do not usually conjure visions of a peaceful resolution of conflict. But after two years of bitter warfare, someone had to propose an end to the hostilities that threatened the business interests of baseball owners and the health of the game. That someone turned out to be Herrmann, who, along with fellow owners Frank Robison of the St. Louis Cardinals and James Hart of the Chicago Cubs, approached Johnson in New York during the Christmas season and suggested a peace conference. "I knew in an instant the purpose of their visit," recalled Johnson, "and after greetings all around they informed me they composed a committee of the old league to wait on me and see if peace terms could be arranged."

The old league, as Johnson called it, dated to 1876. By 1891, the National League owners had vanquished all competition, and as a result they exercised monopolistic control over baseball. But having struggled so valiantly for dominance, the league began to falter. Owners squabbled with one another. They released veteran players, unilaterally slashed salaries, and placed noncompetitive teams on the field. As a result, baseball went into decline. In Philadelphia, for example, the team went from 78–53 in 1895 to 55–77 in 1897; attendance dropped accordingly from 475,000 in 1895 to 265,000 in 1898. By 1899, the Cleveland Spiders set an all-time record for ineptitude by winning only 20 out of 154 games. After that season, the National League contracted to an eight-team circuit by dropping the franchises in Baltimore, Washington, Louisville, and, not surprisingly, Cleveland. In 1900, the editor of *Sporting Life* indicted the National League magnates for their "gross individual and collective mismanagement, their fierce factional fights, their cynical disregard of decency and honor, their open spoliation of each other, their deliberate alienation of press and public, their flagrant disloyalty to friends and supporters and their tyrannical treatment of the players."

The National League had also shown its disdain for the Western League, a minor-league association of eight teams headed by Ban Johnson. Major-league owners refused to pay a fair price to their Western League counterparts for minor-league talent. They also would not agree to a rule allowing Western League owners to hold on to their players for at least two years. As a result, successful Western League teams one year would find themselves decimated the following season with little to show for having developed National League talent.

The actions of one owner in particular roiled Johnson and threatened the competitive balance of the minor league. John T. Brush controlled the Cincinnati Reds of the National League as well as the Western League Indianapolis franchise. He had come to Indianapolis from Boston in 1875, when he was thirty, opened a clothing store, made it a success, and brought a baseball franchise to the city in 1887. In 1893, he assumed ownership of the Reds. At the time, Johnson was still sports editor of the *Commercial-Gazette*, and his reporting placed him at odds with Brush. Peeved that a friend was not awarded the Cincinnati club, he repeatedly referred to Brush in print as "wily," "slick," and "cunning." In response, Brush denied him a press pass to the Reds games, and Johnson had to pay to gain entrance and report on the team.

When Johnson became president of the Western League in 1894, Brush did all he could to weaken Johnson's league. He began to use his minor-league Indianapolis team as a farm system for the National League Cincinnati team, moving players back and forth at will. He also undermined the balance of the Western League by drafting minor-league players for his major-league team and then demoting them to Indianapolis. Writers joked that the franchise should be called "Cincinnapolis," and they denounced the practice of farming players with the epithet "Brushism."

In the context of the decline of the National League, and the specific assault of one National League owner upon the stability of the Western League, Ban Johnson decided that the moment had come to transform his circuit into a rival major-league organization. Other factors played into the decision as well. The agreement between the Western League owners would have to be renegotiated before it expired on October 20, 1900. Meanwhile, rumors circulated that the old American Association, which had been extinguished in its competition with the National League in 1891, was planning to place teams in the cities now open as a result of National League contraction, and Johnson wanted to preempt any move it might make. Finally, the formation of a players' union in June 1900, the Protective Association of Professional Baseball Players, meant that players dissatisfied with the old league might be willing to jump to a new major league that paid higher salaries and offered greater security.

In October 1899, the Western League officially became the

American League and began to plan for the upcoming season still as a minor-league circuit, though one considerably upgraded in terms of franchise locations. Starting in 1900, it entered National League territory by gaining a club in Chicago—the White Sox. Charles Comiskey, a close friend and ally of Johnson's, had made a deal with James Hart, the owner of the National League Chicago Cubs, that permitted Comiskey to shift his minor-league St. Paul club to the South Side of Chicago. In return, Hart received the right to draft two White Sox players. At the same time, the Grand Rapids club of the old Western League moved to Cleveland, newly open territory as a result of National League contraction. Charles Somers, a coal and shipping magnate, not only became owner of the franchise but served as the primary financier of the budding American League by putting up the money for ballpark leases.

After one season as a minor-league circuit, the American League prepared to raise itself to the ranks of a competing major-league organization, starting in 1901. For that season, the franchises in Minneapolis, Indianapolis, and Kansas City were dropped in favor of new clubs in Philadelphia, Baltimore, and Washington. The inaugural season was rounded out with teams in Chicago, Cleveland, Detroit, Milwaukee, and Boston. In 1902, the Milwaukee team moved to St. Louis, and in 1903, the Baltimore one relocated to New York. These eight teams—Chicago, Cleveland, Detroit, St. Louis, Washington, Philadelphia, Boston, and New York—would remain American League fixtures until 1954, when the St. Louis Browns moved to Baltimore.

Starting in 1903, then, the National League was competing directly against the American League in Boston, Philadelphia, Chicago, St. Louis, and New York. Teams in Cincinnati, Brooklyn, and Pittsburgh rounded out its circuit. Stability reigned as well in the National League for half a century, until the Boston Braves moved to Milwaukee in 1953. No one in 1901, however, would have predicted decades of stability and growth for the game of baseball. Rather, it was a war, which observers thought would be fought until the death of one organization or the other. Certainly, in the five cities where the leagues competed directly, it was believed the contest would be for "the survival of the fittest," "a war of magnates for territorial rights, and the prestige of securing the cream of the playing talent of the base ball world."

To field competitive teams that would be attractive to fans, the American League needed talented players, and the natural place to get them was from National League clubs. From the start, Johnson proclaimed that he did not recognize the legality of the reserve clause that National League owners included in players' contracts. The clause, adopted in 1879, gave owners an option on a player's services for the following season on terms theoretically negotiated by both parties, but in reality imposed by the owners, who tacitly agreed not to compete with one another for players reserved by other teams. A ballplayer could hold out for more money, but he risked having nowhere to play for the season. One of the demands made by the Protective Association was to revise the reserve clause. But the National League magnates showed little interest in the players' cause. These men had spent most of their careers battling labor organizers in their other businesses and they weren't about to give in when it came to baseball. The owner of the Boston Braves, Arthur Soden, flatly proclaimed, "I do not believe in labor organizations or unions. When a player ceases to be useful to me, I will release him." Ban Johnson, by contrast, announced that the American League would repudiate the reserve clause, raise the minimum salary, stop the practice of farming out players, and recognize the Protective Association. Players began to pay attention.

Clark Griffith, Cubs pitcher and vice president of the Protective Association, was one of the first to meet with representatives from the new league. For six consecutive seasons between 1894 and 1899, Griffith had won more than 20 games. He did so with a combination of skill and guile, throwing hard, hiding the ball behind his leg as he reared to deliver, and regularly using his spikes to cut the sphere so it would fly off in odd directions. For his wiz-

[handwritten margin note: reserve clause a reason players accept of AL]

ardry on the mound, as well as on the hunting grounds, he earned the nickname the "Old Fox." Sometime in the fall of 1900, Griffith met with Johnson and Charles Comiskey at a café in Chicago. They discussed the possibility of recruiting players to the new league, and Griffith said he would get back to them once he knew the National League's response to the association's demands. That response came in December when, at the league's annual meeting in New York, owners rejected the players' proposals. Griffith quickly informed Johnson, "Go ahead [and] get all the players you want."

In the ensuing war for baseball talent, the American League signed dozens of players from the National League, some of them the premier stars of the day. Griffith left the Cubs and became player-manager for the crosstown rival White Sox, with whom he won the American League pennant in 1901. At the end of 1900, Ban Johnson scored another coup when he and Charles Comiskey arranged a furtive meeting in a hotel room with John McGraw and Wilbert Robinson and persuaded the two players to abandon the St. Louis Cardinals, where they had ended up after the National League folded its Baltimore franchise. McGraw was one of the finest players of the day, and one of the roughest. Between 1893 and 1899 he never hit below .320 (in 1899 he hit .391), and he routinely stole 40 or more bases (with a high of 78 in 1894). He would do anything to gain an edge—curse umpires, bait fans, push and spike opposing players. McGraw was the poster child for what the sporting papers denounced as baseball "rowdyism." Baltimore had embraced him, and now he pined to return east. When McGraw accepted Johnson's offer to play, manage, and own part of the new American League franchise, Johnson had what seemed like a major piece of the American League lineup in place.

At a subsequent meeting in Chicago in January 1901, Johnson and his associates came up with a list of forty-six players who they hoped would jump to the American League. Johnson, Comiskey, Griffith, McGraw, and others went about contacting the players and making the case for the new league. Johnson recalled that they "moved from city to city under cover of darkness" and then slipped out before daylight, undetected by National League owners who were on the lookout for the raiders. In February, baseball fans learned that Nap Lajoie, the remarkable Philadelphia Phillies infielder, had signed a multi-year deal with the crosstown American League rival A's, managed by Connie Mack. Lajoie was only twenty-five years old, and in four full seasons with the Phillies he had never batted below .324 and had twice knocked in 127 runs. Like so many other National League players, he was dismayed by the $2,400 maximum salary. When he learned that his teammate Ed Delahanty, the most feared hitter of the era, had a deal that privately paid him several hundred dollars more than the league maximum, Lajoie jumped for a salary thousands higher than he earned in the National League.

The Phillies' owner, Colonel John Rogers, decided to seek an injunction against Lajoie, as well as fellow jumpers Bill Bernhard and Charles Fraser, to prevent them from playing for the Athletics. But a Philadelphia court ruled against Rogers, stating that the loss of the players would not cause the employer "irreparable harm," and that the standard National League contract lacked "mutuality"—in return for what the players gave up as a result of the reserve clause, they did not receive anything back. Rogers appealed to the Pennsylvania Supreme Court, and a year later, in April 1902, the court unanimously reversed the earlier decision and granted an injunction preventing the men from playing for any team in the state except the Phillies. Ban Johnson was not about to allow the star of the premiere American League season to be lost and, with the cooperation of Connie Mack, Lajoie and Bernhard were traded to Cleveland, where Pennsylvania law did not apply. When the Bronchos, as the Cleveland team was known that season, came to Philadelphia to play the A's, Lajoie and Bernhard whiled away their time on the beaches at Atlantic City, New Jersey, out of reach of the jurisdiction of Pennsylvania's courts.

Lajoie electrified fans in 1901 and gave the American League a potent presence in Philadelphia, a city where it competed directly with the National League. The Athletics drew more than 200,000 people in their inaugural season, almost as many as the Phillies. And Lajoie had one of the greatest offensive seasons ever recorded, batting .426, hitting 14 home runs in an era when the long ball was a rarity, and knocking in 125 runs. He was so feared at the plate that during a game in May against the White Stockings, the pitcher walked him intentionally with the bases loaded.

In Chicago, St. Louis, and Boston, in 1902 the three other cities where the two leagues competed directly for fans, the story was much the same. In Chicago, the White Sox outdrew the Cubs; in St. Louis, the Browns outdrew the Cardinals; in Boston, the Americans outdrew the National League Braves. The success of the new Boston franchise hinged on the acquisition of two players who jumped in 1901. Jimmy Collins left the crosstown rivals to become the player-manager with the Americans. He redefined the position of the third baseman, showing range away from the bag and charging in to field bunts bare-handed as he threw off-balance to first. In 1900, he had 601 total chances at his position (he committed 40 errors, for a fielding percentage of .935, 40 points higher than the league average). As a batter, he showed power (he led the NL with 15 home runs in 1898) and hit for average.

What made Collins's life as manager easier, besides the $4,000 for which he signed, was the knowledge that Cy Young had also jumped over to Boston. Denton Young got his nickname, it was said, because whenever the ball got past the catcher it splintered the wooden backstop into pieces, as if a cyclone had hit it. Raised in Ohio, Young embodied the stereotype of the strong country boy who could throw an overpowering fastball and back it up with a "drop ball" that froze the hitter. In 1901, Young was already thirty-four years old and had been pitching since 1890. In 1893, the distance from the pitcher's mound to home plate was increased from 51 feet to the modern distance of 60 feet 6 inches.

The change ruined many a pitcher's career and led to an offensive explosion in the National League. But Young won 34 games that year, one of nine consecutive seasons of 20 wins or more. That string was not broken until 1900, when Young won 19 games. Young had become unhappy with the St. Louis Cardinals. He despised the owner, Frank Robison, whom he held responsible for the Cleveland Spiders' disastrous season of 1899. In 1898, Robison had purchased the St. Louis franchise and shifted all his star Cleveland players there, including Young. The pitcher encapsulated the feelings of many an aggrieved National League player when he told his former owner, "Your treatment of your players has been so inconsiderate that no self-respecting man would want to work for you if he could do anything else in the world."

The American League had managed to acquire an astonishing forty-five of the forty-six players on their initial list. The one star who eluded their grasp was Honus Wagner. John Peter Wagner (called Honus or Hans because it was short for Johannes) came to baseball out of the Pennsylvania coal mines where he had gone to work when he was twelve years old. "I went down into the mines when it was dark and when I came out it was the dusk of evening," he recalled. But baseball, he said, was in his blood. He went from making $14 a month in the mines to $35 a month as a nineteen-year-old playing for a minor-league team in Ohio. Two years later, in 1897, he found himself in Louisville, a member of Barney Dreyfuss's National League Colonels.

Wagner quickly established himself as a potent offensive threat (he hit .335 as a rookie) and the best defensive player in baseball. Wagner had huge hands on a compact frame—one sportswriter called him a "human crab." He enjoyed telling the story of the time he was playing first base, took his glove off his left hand, and reached into his back pocket for some chewing tobacco. The batter hit the ball to second and Wagner tried to get his hand out, but it was stuck. He caught the throw with his bare right hand and then went to the bench to have his pocket cut open. Wagner's hands were so big that whenever he made an infield play, he scooped a handful of dirt along with the ball, and Kitty Bransfield said that he simply caught the largest object hurtling his way. His throwing arm was so strong that one writer insisted that "there is not another man playing ball who can stand back so far and get the ball to first base ahead of a fast runner." Wagner also showed deceptive quickness in getting to the ball as well as in running the bases, an attribute that earned him his nickname "the flying Dutchman." He played outfield as well as infield, but, starting in 1903, he settled in at shortstop, the most demanding position on the field.

Wagner came to the Pirates in 1900, after the National League dropped the Louisville franchise. Owner Barney Dreyfuss essentially merged the Louisville Colonels with the Pittsburgh Pirates and took over as president of the team. Along with Wagner came Fred Clarke, Tommy Leach, Deacon Phillippe, and nine other Colonel players. In his first season with the Pirates, at age twenty-six, Wagner hit .381 and drove in 100 runs. The American League came calling.

In retirement, Wagner would claim that Clark Griffith had come to his home in Carnegie, Pennsylvania, and placed twenty $1,000 bills on the table in an effort to induce him to jump leagues. Instead, Wagner re-signed with Pittsburgh for $2,700 in 1901; he earned $5,000 in 1903, and for the rest of his career he simply signed a blank contract during the winter and Dreyfuss filled in whatever amount he pleased. Wagner loved playing for the Pirates and before the hometown fans. "They meant much more to me than money," he explained.

As it turned out, few Pirates defected to the American League in 1901 and 1902. One reason was Dreyfuss's benevolent owner-ship; players thought him fair, and he signed them to extended contracts. Another was that Ban Johnson hoped to lure Dreyfuss to the American League or gain territorial rights to place a competing team in Pittsburgh. Some sportswriters at the time speculated that the wily Johnson sought intentionally to leave one potent team intact in the National League so that there would be no pennant race and fans would lose interest. If that is the case, Johnson calculated correctly: the 1902 Pirates went 103–36 and beat out the second-place Brooklyn Superbas by a full 27 games. They are the only team in baseball history to complete a full season without three consecutive losses.

In fact, Johnson tried but failed to recruit many Pirates. In several cases, he was simply outmaneuvered by the Pirates' organization. Dreyfuss and club secretary Harry Pulliam engaged in counterespionage. On one occasion, they learned from a wire operator, who was a friend, that Ban Johnson and Charley Somers had taken rooms at the Lincoln Hotel in Pittsburgh. The Pirates' officials occupied rooms on both sides of the American League magnates and eavesdropped through the ventilation system. They overheard six of their players agreeing to jump to the American League, and later intervened to prevent four of them from departing. On another occasion, Kitty Bransfield was sent home to Worcester with an injury, and Dreyfuss learned that Ban Johnson was headed there to encourage the player to jump. Pulliam quickly boarded a train to Massachusetts, and as it turned out, he was on the same overnighter as the American League president. That night Pulliam somehow got hold of Johnson's shoes and hid them. The next morning Johnson searched the train while Pulliam hurried to Bransfield's house and signed him to a new contract.

Although Wagner and most of his teammates remained Pirates, former National League stars such as Lajoie, McGraw, Collins, and Young gave the American League instant legitimacy in the eyes of the fans. While National League attendance in 1901 reached 1.9 million fans, the American League did nearly as well, attracting 1.6 million. The following year, with thirty-seven additional players jumping to the new league, including Ed Delahanty, Rube Waddell, Jesse Burkett, and Bill Dinneen, American League attendance soared to 2.2 million, whereas National League attendance dropped to 1.7 million. And the new league accomplished the feat in eight cities whose total population was nearly 3 million less than in the eight National League cities.

Part of the American League's popularity stemmed from a significant rule difference from the National League: for its first two seasons, it did not count foul balls (except for bunts) as strikes, and as a result, its teams produced more runs than National League teams: 5.35 per game as compared to 4.63. Fans enjoyed seeing runs scored, and the offensive explosion in the American League, as well as the star players on the field, attracted people to the ballpark.

Wars are fought in two directions, and the National League owners plotted ways to persuade players to return. Davy Jones, a coveted prospect in 1901 after he hit .384 for a minor-league team, was sold to the Cubs, but jumped even before he reported when Milwaukee made him a better offer. The following year, the Milwaukee franchise relocated to St. Louis. Several weeks into the season, the Browns were playing the White Sox in Chicago and Jones got a call from James Hart, the Cubs owner. The next day the two men met.

"You know," Hart said, "I've lost a lot of good ballplayers to the American League, men like Clark Griffith and Jimmy Callahan, not to mention yourself. I'd like to try to get some of you fellows to move the other way. What would you think about jumping back?"

"What have you got to offer?" Jones asked.

"How about a two-year contract for $3,600 a year, the highest salary on the club, plus a $500 bonus you can have right now?"

Jones took the cash, went back to the hotel, packed, and that afternoon reported to the Cubs. His decision to return to the National League was a minor skirmish in the baseball wars. (By 1906, Jones was back in the American League with Detroit, and he ended up having an average career spent primarily as a backup outfielder.)

But another player who rejoined the National League in 1902

exploded a bomb that effectively destroyed an American League franchise. John McGraw and Ban Johnson should have realized in 1901 that the two would never get along, but their agreement at the time was to the benefit of each. The two battled throughout the first season. McGraw advised his former teammate, and friend, Hugh Jennings against playing for the Philadelphia Athletics, though the former Baltimore star, who hit .401 in 1896, would have been an asset to the new league. Both Ban Johnson and Connie Mack became furious. And time and again McGraw and his players cursed umpires, provoked fans, and intimidated other teams. "He had the most vicious tongue of any man who ever lived," recalled one player who remained loyal to him despite the tirades. But Ban Johnson, trying to run a clean, respectable league free of accusations of rowdyism or anarchy, could not tolerate the behavior of his Baltimore manager.

McGraw was ejected from the first game of the 1902 season, and Johnson soon suspended him for a separate incident in which he incited an attack on an umpire. McGraw felt singled out by the umpires and Johnson. By the summer, he had had enough, and he orchestrated his escape from Baltimore. He was aided by John Brush, who had secretly met with the player-manager a year earlier. Brush was in the process of buying an interest in the New York Giants from the owner, Andrew Freedman, a member of Tammany Hall and one of the most powerful men in New York, and he wanted McGraw to manage the team. In July 1902, McGraw met with Freedman in New York and signed a contract for $11,000 a year, making him the highest-paid player or manager in baseball. At the same time, Freedman bought shares of stock in the Baltimore franchise. The ownership promptly released six of the fourteen Baltimore players: Joe McGinnity, Roger Bresnahan, Dan McGann, and Jack Cronin jumped to the Giants, while Joe Kelley and Cy Seymour went to the Reds. Employing his powers as president of the league, Johnson ruled that because the owners failed to field a team, they would have to forfeit ownership of the Baltimore franchise. With the league in control, minor-league talent was brought in, and the Orioles managed to finish the season with a woeful record of 50 and 88, going 24 and 57 after McGraw left.

McGraw's apostasy left a gaping hole in the American League that Johnson barely managed to fill. But it had the beneficial effect of accelerating the league's move into New York. McGraw's act, Johnson said, "utterly killed baseball in Baltimore" and motivated him to prepare "for a New York invasion."

Invasion and war were still very much the talk of the day when the annual National League meeting took place in December of 1902. Harry Pulliam was elected president, replacing an executive committee headed by Brush. With the new leadership came a changed attitude toward conflict with the American League. Besides, the word was that despite the machinations of Freedman's cronies, the American League had found a location for a team in New York—a high, rocky patch of land in Washington Heights, at the northern tip of Manhattan. The National League's best efforts had failed; their rivals would have a presence in the most populous city in the nation. Having lost scores of players to the American League and having been defeated at the box office, the majority of National League owners faced the reality of a thriving American League. The time for a peace conference had arrived.

GAME TWO, FRIDAY, OCTOBER 2

HARRY PULLIAM, newly elected president of the National League, encapsulated the feelings of all Pittsburgh fans when, following the Pirates' 7–3 victory in Game One, he said, "Today held the happiest hours of my baseball life. I saw the champions of my league show their superiority over their rival champions of the American League. . . . No matter how the remaining games of the world's championship series terminate, Pittsburg's baseball team, the greatest in the country, cannot be deprived of the glory earned on the diamond here." After the game, the Pirates returned to the Hotel Vendome, had dinner, and then journeyed out for an evening's entertainment. They were a loose and happy team, thrilled to have come into Boston and taken the first game of the series. A group of players went to Keith's Theatre, where the proprietor had reserved several boxes for them. Showing their admiration for the way the Pittsburgh nine played, the audience applauded as the athletes took their seats. Keith's offered the latest in vaudeville. The players watched the trapeze performer Mademoiselle Amoros, "as handsome and graceful as she is daring," and the English whistler and mimic Charles Mildare. A comedian performed a monologue, and a duo entertained with "a melange of laugh-provoking nonsense and topical songs." It was an enjoyable way to close out the day and to bask in victory.

The Pittsburgh rooters who had come to Boston were "jubilant and kept the sedate old town in a whirl of excitement . . . by their celebration . . . while Boston fandom was in sackcloth and ashes." The only problem was the eleven o'clock curfew, "which is strictly enforced in this puritanical town." Having been compelled to retire prematurely, the Pittsburgh fans were up early Friday morning, eager for the second game of the series to get under way.

The day dawned cloudy after an evening of showers. At two in the afternoon, light rain trickled down, but it had stopped by game time. Because of the weather and the disappointment from the previous day's results, only 9,500 fans paid to attend the second game of the series. Several hundred more got "fence" admissions, free entrance by climbing the outfield wall and standing along the terrace. Still, all the seats in the grandstand and bleachers were full, and many of the same celebrities assumed their front-row positions. The only space that looked less congested than the day before was the area behind the outfield ropes. Henry Killilea arrived from Milwaukee and joined the other baseball magnates. Ban Johnson sent Jimmy Collins a telegram: "Go after them today and victory will be yours."

Bill Dinneen took the mound for the Americans. The six-foot-one-inch righty, who had jumped from Boston's National League team in 1902, had gone 21–13 during the season. Observers admired his physique and pitching motion: "he takes a full swing and a long step, gets his body into the pitch and follows her through." After retiring in 1910, the Syracuse native would become an American League umpire, and over his career would officiate in forty-five World Series games. But none of those would compare to the work he had before him today.

From the first pitch, Dinneen looked fast. After opening with three consecutive balls, he came back to strike out Ginger Beaumont. He walked Fred Clarke, but then struck out Tommy Leach, Pittsburgh's pesky third baseman who had gotten four hits the day before. Dinneen's "hypnotic curves" were starting to break over the plate, and the crowd roared its approval. With two out and Honus Wagner up, Clarke thought about stealing second, but he got careless and was picked off by Dinneen, who threw to first base. Candy LaChance fired to Hobe Ferris for the out at second, and the side was retired. At least today, Boston would not lose themselves, or the game, in the first inning.

Pittsburgh sent righty Sam Leever to the mound. Leever had a career year, going 25–7 with a league-leading ERA of 2.06 and 7 shutouts. But the unassuming pitcher, who had been a schoolteacher in Ohio before becoming a professional ballplayer, had hurt himself in September when he went trapshooting and the rifle recoiled into his shoulder. As "Schoolmaster" Leever took the mound, Clarke had no idea what he would get from his ace.

It did not take long to find out. Patsy Dougherty stepped in. The day before, he had been visibly nervous and struck out. The lefty batter looked for a good pitch to drive, and he got it. He smashed the ball almost to the ropes in right-center field. As he rounded the bases, the fans rose, their wild screams propelling him forward. The Pirates fielded the ball perfectly and hit the cutoffs. As Dougherty rounded third and headed for home, the throw came to the plate. Boston's fastest man dove headfirst. "Safe!" screamed umpire O'Day. Dougherty's inside-the-park home run gave the Americans their first World Series lead.

Boston was not done. Jimmy Collins flied out deep to Clarke in left. But Chick Stahl doubled to center and scored on Buck Freeman's base hit up the middle. Fred Parent flied hard to left, but LaChance walked. Leever was in danger of giving up the game in the first inning. It was clear that his arm was not right; even the outs were well hit. Although the inning ended when Ferris grounded weakly to Wagner, Boston had made a statement. They had reversed the first game opening and demonstrated that they could hit and run. They were ahead 2–0. Now it was up to Dinneen to prove that he could continue to pitch effectively.

Dinneen breezed through the second and third innings, striking out three of the six men he faced and allowing the others nothing but pop-ups. Big Bill was sharp, and the crowd sensed it. The Pirates removed Leever from the game after the first inning. It was clear that "he had absolutely nothing, neither speed, curves nor control." Clarke put in Bucky Veil, a twenty-two-year-old righty who had thrown only 71 innings all year. The reliever got through the second and third innings, aided by two nifty defensive plays by Wagner at short. All Veil had to do was keep Pittsburgh in the game and allow the offense a chance to erupt, and so far he was up to the task.

For Boston, the "crisis of the game" came in the top of the fourth inning. Beaumont, after swinging at two curve balls out of the strike zone, showed some discipline and walked to lead off for Pittsburgh. At third base, manager Collins kicked the dirt; he knew all too well that no good ever came of leadoff walks, especially when issued to the top of the order. On the next pitch, Clarke singled over second base for the Pirates' first hit of the game. Beaumont saw Stahl field the ball quickly and did not try for third; he was not going to make the first out of the inning on the bases and kill a rally.

The crowd pleaded for the home team to extinguish the threat. To those standing outside the Huntington Avenue Grounds it sounded like a stampede. But in the stands all one could hear was the screech of echoing voices: "Hold them down! Hold them down!" implored the fans. William Henry Moody, the Secretary of the Navy, who was in attendance, rose half out of his seat, his face crimson with excitement.

Right-handed hitter Tommy Leach, Boston's nemesis in the first game, stepped in. There were two runners on base with no one out, yet Dinneen appeared "perfectly calm and steady, even to the point of indifference." His first pitch was a fastball for a strike; the second was high and inside. Dinneen threw a curve, and Leach bunted the ball slowly back to the pitcher. "Quick fielding and a lightning throw" got the speedster by a step at first, though Leach protested that he was safe.

The Pirates in their dugout. Honus Wagner is fourth from the left
MCGREEVEY COLLECTION, BOSTON PUBLIC LIBRARY

Runners were on second and third, in scoring position, with Wagner due up—the "mighty Wagner," the "surest batsman on the Pittsburg team," the "terror to every pitcher in the National League."

Wagner swung at the first pitch and missed. The crowd howled.

Undeterred, Wagner swung at the next pitch as well, and he connected for a vicious shot that curved foul into the first-base bleachers. The "grand stand quivered with excitement."

Again, Dinneen delivered a pitch over the plate; he wasn't going to give in to the slugger, not even with first base open. Wagner turned on the pitch and "with a sharp crack the ball left the bat, headed for right [center] field, while two flying Pittsburg runners were tearing round the circuit for home."

Hobe Ferris leaped, pulled the ball out of the air, and, in one motion, stepped on second to double up Clarke and end the threat. Ferris had "atoned nobly for his costly errors of the day before." As he jogged off the field, he doffed his cap toward the crowd. Boston had escaped "from a tight place . . . and the crowd rose as one man."

The score remained 2–0, but Boston threatened in nearly every inning. With one out, in the bottom of the fourth, Veil committed the sin of walking the opposing pitcher, Dinneen. Dougherty grounded into a fielder's choice. Collins followed with a single past first, and Dougherty took third. Collins then stole second, but Dougherty remained at third, as the Pirates had the catcher throw back to the pitcher, rather than to second base, in order to prevent a double steal. Stahl grounded out to end the inning, but it seemed inevitable that Boston would score more runs against Veil.

In the bottom of the fifth, the Americans loaded the bases with no one out. Freeman had doubled, Parent walked, and Veil made an error on LaChance's bunt. Ferris hit the ball to Leach and the third baseman threw home for the force. The crowd squirmed. They knew how important it was to tack on a run or two, and this was their best opportunity since the opening of the game.

Criger came up to bat. For two days Criger had been impotent at bat. Now he hit the ball hard, but right at second baseman Ritchey, who flipped to Wagner, who fired to Bransfield for an inning-ending double play. The Pirates' defense was keeping them in the game.

The Pirate hitters, however, could not solve Dinneen, who retired the opposition in order in the fifth and sixth innings. He had struck out nine up to that point. The pitcher came up to bat to lead off the bottom of the sixth; the crowd applauded wildly. He grounded out to first, leaving the hitting to the top of the order. Dougherty's first-inning home run still stood as the only score

Boston needed, but no Boston player or fan felt comfortable with even a two-run lead.

Dougherty worked the count full, and then sliced the ball deep into left field, where, to everyone's amazement, it disappeared over the fence for his second home run of the game. It was one of the longest shots ever hit at Huntington Grounds, and only the second time anyone could remember a ball leaving the park in left field. The fans "danced and they shrieked and it was minutes before they came down to earth again." After the game, Collins called the blast "the greatest hit I ever saw by a left-handed batter." Unnerved by the home run, Veil walked Collins, who promptly stole second and took third when backup catcher Harry Smith, who started the second game behind the plate, threw the ball past Ritchey. But Collins was left stranded when Stahl struck out and Freeman fouled out to first. Still, Boston had added a run and now led 3–0. The Pirates were running out of time.

Boston Americans Pose for a Herald Photographer While Seated on Their Bench in the Seventh Inning.

This photograph was taken by a Herald staff photographer at the Boston-Pittsburg game yesterday while Parent was at the bat in the seventh inning. It will be noticed that Lachance has his bat in hand ready to take his next turn, and that Ferris is selecting his stick, as he is to go to the bat in the inning.

The seventh inning came and went in a flash as both teams went down in order. The Pirates had a chance in the eighth, when Ritchey led off with a drive that reached the left-field corner. It was only the Pirates' third hit off Dinneen. Ritchey rounded first and headed for second. Dougherty, the offensive hero, showed he could also play defense. Scooping the ball up on a bounce, the left fielder fired "a rifle shot" to Ferris, who easily tagged out Ritchey. Whatever lift the hit might have provided the Pirates collapsed like a kite without wind. Sebring promptly struck out and Smith hit weakly back to the pitcher.

In the bottom of the eighth inning, Wagner and Ritchey turned their second double play of the game, erasing yet another Boston scoring threat as Criger, who had walked to start the inning, was left at third.

Veil, who had pitched ably in relief, was due to lead off the ninth, and Clarke pinch-hit Ed Phelps, but the catcher in Game One struck out. Beaumont popped up to Parent, and Clarke ended the game with a groundout to short. Boston had tied the series with a 3–0 victory. Once again, the first inning had proven fateful. Boston had "completely revers[ed] their form of the day before." The Boston infield "proved stone walls through which no Pittsburg drive could force its way." Dinneen pitched "one of the best games of his long career. . . . His speed was terrific and his curves broke just right." Only twenty-nine Pirates came to bat, and only one of them reached third base. Everyone but Wagner and Smith struck out at least once. Dinneen pitched "gilt-edged ball from start to finish" and accomplished "what 'Cy' Young could not do" the day before. After the game, Fred Clarke put it simply: "Dinneen's pitching was first class." Frank M'Quiston of the *Pittsburg Dispatch* quipped that Boston made the Pirates look like "last summer's straw hat and feel worse."

The game, reporters concluded, was "a battle of giants, . . . one of the most brilliantly played and fiercely contested battles that has yet been fought out." "It was one of the prettiest ball games ever seen," acknowledged a Pirate partisan. No balls went past the ropes into the crowd, and "in every way the game passed off smoothly and cleanly."

The fans had served as a tenth man for the home team: "That great crowd, moved by a single thought, acted as one man. The bleachers and the grandstand and the outfield occupants breathed together and shouted together. When, in the second inning, Dinneen lay off second base and Veil made a bluff throw to Wagner to catch him, 9,000 voices shouted a warning. Nine thousand 'ohs' and 'ahs' burst on the air as one's hopes rose or fell. . . . How the crowd cheered Dinneen and Dougherty and Ferris, when the latter made a sensational catch of Wagner's fierce liner with two men on base completing, unaided, a double play and pulling Boston out of a hole. These things can never be properly told, but they will go down in history with the spectators who heard and saw them."

Even though Pittsburgh had lost the second game, its fans came away confident about the team's chances in the series, and they backed their feelings with cash. At hotels around town that night, "money was wagered in big and little bits as freely as sarsaparilla and peanuts at a county fair." The way Pirates supporters saw it, all Boston could muster offensively was two runs off an injured pitcher and one off a substitute. In reviewing the game, fans contemplated the contingency of baseball. At any time during the afternoon, "a couple of hits or misplays would have tied the score." Wagner's shot in the fourth was the one that everyone talked about. It was a lucky break that Ferris was in the right spot. But no one wanted his team's fate to rest in luck's hands. And those double plays turned by the Pirates' defense were something at which to marvel, "worth travelling miles to see." Some thought the Pittsburgh infield a little too flashy "to please the real old-timers who like the get-there without the calcium light effects." But this was the twentieth century, and these players could perform wonders on the field. "Nothing short of a miracle," thought the *Pittsburg Leader*, "can rob the redoubtable 'Pirates' of their reputation as the best ball team in the country."

Tim Murnane also had luck on his mind. Murnane was the baseball correspondent for the *Boston Globe* and had a weekly column that appeared on Sundays under the title "Murnane's Baseball." Murnane knew baseball and he knew Boston. He had played for a number of teams in the 1870s, including Boston, and in 1884 he managed and played for Boston's entry into the Union Association. Shortly after leaving the field as a player, he reentered it as a writer and began offering daily accounts of the National League games. He also remained a devoted fan and Royal Rooter.

Murnane, who served as official scorer for the games at Huntington Avenue, had never seen anything like this series, and his newspaper took advantage of the commotion. "The interest taken in the Pittsburg-Boston series for the championship of the world is greater than has ever before been shown in baseball," he asserted. The *Globe*, a morning paper, began to issue baseball extras in the early evening following every game. Writers tried to interview the players and often featured their quotes boxed in bold type. Editors in Boston and Pittsburgh had discovered that the World Series sold papers. For the first time, baseball news became front-page news.

After the second game, Murnane praised the fans for their fair treatment of the opposing team and expressed concern that it might be different in the smoky city where a less congenial disposition prevailed. He reminded readers that "luck enters largely into baseball. A pebble on the field may change the course of a ball, and lose or win a game."

Local rooters were happy for the victory over Pittsburgh, but as night fell they pondered "if Boston has to play such wonderful ball, with two home runs, to win out by only three runs, with a second-string pitcher working, what can she do when her own pitcher is being hit?" They would not have long to wait for the answer.

THE SECOND GAME

BOSTON.	AB.	R.	B.	P.	A.	E.
Dougherty, lf.....	4	2	3	0	1	0
Collins, 3b........	4	0	1	1	1	0
Stahl, cf..........	4	1	1	1	0	0
Freeman, rf.......	4	0	2	0	0	0
Parent, ss.........	3	0	1	3	3	0
La Chance, 1b.....	2	0	0	6	1	0
Ferris, 2b.........	4	0	0	5	0	0
Criger, c..........	3	0	0	11	0	0
Dineen, p.........	2	0	1	0	3	0
Total..........	30	3	9	27	9	0

PITTSBURG.	AB.	R.	B.	P.	A.	E
Beaumont, cf......	3	0	0	3	0	0
Clarke, lf.........	3	0	1	3	0	0
Leach, 3b.........	3	0	0	0	2	0
Wagner, ss........	3	0	0	3	3	0
Bransfield, 1b.....	3	0	0	9	1	0
Ritchey, 2b.......	3	0	1	3	3	0
Sebring, rf........	3	0	1	1	0	0
Smith, c..........	3	0	0	2	1	1
Leever, p..........	0	0	0	0	0	0
Vail, p............	2	0	0	0	0	1
*Phelps...........	1	0	0	0	0	0
Total..........	27	0	3	24	10	2

*Batted for Vail in ninth.

Boston...................	2	0	0	0	0	1	0	0	x—— 3
Pittsburg................	0	0	0	0	0	0	0	0	0—— 0

Earned runs—Boston 3. Two-base hit—Stahl. Home runs—Dougherty 2. Double plays—Ferris unassisted; Ritchey, Wagner, Bransfield; Wagner, Ritchey, Bransfield. First on balls—Off Dineen 2, Vail 4, Leever 1. Stolen bases—Collins 2. Hit by pitcher—By Vail 1. Struck out—By Dineen 11, Vail 1. Time—1.47. Umpires—O'Day and Connolly. Attendance—9,415.

PEACE

THE PEACE CONFERENCE of January 1903 had come as a surprise. The *Sporting News* reported that "the movement for peace was a case of spontaneous combustion." Exhausted owners in the National League did not so much take action as succumb to it. St. Louis Cardinals owner Frank Robison said offhandedly that he was tired and wanted to avoid a repeat of 1902, in which six National League clubs lost money. Colonel Rogers, the Philadelphia Phillies owner, agreed. Jim Hart of the Chicago Cubs said, "Well, what's the use of fighting anyway?" Garry Herrmann, the Reds owner, seconded a motion to seek a peace conference. "The American League is here to stay," he conceded. With John Brush no longer heading the executive committee, the motion passed. Sportswriters speculated that the National League sprang the peace offer to "make a good grandstand play and save some of its honor." But it was a mystery, they thought, how the leagues would possibly "reach any compromise which will reconcile all the many conflicting claims of the warring clubs." And they warned that the sores on each side were so raw that any misquoting or misunderstanding would "produce a breach so wide that it will take all the skill of the best base ball surgeon to heal it this winter."

The National League negotiating committee consisted of President Henry Pulliam, Robison, Hart, and Herrmann. The American League prepared to send President Ban Johnson and owners Charles Comiskey of Chicago, Charles Somers of Cleveland, and Henry Killilea of Boston. But, as feared, even before it started, the conference nearly derailed over the issue of delegate powers. The American League delegation received "plenary powers" from the owners and could therefore bind the league in any negotiations. Johnson threatened not to meet unless Herrmann had similar power to act. Johnson also made it clear that an amalgamation of the two leagues into one twelve-club league, something some National League owners desired, was unacceptable to him. The result of all the pre-conference wrangling was "estrangement, misunderstanding and coolness on the part of the rival committeemen." But after coming under attack from the press for showing a lack of sincerity and good faith, and with reassurances from Garry Herrmann that he had authority from the majority of National League owners, Johnson backed off his threats and the peace conference opened in Cincinnati on Friday, January 9.

In addition to the eight official delegates, others sat in on the discussions. Barney Dreyfuss, owner of the Pirates, and some of the stockholders from the Browns and Giants attended the conference. A couple of minor-league managers from the Western and New England League listened in as well, and several players found their way to Cincinnati, most notably Sam Leever, the established Pirate pitcher, who said that he came out of curiosity and a desire to see "a settlement that would put an end to the contract-jumping and other evils, which a base ball war breeds."

The conference began at ten-thirty in the morning and the delegates worked until ten in the evening. They took lunch in the committee room but dined in the restaurant at the St. Nicholas Hotel, which was known throughout the city for its gourmet chef. As discussions proceeded, the meeting room filled with cigar smoke. James Hart, proclaiming that the "assembly chamber resembled a smokehouse at hog-killing time," periodically escaped to the lobby for fresh air. But amidst the thickening air, the delegates made quick progress on the general issues before them. They rejected the idea of merging the sixteen teams in two leagues into one twelve-team circuit, and, in cities with two ball clubs, they proscribed the idea of collapsing them into one franchise. They agreed that all contracts thereafter entered into by the clubs of either league with players, managers, or umpires would be valid and binding. They also reaffirmed the reserve clause and adoption of a uniform contract. Territorial issues were settled, with the American League receiving the right to place a team in New York and agreeing not to seek a franchise in Pittsburgh.

So far, so good. By the end of day, however, questions arose about the disposition of specific players whose contracts were in dispute because they had taken money from more than one team. Tempers began to flare. Henry Killilea triggered the fireworks when he denounced the National League for tactics that led Ed Delahanty and George Davis, two of the most prominent players who jumped to the American League in 1902, to sign National League contracts for 1903.

Ed Delahanty was a thirteen-year veteran in 1901, with a private deal that paid him $600 above the $2,400 National League maximum. His Philadelphia Phillies teammate Nap Lajoie thought he had the same deal, but when he found out that he was being paid $400 less than Big Ed, he jumped to the new league. Delahanty, however, could afford to wait and see how matters fared with the new league. He had hit over .400 three times and powered in more than 90 runs for 9 consecutive seasons. One pitcher, when asked how to pitch to the slugger, answered, "When you pitch to Delahanty, you just want to shut your eyes, say a prayer, and chuck the ball. The Lord only knows what'll happen after that."

Delahanty continued to produce for Philadelphia in 1901, but with the Phillies slipping in the pennant race, and the money offered by the American League proving no illusion, the blandishments of the new league seemed appealing. In August, he met with manager Jimmy Manning of the American League Washington Senators. Perhaps in retaliation for Colonel Rogers's suit against Lajoie, the American League had targeted the Phillies. By year's end, Al Orth, Elmer Flick, Jack Townsend, Harry Wolverton, and several others would jump. So, too, Delahanty, who signed with Washington for two years at $4,000 per year, and then helped Griffith and McGraw recruit others to the new league.

Delahanty did not disappoint. In 1902, he hit .376 with 10 home runs and 93 RBIs. Playing on a weak Washington team that finished 22 games out of first place, he still managed to lead the league in on-base percentage and slugging percentage. He lost the American League batting title by only two percentage points to his former teammate Lajoie. And because of the decision of the Pennsylvania courts, Delahanty, like Lajoie, could not play in Philadelphia.

Even before the season ended, rumors circulated that Delahanty's services would be available to the highest bidder for 1903, even though he had already signed a contract with the Senators for that year. During the fall, Big Ed could be found at the racetracks in New York, where he regularly lost money and then requested, and received, advances on the following year's salary from the Senators. Sporting papers reported that Delahanty had received several offers, but the star outfielder continued to deny any intention of deserting Washington.

On more than one occasion that fall, Delahanty ran into another horse player at the racetracks in New York and Washington. John McGraw knew the ponies almost as well as he knew what motivated ballplayers, and the prospect of adding the Senators star to his Giants outfield seemed like an excellent bet. McGraw apparently gave Delahanty a $3,000 advance and signed him to a contract reported at $6,000 per year. According to the deal, Big Ed would get the money whether he played or not. "I have no reason to fear the American League," McGraw said.

At the conference, Killilea also denounced the way McGraw had persuaded shortstop George Davis to abandon the White Sox to return to the National League Giants, the team from which he had jumped in 1901. A steady .300 hitter, Davis also showed power and speed. In his best Giants season in 1897, he hit .353, smacked 10 home runs, drove in 136 runs, and stole 65 bases. He had less success, however, as a manager than as a player. After the Giants went 52–81 in 1901, Davis and the team were ready to go their own ways. The star shortstop jumped to the White Sox for a two-year contract at $4,000 per year. Davis had John Montgomery Ward, the former player and organizer who had challenged the National League in 1890 when he organized the Brotherhood of Professional Ball Players, examine the contract, and Ward told him that it was legally binding to both parties. Davis had a good year for the White Sox in 1902, but that fall McGraw came calling. He told Davis that the reserve clause in his old Giants contract still applied and he offered the player an advance of $2,700 on a $6,300 salary. Davis accepted McGraw's word over Ward's judgment, and he took the money and jumped back to the Giants.

Killilea's tirade against Delahanty and Davis did not go unanswered by the National League delegates. After all, their teams were the ones that had initially been decimated by the American League raiders. Even the Pirates, previously untouched, had recently lost two of their star pitchers: Jack Chesbro (who had won 28 games in 1902) and Jesse Tannehill (who had won 20). Accusing the American League owners of hypocrisy and unsportsmanlike conduct, the National League delegates threatened to walk out. At this juncture, Garry Herrmann asked for calm. Saying he had to attend a social function, he called for everyone to get a good night's sleep and return in the morning to consider the "vexatious problem" of disputed player contracts.

PEACE DELEGATES AT HERRMANN'S DINNER PARTY.

HART. PULLIAM. KILLILEA. SOMERS. JOHNSON. HERRMANN. DREYFUSS. COMISKEY. ROBINSON.

Saturday's session started no better. Ban Johnson denounced Delahanty for his actions and sought to have the player banned from baseball. Nearly all the other American League delegates agreed. Charles Comiskey, however, opposed such a move, saying that contract jumping was not so much the fault of players as of the ruthless "men of influence" who connived and cajoled. He had in mind McGraw and Giants owner John Brush, whose handiwork was evident in luring players back to the National League. In opposing the blacklist of Delahanty, Comiskey also had his own interests at stake. If Big Ed was thrown out, George Davis would not be far behind. Johnson came around to his friend Comiskey's point of view. "The magnate who makes a contract jumper," he concluded, "is just as culpable as the player." In the end, the delegates compromised and agreed to consider each player on a case-by-case basis. One writer reported that "both sides sensibly concluded that a few players were not worth fighting for, and in case of a continuation of the war neither claimant would have a certainty of securing the man who had signed two contracts."

Still, it would take one owner to go first and display an un-selfish attitude in order for the player problem to be settled. That owner was Garry Herrmann. "I am here for peace," he said, "not because it is to the advantage of the Cincinnati Club from a fi-nancial standpoint, but because the people's pastime should be placed on a higher plane." With that, he relinquished any claim to Sam Crawford, the young Cincinnati lefty who, in 1901, hit 16 home runs and drove in 104 runs, but who had signed contracts with Detroit and Cincinnati for 1903. Barney Dreyfuss then of-fered to give up Jimmy Sebring, whom Detroit also claimed, but while Johnson applauded the spirit of compromise, he displayed his own magnanimity in ruling that Sebring belonged to the Pi-rates. As a result of that ruling, Sebring would make history in the first World Series.

One by one, the delegates settled the cases of the fifteen play-ers who were in dispute. A scorecard would show that American League teams were awarded eight players and National League clubs seven, but the numbers were deceptive. Some of the best players of the day, future Hall of Famers Delahanty, Davis, Craw-ford, and Willie Keeler, ended up in the American League, along with solid stars such as Kid Elberfeld and Bill Donovan. Others, such as Lajoie, were not considered in doubt by the conference and therefore remained where they were. Wid Conroy and Doc White rounded out the eight players awarded to the American League. The National League retained only two outright stars: Christy Mathewson, a remarkable talent, and Pirate Tommy Leach, considered by some "the greatest third baseman in the country." Vic Willis, Harry Smith, Frank Bowerman, Jack Warner, and Rudy Hulswitt comprised the rest.

That evening, the delegates issued a document outlining the terms of the peace treaty and then adjourned. "The major league child has been born," announced the *Sporting News*, "and it's twins." Commentators quickly declared the American League the victors and thought there "would be h—ll to pay in the National." The junior circuit "won more than they started out to win," because they not only obtained "equal rights and two major leagues," but also "have a stronger circuit than the National." The Brooklyn Superbas, who lost Donovan and Keeler, were proclaimed dead. And John T. Brush, who before the meeting had announced that no agreement would be considered in which his Giants did not get Delahanty, discovered that "his once aristocratic power in the league has dwindled down to nil." All the National League got, observers sneered, was "Peace and Leach."

National League owners called for a meeting to be held in Cincinnati on January 20 to ratify the agreement. Brush was not yet ready to surrender, however. He got a temporary court injunction restraining Pulliam from ratifying the work of the peace delegates. His actions divided the National League between the East and the West, and there was even talk of the western franchises in Pittsburgh, Chicago, St. Louis, and Cincinnati jumping to the American League. Brush arrived in Cincinnati, according to one correspondent, prepared "to shoot the tail feathers out of the dove of peace." But after a day of discussion, in which it became clear that if he persisted with his injunction he would go bankrupt, Brush dropped his suit. "You may make me eat that agreement," he said, "but you can't make me say that I like it." One reporter speculated that Brush "swallowed his bitter defeat" and retreated, in all likelihood, to plan his revenge. When the National League adjourned with an agreement on January 22, the owners gathered together in the late afternoon and sang "In the Good Old Summer Time." Saying he had to catch a train, Brush did not participate in the festivities.

With peace finally in place, thoughts over the next few weeks turned to the schedule for the upcoming season and whether there would be any interleague games to decide "the world's championship." To the owners, it was natural to discuss such a possibility. Most of them remembered, and some of them had played in, the postseason events of 1884–1890 between the National League and its competitor at the time, the American Association. Those contests were desultory affairs, played at different locations and with differing numbers of games, and according to rules that predated the modern game (a pitching distance of 50 feet, the shape of home plate a twelve-inch square, various ball and strike rules). One aspect only from those games carried over into the twentieth century: the idea that the event constituted a "World's Championship Series."

No one doubted that a postseason series between the National League and American League pennant winners would prove hugely successful. Owners and players only had to look back to October 1902, when the champion Pittsburgh Pirates faced a group of American League all-stars in four exhibition games to be held in Pittsburgh and Cleveland. The American League team featured Cy Young, Addie Joss, Harry Davis, Monte Cross, Bobby Wallace, Fielder Jones, and Topsy Hartsel. Nap Lajoie would play only in the games held in Cleveland because he still faced an injunction in Pennsylvania. In the first game, Sam Leever outpitched Cy Young, who relinquished a leadoff triple to Ginger Beaumont, followed by a base hit from Fred Clarke. The Pirates won 4–3; Leever had taken a shutout into the ninth inning. In the second game, Deacon Phillippe dazzled everyone by shutting out the American League all-stars 2–0. The scene shifted to Cleveland, and Sam Leever battled Bill Bernhard through eleven scoreless innings before the game was called because of darkness. In the fourth and final contest, Cy Young got the best of Deacon Phillippe and narrowly defeated the champion Pirates in a 1–0 game. Crowds of four and five thousand fans thrilled over the series, which seemed to show that Pittsburgh "outclassed the Americans." But observers pointed out that the all-stars were a picked group that did not play together and therefore were "deficient in the team play so necessary to stand off a well-drilled organization." The financially successful series highlighted the "regret that the National and American champions did not come together" and built enthusiasm for a series in which the pennant winners would face off against each other.

Peace between the leagues altered the landscape of possibility. As players prepared for the opening of the 1903 season, owners discussed a suggestion made by Garry Herrmann for a round-robin series of interleague games in which every team from each league would play six games against one another for a total of forty-eight games divided between the spring and fall. The team with the highest winning percentage would be crowned the national champion. While the plan excited interest because interleague competition would be a boon at the box office, several owners opposed it because they thought games played in the spring would reveal the weaknesses of some franchises and have the effect of lessening fan interest in their home team. Herrmann's plan, while admired, was quietly dropped by the schedule makers as too radical.

Other ideas began to circulate. One reporter thought that the owners could arrange a series between the first-place finishers in each league for "the championship of the world." Given the uncertainty of the new peace and the resentments left over from years of war, the possibility of such a series, as of January 1903, seemed remote. For now, fans rejoiced that "a new era in the history of professional base ball" was about to begin.

GAME THREE, SATURDAY, OCTOBER 3

FANS WHO PURCHASED THE *BOSTON GLOBE* on Saturday morning, October 3, were treated to an editorial that praised them for their good behavior and "love of the sport for its own sake." The editors marveled at the public's devotion to baseball and proclaimed that the series "cannot but be regarded as marking the epoch of the highest development of America's national game." By late afternoon, they undoubtedly wished that they could have retracted their opinion.

Excited by the two games played so far, and stimulated by the balmy weather, not to mention the extra money in their pockets from a Friday payday, fans turned out by the thousands for the Saturday afternoon contest. By 11:00, hundreds of people stood outside waiting for the gates to open. Hour after hour, packed streetcars unloaded fans at the park. The single long lane that led to the ticket office was clogged with fans inching forward, eager to buy tickets for the third game in Boston before the series shifted to Pittsburgh for four games. The ticket sellers had no time to place the dollars and coins in the box, so they simply threw the money to the floor. Later, once the game started, there would be time to gather it.

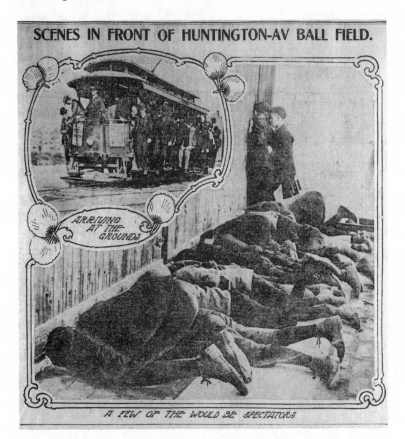

SCENES IN FRONT OF HUNTINGTON-AV BALL FIELD.

ARRIVING AT THE GROUNDS

A FEW OF THE WOULD BE SPECTATORS

At noon, the gates opened, and a "surging, struggling mass" rushed into the park. By 1:15, all the seats had been sold and the area behind the outfield ropes continued to swell with people who jostled for position. At 2:00, fans covered the outfield, occupied the terrace, climbed the fences, even found their way to the roof. Ticket speculators made a fortune, offering general admission bleacher tickets for $1–$2 and reserved grandstand seats for as high as $10. Even the peanut vendors and scorecard boys made out by selling buckets and boxes for people to stand on for $1

Fans gaining "fence admission" to the third game of the World Series

MCGREEVEY COLLECTION, BOSTON PUBLIC LIBRARY

apiece. The ticket office closed, and the speculators ran out of seats. Yet people were still arriving. Some 3,000 fans clustered outside the Huntington Avenue Grounds and clamored for admission. Once the game started, those in the bleachers called out to those in the street, reporting what was happening on the field.

The official attendance was put at 18,801, but that figure was low. Probably between 20,000 and 25,000 people jammed themselves into the park. The situation seemed unstable. Anticipating a larger Saturday crowd, Boston's business manager had arranged for 50 policemen, up from the 35 at the previous game. But as many as 150 officers would have had trouble containing this gathering. As the crowd swelled, it vibrated back and forth in waves. Fans stood ten deep in the outfield. Suddenly, at a little after 2:00, a few men slid past the ropes in center field. Others started to press toward the field from the third-base bleachers. Within seconds, a stampede began. Thousands broke through the ropes and covered the entire field. They "tore across the diamond . . . drove the two teams from their benches, swept restlessly around and around the entire lot, and they determined to get as close to the play as possible." "A surging, struggling, frantic crowd," reported the *Boston Post*, "a sea of faces, a perspiring mass of humanity that fringed the fences, packed and jammed the stands, encircled the diamond and fought both police and players."

The scene on the field prior to Game Three
MCGREEVEY COLLECTION, BOSTON PUBLIC LIBRARY

The scene was unfathomable. In their desire to get closer to the action, the exuberant fans, described as "good natured," threatened the game, the players, and their own physical welfare. The police, aided by several players, struggled to prevent the mob from invading the reserved grandstand section. Two women, caught in the crush, were rescued by Chick Stahl and several policemen. The fans packed the field, and the police began trying to move them from the infield. Time and again the police would charge, with their clubs drawn, only to discover that the crowd would rush back to fill each area shortly after it was cleared. Boston's business manager raced into the dressing room and returned with an armful of bats for the police, who used them against the shins and skulls of unruly fans. The victims grabbed themselves as if poked with a "white, hot brand." Some fans saw "stars which no astronomer has yet mapped."

The police could not restore order and clear the diamond. The game would have to be postponed, or worse, forfeited to the Pirates. At 2:45, a hundred additional officers rushed to the grounds, although the mounted unit the police had requested never arrived. One policeman, who weighed nearly three hundred pounds, had a "unique method of pushing back the crowd." He would "throw his arms in the air and then run like a mad bull into the midst of the encroachers. His efforts had great effect." A patrolman brought out a long length of rubber hose and, with four men on each side, the police used it as a battering ram to force the crowd back. With a concerted push, they cleared the diamond. Then they moved to the outfield where "inch by inch the swaying mass fell back. . . . Forty feet was gained in 20 minutes." At the same time, "the members of both nines, anxious to get together in the decisive battle of the local series, were using their bats in much the same manner as the police did the hose."

The best the police could do was to move the crowd about fifty yards behind the diamond. Along the baselines on first and third, the crowd was packed to within fifteen feet of the playing field. Behind the catcher, a space of about thirty feet was cleared, and men lined up ten deep in front of the backstop. The players were closed off from their benches and sat on the grass to the side of the catcher. The fans who crowded in front of the stands would be dangerously close to the action, but the patrolmen decided to leave them there, "knowing that a few foul balls would clear this part of the field better than the most strenuous suasion."

The Pirates came out to warm up. Second base was missing. Fred Clarke threw his cap down as a substitute, much to the

POLICE CLEARING THE DIAMOND.

RUBBER HOSE MADE TO DO SERVICE AS A ROPE.

amusement of the crowd. Finally, a "230 pound policeman gained fame by rescuing [the bag which] had been stolen by a 57-pound newsboy." After a few hit balls, the fans again drifted onto the field. The bell rang for Boston's turn, and the Pirates finished their warm-up having handled fewer than twenty chances. Screaming and waving his arms, Jimmy Collins urged the crowd to give the home team more room. A little after 3:00 p.m., Collins, Clarke, and umpire Connolly met to discuss ground rules. Connolly once remarked that "the constant woes of an umpire's life are the height of a pitch, rain, and darkness." He neglected to mention the fans. The group decided that balls hit into the outfield crowd, which stood only about 150 feet beyond the base paths, would count for doubles.

Remarkably, the game began only fifteen minutes late. Boston sent the young righty "Long" Tom Hughes to the mound. The six-foot-one Hughes was coming off his best year, in which he

NEVER BEFORE WAS SUCH A VAST CROWD SEEN AT A
BALL GAME IN BOSTON AS AT YESTERDAY'S CONTEST.

had won 20 games and lost only 7. Hughes hailed from Chicago and broke in with the National League Cubs in 1900, but he signed with the American League in 1902. He was a control pitcher who used a change of pace to fool the hitters.

To start the game, Hughes disposed of Beaumont, Clarke, and Leach on three groundouts, two of them snappy plays made by Collins at third. So far, the Americans seemed untroubled by the fans, who loomed closer to the action than ever before.

The Pirates brought back Deacon Phillippe on only one day's rest. They had no choice. Lefty Ed Doheny had deserted the team at the end of September, and while Clarke hoped to have him available for the games in Pittsburgh, he still had not returned. And thirty-five-year-old "Roaring" Bill Kennedy was nursing an injured hip. So Phillippe took to the slab in an attempt to repeat his outstanding work of two days earlier, while Boston came to bat "confident that history would not repeat itself." But Boston, like Pittsburgh, went down in order in the first on two ground-outs and a fly ball.

In the second, Wagner led off and grounded to Ferris. That brought the Worcester, Massachusetts, native William "Kitty" Bransfield to the plate. Bransfield's father had lost his leg at the Battle of Gettysburg, and Kitty grew up working in a metal factory. He got his nickname as a child when his friends, looking at the *Police Gazette*, decided that William looked just like Billy the Kid. They started calling him "the kid," which was eventually corrupted to "Kitty" through the accent of a German woman who worked at the candy store frequented by the boys.

Playing in front of family and friends, Bransfield had so far managed only one hit in seven at-bats. Hughes delivered, and Bransfield smashed a hard ground ball to Collins, who, "with his wonderful stops and lightning throws to first, shortened the career of many an ambitious base runner." Two outs. Ritchey came to bat and lifted a ball into the crowd in center field, a ground-rule double. The ball fell only a few yards from the outfielders. The fans groaned, perhaps in self-reproach, because Dougherty or Stahl would have caught the ball easily had the crowd not shrunk the dimensions of the field. Sebring walked, and Phelps hit the ball into the left-field crowd for another double, scoring Ritchey. Phillippe grounded out, but his team now held a one-run lead.

In the bottom of the second, LaChance mustered a two-out double, but was left stranded. Many thought that had the fans been back where they were the previous two days, LaChance's shot would have gone for at least a triple, if not an inside-the-park home run.

In the top of the third, Hughes started to come undone. Boston's number-three hurler walked Beaumont on four consecutive pitches to begin the inning. Clarke then doubled into the crowd in left. Leach quickly singled, scoring Beaumont. Wagner was due up, with runners on first and third, and nobody out. The score stood 2–0, and Collins had seen enough. He started arguing with the umpire in a ploy to buy some time for a relief pitcher to warm up. As the argument concluded, the crowd that was jammed against the grandstand "trembled, then parted with a loud sound." Out walked a large man with tawny hair. The fans recognized him at once. "In a second every one of that gang of 25,000 was swinging hats wildly and yelling 'Cy! Cy!' and it was he, Young was rushing to the rescue."

Collins needed the extra time because, while Hughes was getting into trouble, Young had been sitting in the club's office, still in street clothes, helping to count the day's take. Hughes would not appear again in the series. Indeed, Collins kept *him* in street clothes and said he would use Norwood Gibson as a substitute if he had to. The *Globe* reported that "Hughes had the chance of his life to make good, but lost his opportunity in Boston being too sporty," a reference to Hughes's gambling and Collins's suspicion, perhaps, that the pitcher's performance was not on the level.

When play resumed, Wagner stepped in. Young's first effort was a wild pitch that put Leach on second, but did not roll far enough away to allow Clarke to score from third. Wagner fell behind in the count with two strikes. Young then came with a hard curve ball that failed to break early enough and drilled the superstar in his left shoulder. Wagner's face "crinkle[d] like an old ash-dump boot," and he stormed around for a few moments.

"Hully gee," yelled a young man, "but Wagner must be hard as nails to take such a swat as that." Another cupped his hands together and screamed "Kill 'em, Cy, that's the only way they can be done up today." The shortstop said his arm went to sleep. If so, remarked one writer, "it was the only part of Hans that did any sleeping during the remainder of the game." Young stood motionless. He retrieved the ball, rubbed it in his glove, glared at first, and "began swaying like a Sioux squaw in a death dance, for another delivery."

Bases loaded, no one out. Young induced the struggling Bransfield to foul out to first. Ritchey hit a hard shot to third, which Collins handled and threw to Criger to force Clarke at home. The bases were still loaded, but now two were out. It looked as if Young would escape from the jam. Sebring had two strikes on him when he hit a swift, skipping shot to Parent. The shortstop partially stopped the ball. Leach scored, but Wagner got caught rounding third and was tagged out by the catcher in a rundown. The Pirates had jumped ahead 3–0. And Phillippe seemed to be gaining strength. He retired Criger, Young, and Dougherty in order in the bottom of the third, the last two on strikeouts.

In the fourth, Phelps led off and hit an otherwise catchable ball that went for a double into the center-field crowd. Phillippe grounded back to Young, who caught Phelps trying to go to third. Beaumont popped to center and Clarke hit into a fielder's choice. Young looked sharp, and there was every reason to believe he would hold the Pirates to three runs. But would the Boston bats come alive?

As the players changed sides, the police managed to move the outfield crowd back another thirty feet. The Boston partisans couldn't help thinking that had the police done so in Pittsburgh's second or third time up, "a different tale would possibly have been told." Collins led off the fourth inning with a single up the middle. Phillippe then walked Stahl. The crowd came alive, tooting horns and screaming encouragement.

That brought Buck Freeman to the plate. Standing only five feet nine inches and weighing about 160 pounds, Freeman could wallop the ball. In 1899, when he set the single-season record with 25 home runs, he also had 25 triples. Freeman had hit the ball well the first two games, and the gamblers who gathered in the pavilion area loved betting on the right fielder. With each at-bat, hundreds of dollars at even money were wagered on whether he would get on base. But this time Freeman hit a bouncing ball back to Phillippe, who threw to first for the out.

The groundout did not win Freeman's backers any money, but it did advance Collins and Stahl into scoring position with only one out. Parent flied out to Sebring in right, and Collins prepared to tag up. Leach was well known around baseball for distracting the umpire by yelling "Watch his feet," and then giving a little tug on the runner's belt to slow him down. In fact, a few years later, Del Howard, wise to Leach's tricks, would unbuckle his belt while standing at third and leave Leach holding it in his hands as he ran home. Collins encountered no difficulty, however, with his counterpart at third, and scored Boston's first run. LaChance walked, and almost got picked off when catcher Ed Phelps threw down to first, but Bransfield dropped the ball. Ferris struck out to end the inning.

Boston had broken through to make the score 3–1, but was unable to build any momentum as Young and Phillippe settled into a pitcher's duel. The fifth, sixth, and seventh innings went quickly, with each side retired in order. When Phillippe came to bat in the seventh, the fans applauded him. Again he had been masterful, relinquishing only two hits to that point.

In the top of the eighth, Leach flied out to Freeman. Wagner followed with a double into the right-field ropes. Bransfield then bunted, Young misplayed the ball, and the runners were safe at first and third. Ritchey smashed a shot to third, the only one of the game that was too quick for Collins to handle, and Wagner scored to put the Pirates ahead 4–1. A clear error by Young, and a debatable one by Collins, had cost Boston a run. Sebring flied out to Dougherty in left, and Ritchey tried to advance to third after the catch. But Collins made a one-handed scoop of Dougherty's throw and simultaneously tagged Ritchey to end the inning.

Young had also pitched brilliantly, erasing any questions that lingered from the first game, and the fans cheered as he led off the bottom of the eighth. The pitcher smashed the ball fifteen feet to Phillippe's left. Second baseman Ritchey had no chance to get to the ball, and it looked as if the hit would stick for a leadoff single. But Wagner got to it from his shortstop position "on the dead run with one hand after making a 30-foot dive for it, and after nailing it threw Young out with his left hand," his glove hand. It was an impossible play, an unimaginable play, but it had just happened. "The crowd went wild," reported M'Quiston. "For half a minute the grandstand was a sea of hats and the roar was awful. Thousands in the outfield forgot religion, home, and the policeman's clubs and jumping to their feet cheered wildly, almost insanely." Wagner stood at short, modestly dusting off his pants.

The gloves of the era helped make Wagner's play possible. They had no pocket and only minimal stitching to separate the thumb from the fingers. Tommy Leach recalled that "we used to catch the ball with our hands, in the fingers." To add even greater control, Wagner would cut out the leather from the palm of the glove. Eventually, pockets, webs, and lacing would transform the ways in which gloves were utilized. But players in 1903 relied more on their hands than their gloves to field the ball.

Dougherty struck out, and with two outs in the eighth, Collins doubled. Stahl singled to make the score 4–2, but Freeman again cost his supporters in the stands by grounding into a force play that ended the brief uprising. If the Americans did not realize before Wagner's acrobatic play that the day was not to be, they did now.

In the ninth, after Pittsburgh went down in order, few thought a rally against Phillippe, who had kept the ball down in the strike zone all afternoon, was possible. And it wasn't. Parent popped up to second. LaChance grounded to Wagner. Ferris struck out, but won a momentary reprieve when Phelps dropped the ball. An instant later, with the throw to first, his at-bat, as well as the game, came to an end.

No one had left the grounds before the final out. Whereas, prior to the game, some fans on the field had tried to climb into the stands, now those in the stands emptied onto the field. For ten minutes, "it was impossible to see one bare inch of turf." As the fans shuffled away from the grounds, "gloom and silence" marked their demeanor. They admitted that the "Pittsburg aggregation is almost in a class by itself," and conceded that "Boston's chances for the championship look very dim indeed."

If the commotion prior to the game had turned the contest into a battle of nerves, then Phillippe demonstrated that he could not be shaken. Twice a hit would have led to runs for Boston, and twice the Deacon "showed his ability, once by a strike-out and the second time by compelling the batsman to hit a grounder to the infield." He was pitching from inside "a great ring of humanity, 40 deep, sitting, standing or lying around the entire field within 200 feet of the bases, yet in nine full innings he allowed only two balls to be hit into the crowd." Hughes, by contrast, became rattled when he saw "those dumpy, illegal hits" fall no farther than ten feet from his outfielders. The Pirates also "backed up their pitcher at every point, and time and again cut off seeming base hits by apparently impossible plays." Wagner alone "was everywhere and anywhere [and] three of his stops were labeled sure base hits." Pittsburgh had spent the afternoon "outbatting, outfielding, and, yes, 'outnerving'" their opponents.

Some would say "outlucking" them as well. "Luck is Quite a Factor," claimed a headline in the *Boston Globe.* "Luck, that inscrutable dogma of the fatalists, was romping" with the Pirates all day long. The problem was the ground rule established prior to the game. "Right here," reporters noted, "was where Boston lost the game before ever it was started." Of four Pirate base hits in the first three innings, doubles into the crowd by Ritchey, Phelps, and Clarke would have been easy outs. The two runs resulting from these hits, went one analysis, was the margin of the loss. A third run as well, scored in the eighth, came off yet another "fungoe," a lazy fly ball hit by Wagner just beyond the outfielder. And LaChance's shot in the bottom of the second "would have been a clean home run" rather than a ground-rule double. "With a clear field," thought one writer, "the final score would have been three to one in favor of Boston." Difficult as it was to admit, the fans' behavior prior to the game had to be viewed as "the main cause of the local team's defeat."

There were "plenty of excuses and ifs to offer" for the results of the game. If only Young had started, many thought Boston would have won. If only the Boston bats had broken through in the fourth and the eighth innings, they might have emerged victorious. If Young and Collins had not made those errors in the eighth, the Pirates would have had one less run. If only the crowd had been a few feet farther back. It was a game of feet. "Baseball is full of uncertainties," reasoned one writer.

Some chose to read uncertainty and luck as corruption. Rumors spread around town afterward that the Americans had intentionally thrown at least one of the two games they had lost, that the games were "not on the level." Because they would share in the gate receipts, the Boston players had a financial stake in extending the series and drawing large crowds in Pittsburgh. The errors in the first inning of the first game had seemed suspicious. In the third game, Hughes had pitched poorly, though to be fair, he was victimized by the ground rules. To refute the rumors, the newspapers insisted that "all three games have been for blood," and anyone who thought otherwise had not been watching.

Although disheartened by the loss, Boston fans soon regained their confidence. The teams seemed evenly matched, that much was clear. And Collins's boys had a history of doing well on the road. It would be hard for the Pirates, given their pitching, to win three straight and take the series before returning to Boston. A victory in Pittsburgh on Monday would even out matters. If it was true that luck "seldom breaks even but will follow one club for a while and then flirt with the next-door neighbor ready to change its abode at any moment," then maybe the change of scenery would bring the Americans some good fortune of their own. In the morning, fans read that, during the game, a small fire was blazing beneath the third-base bleachers but two fans, looking for a better view of the game, discovered and extinguished it. Sometimes luck strikes and, at the time, you don't even know it.

The train to Pittsburgh was scheduled to leave South Station at 10:15 Sunday morning. More than one hundred Boston fans had already purchased tickets for the trip. Reflecting on Saturday's events, one observer sighed and marveled at "the wonderful hold baseball has on the American public."

THE THIRD GAME

PITTSBURG.	AB.	R.	B.	P.	A.	E.		BOSTON.	AB.	R.	B.	P.	A.	E
Beaumont, cf.....	4	1	0	1	0	0		Dougherty, lf.....	4	0	0	1	1	0
Clarke, lf.........	4	0	1	0	0	0		Collins, 3b........	4	2	2	2	6	1
Leach, 3b.........	4	1	1	0	1	0		Stahl cf..........	3	0	1	2	0	0
Wagner, ss	3	1	1	0	7	0		Freeman, rf	3	0	0	1	0	0
Bransfield, 1b.....	3	0	0	15	0	0		Parent, ss	4	0	0	0	7	0
Ritchey, 2b.......	4	1	1	2	2	0		LaChance, 1b.....	4	0	1	15	0	0
Sebring, rf........	3	0	1	4	0	0		Ferris, 2b.........	4	0	0	2	2	0
Phelps, c	4	0	2	5	1	0		Criger, c..........	3	0	0	4	1	0
Phillippe, p.......	4	0	0	0	4	0		Hughes, p	0	0	0	0	0	0
								Young, p	3	0	0	0	2	0
Total	33	4	7	27	15	0		Total...........	32	2	4	27	19	2

Pittsburg.......	0	1	2	0	0	0	0	1	0—	4
Boston..................	0	0	0	1	0	0	0	1	0—	2

Earned run—Boston. Two-base hits—Collins, LaChance, Clarke, Ritchey, Wagner, Phelps 2. Stolen base—Leach. Double play—Dougherty, Collins. First on balls—Off Hughes 2, Phillippe 3. Hit by pitcher—By Young 1. Struck out—By Phillippe 5, Young 2. Passed ball—Criger. Time—1.50. Umpires—O'Day and Connolly. Attendance—18,801.

FANS REJOICED when news of baseball peace made headlines in January 1903, and they began to warm themselves with thoughts of late afternoons at the ballpark. The schedule makers announced a 140-game circuit that would run from mid-April to the end of September. In locales with one team from each league, the possibility of preseason interleague contests that would lead to city bragging rights generated additional excitement. But before any games could be played, the terms of the peace agreement had to be implemented.

Through the winter, baseball leaders faced multiple controversies, any one of which might have threatened the tenuous pact. An immediate problem to be dealt with was the refusal of several players who had been awarded back to their original teams to return the advance money they had received from other owners. Some players complied quickly and readily. Sam Crawford, for example, awarded to Detroit, returned $300 to Cincinnati. But Ed Delahanty and George Davis, who tried to jump from the American League to the National when McGraw's Giants came calling, but were assigned back to Washington and Chicago respectively, remained obstinate. One reason was the amount of money each owed. Delahanty had received nearly $4,500, the same figure as his Washington salary, and he had already taken an advance on it. To return the money to the Giants would leave him playing the season at a loss. Davis owed $2,775 and believed that the contract he had signed with the Giants guaranteed his salary.

But there was another reason behind the players' recalcitrance. "There is a well-founded suspicion that John T. Brush is responsible for the rebellious spirit shown by Delahanty and Davis," reported the *Sporting News*. Although he signed the peace agreement, Brush was still looking for ways to subvert it. He encouraged the players to initiate legal proceedings to prove the validity of the contracts with New York, though journalists pointed out that even if the courts ruled in favor of the Giants, the result would be that the team would win the right to pay salaries to two men who would never be permitted to play for them. Already owners such as Garry Herrmann of the Reds and James Hart of the Cubs had proclaimed that if Delahanty and Davis were on the Giants roster, their teams would not play any games against them. It looked as if the new arrangement in baseball was coming undone.

The league presidents reacted by placing Delahanty and Davis on the ineligible list until they settled their debts. In March, George Davis appeared at Giants spring training in Savannah. Ban Johnson and Harry Pulliam were outraged. Johnson declared that the peace treaty "is ironclad and will govern professional baseball in this country." And Pulliam observed that the National League, in ratifying the peace conference, showed its "desire to restore order in base ball instead of anarchy, and to put this professional sport on a clean, sportsmanlike and honorable basis and save organized base ball from impending ruin." Delahanty and Davis would play for Washington and Chicago in the American League, or they would not play at all.

Facing no salary for the coming season, Delahanty finally reported to Washington on March 24, with spring training well under way. Tom Loftus, the manager, refused to let him take the field unless the money he owed the Giants was repaid. But Delahanty was broke, having squandered his advances and more on the ponies. Finally, he made a deal whereby the club would reimburse the money on his behalf, but it would be deducted from Delahanty's salary over two seasons.

Davis, however, refused to give in. He continued informally to work out with the Giants, and, although he was banned from playing in games, he received half of his salary from Brush in agreement for not playing anywhere else. George Davis, remarked a reporter, "wanders sadly about the New York grounds every day like a soul lost in the suburbs of paradise."

The American League faced an even more formidable problem than the fate of two players who did not want to play. It had to make good on the claim that it had a location and a stadium for its new franchise in New York. If it failed, it would abrogate the peace agreement which stipulated two eight-club leagues, with New York as one of the American League cities. Ban Johnson's initial attempts to secure grounds were thwarted by the behind-the-scenes political machinations of Brush, McGraw, and the Giants' former majority owner Andrew Freedman. Freedman wielded power with Tammany Hall and the capitalist leaders of New York. When he had controlled the Giants, he was despised by both fans and players for his autocratic ways. He changed managers twelve times in eight years and refused to reimburse a star pitcher, Amos Rusie, for unwarranted fines levied in 1895, leading Rusie, who won at least 30 games a year between 1891 and 1894, to sit out the entire 1896 season.

Freedman was more than happy to help his partner Brush keep competition out of New York. The multimillionaire took leases on much of the vacant property in the city. When Johnson found property on Lenox Avenue between 142nd and 144th streets the city denied permission to close 143rd Street. Freedman also intervened with the financier August Belmont to keep the newly formed subway corporation from leasing property to the team. McGraw cackled with delight: "I have gone from one end of Manhattan Island to the other and feel prepared to say that there is no place where the American league can locate a ball ground."

McGraw's canvas took him from the Battery up to the Polo Grounds, and as far as the viaduct at 155th Street. There was no room for a ballpark. North of where he stopped rose Washington Heights, a terrain so craggy that there was no reason, he believed, to continue his survey any farther.

Though disappointed by the loss of the Lenox Avenue site, Johnson persevered. He found an appealing location in the Bronx, the old Astor estate at 161st Street and Jerome Avenue, but he thought it imperative that the American League make its base in Manhattan. Twenty years later, the Bronx site would become the home of Yankee Stadium. Johnson instead took out a ten-year lease on property owned by the New York Institute for the Blind. It was located between 165th and 168th streets from Eleventh Avenue to Fort Washington Road in the Washington Heights section of Manhattan. In his journey across the city, McGraw had not wandered far enough north.

But New York's National League interests were not ready to surrender and they made one last attempt to derail proceedings. A petition was submitted to the Board of Improvements that called for cutting across 166th and 167th streets, and claiming that if the ballpark was approved, Washington Heights would fall victim to rowdyism, saloons, and depreciated property values. The American League responded with a petition of its own from 120 business leaders in the neighborhood who favored the park. The board went into executive session. When the members emerged, they announced the vote: the motion to open the streets by cutting across the property was defeated 3–2.

The American League had invaded Gotham. National League owners who had privately bet against the American League paid off their debts. Charles Comiskey of the White Sox won three suits of clothes from Charles Ebbetts of the Brooklyn Superbas.

And Barney Dreyfuss, Pittsburgh's president and inveterate gambler, reportedly "lost big money betting that the American [League] would not locate on Manhattan Island."

But while the league had grounds, it had no ballpark. It was mid-March before all the details were finalized, and the home opener for the as yet unnamed American League team was scheduled for April 30. Clearing the land and constructing the stands in six weeks seemed inconceivable to those who visited the site, a "Herculean task," they said. One reporter described it as "a plot of hilly ground, dotted by large and small boulders and trees, many of them dead, with a pond extending along the Broadway side that will have to be filled in. Masses of rock are grouped where the grandstand is to be erected. There is not a level spot ten feet square on the whole property."

The Greater New York Base Ball Association was incorporated on Saturday, March 14. Joseph Gordon, former New York deputy superintendent of buildings, served as figurehead leader for the actual owners: poolroom, casino, and racetrack entrepreneur Frank Farrell, and the former New York City police chief William Devery. By noon on the same day, wagons appeared at the site and began to unload wheelbarrows, picks, shovels, and drills. "We will have to blast out about 5,000 cubic yards of rock before we can get the field in level shape," declared the contractor. The grounds were the largest of any ballpark in the country. It is "a field of heroic proportions," exclaimed one writer, one "where art would have a hard time vying with nature in supplying attractiveness for the eye." From the grandstand, the park promised to offer stunning views of the Hudson and the Palisades. No name had yet been given. Some referred to it merely as the "American League Park." Others called it the "Washington Oval." But, perched atop the Heights, it became Hilltop Park and, for the ten years they played there, the team was known as the Highlanders, a name that paid homage to the terrain and honored the British regiment known as the Gordon Highlanders.

It looked as if the American League would be ready to play

ball, but one last controversy emerged that threatened to violate the spirit of the peace agreement. In an attempt to unify the playing rules of the two leagues, American League owners had to vote on the adoption of the foul-strike rule. The rule made foul balls hit with fewer than two strikes count as additional strikes.

The National League first adopted the rule in 1901. In part, the owners wanted to shorten the length of the games. Counting fouls as strikes both accelerated the action and, as it turned out, reduced the offensive numbers, though the rules makers initially speculated that it might increase hitting because it would induce batters to swing at the first good pitch that was offered. Owners also wanted to take some of the discretion out of the game. Before the rule was adopted, umpires could call pitches that they deemed intentionally fouled off as strikes. Often players would protest, and games would be slowed even further. By making the foul ball a first or second strike, regardless of intention, the league made the umpire's job a bit easier and removed a spur to the rowdy behavior of players.

For two years, the National League played with the rule and the American League played without it. Owners attributed part of the popularity of the new league to the increased offense that resulted from not having any fouls count as strikes. Several American League owners steadfastly opposed the recommendation of the rules committee that Rule 44, relating to foul strikes, be adopted. Cleveland's owner, Charles Somers, threatened that if it was passed, the organization might, after a few weeks' trial, decide to go back to the old rules. And Henry Killilea, the Boston owner, predicted the rule would lapse into disuse after several weeks.

Writers agreed that "it may be a good thing to have uniform rules." "But," they added, "it does not look to be a good thing for baseball in general to perpetuate such an obnoxious rule." "Let us have more lagging, more hitting, more run getting and more base run getting rather than more strike outs," one columnist opined. "The aim of the game," another said, "should be to encourage the batsman as much as possible, not to operate against him." As to the argument that games were too long, journalists responded that "there is nothing more wearisome to the average fan than the game where batters go out in one, two, three order no matter if the score is 1–0 all the way. Twenty minutes of that kind of game is too long, while two hours of play with something happening all the time is too short." In the end, critics concluded, "no amount of eloquence can alter the fact that a foul is not a strike, any more than it is a strawberry shortcake."

The "foul-strike bugaboo" was debated back and forth. Some suggested a compromise "whereby the pitcher will be penalized to equalize matters by allowing the batter his base on three instead of four balls," but it was never considered seriously. American League owners met in March to vote on the foul-strike rule. Cleveland, Boston, and Chicago voted against it; St. Louis, Detroit, and Washington were for it. Philadelphia refused to vote, and New York was not yet officially organized as a club. It was left to Ban Johnson to cast the deciding vote in favor of the rule. He had worked too hard to achieve peace to allow non-uniform playing rules to threaten the success of the baseball enterprise. Perhaps, in 1972, when the offensive-minded American League adopted the designated hitter rule allowing a player to bat for the pitcher (a rule proposed but discarded by both leagues in 1903), it was exacting some small revenge for being forced, in 1903, to adopt the rule that made fouls count as strikes.

As players prepared to report to their clubs in March, they chatted about the changes in personnel, clubs, and rules. Most were still shocked over the death of Win Mercer, the Detroit pitcher and manager-elect, who had committed suicide in San Francisco in January. Plagued by problems with money and women, and disturbed over his brother's tuberculosis, Mercer connected a tube to a gas jet and placed it in his mouth. His death weighed heavily on players and fans alike. But as the weather warmed, so too did the spirits. By mid-March, players were on their way to spring training sites. Lest they bring themselves bad fortune, no team set off for the South on the thirteenth.

It is unclear when the annual migration of teams to warm climes for a month of workouts and practice began, but the very first issue of the *Sporting News*, published in 1886, reported on the Chicago White Stockings' trip to Hot Springs, Arkansas. Many players hailed from southern and western states and made their winter homes there. The relationship between good weather and good baseball was evident. As teams became increasingly professional and competitive, owners sought every advantage. With player contracts not beginning until the first game of the season, management needed a way to cajole the athletes into shedding their layers of winter fat and coming together as a team. The promise of several weeks in a hotel in a sunny locale did the trick.

In March 1903, every team in baseball except the Washington Senators traveled south or west to prepare for the coming season. "There is not another country on the globe," marveled one reporter, "where men travel such long journeys to take part in athletic contests or become members of athletic teams." In the National League, the Pirates headed to Hot Springs, Arkansas. The Braves, Giants, and Reds journeyed to cities in Georgia. The Phillies traveled to Richmond, the Cardinals to Dallas; and the Cubs were the envy of all the sportswriters, if not the players, for blazing a path to Los Angeles. In the American League, the Athletics headed to Jacksonville. The White Sox, Browns, and Tigers found sites in Louisiana. The Highlanders went to Atlanta, the Naps settled in Birmingham, and the Boston Americans took up residence at Mercer University in Macon, Georgia, in part because Cy Young spent part of the winter coaching the college baseball team there.

Typical of the journeys south was the one taken by the Pirates, who left Pittsburgh on March 17. The *Dispatch* called it "the greatest training trip in the world" and covered the route in detail. Most of the team had already reported to Pittsburgh, and they gathered at the station to board the Pennsylvania Southwestern Limited, scheduled to depart at 9:21 in the evening. The team had a sleeping car all to itself. Honus Wagner, Deacon Phillippe, James Sebring, Sam Leever, Ed Doheny, Tommy Leach, Claude Ritchey, Fred Veil, and even the newly signed William Kennedy were among those on hand. Ginger Beaumont would go to Hot Springs directly from Chicago. Wagner, reluctant to leave his Carnegie home until the last moment, came racing to the station late, causing the owner "the usual amount of heart disease."

About 300 fans gathered to see the team off. They shouted to Wagner, the best known and most recognizable of the group, and tried to identify the players in their civilian clothes. Some of the players brought their wives along. The day before, Fred Clarke had been called home for an emergency, but he promised to meet the team in St. Louis. Barney Dreyfuss boarded the train and handed the boys two boxes of cigars. Dreyfuss, the son of an American citizen, was born and educated in Germany and emigrated to the United States in 1881. At the age of sixteen, he found work scrubbing whiskey barrels in a distillery in Paducah, Kentucky. He took to baseball, and organized a semipro team on which he played second base. In 1888, Dreyfuss moved to Louisville along with the distillery for which he worked, and purchased stock in the Louisville club. By 1890, he was treasurer. At the end of a decade, Dreyfuss seized an opportunity to purchase the Pittsburgh club, thus placing himself in the position to move most of the Colonels players to the Pirates when the National League contracted after 1899. "Baseball is my business," he said.

Boarding the train for Hot Springs, Dreyfuss occupied berth number 13, traditionally Wagner's berth. Ballplayers are a superstitious bunch, and Wagner feared the worst. Even more troubling, his best friend on the team, second baseman Claude Ritchey, was now married. Everyone joked that Wagner moped all day and "went to bed with the chickens," while others stayed up late singing songs and playing poker.

The two-time defending National League champions arrived

in Hot Springs early in the morning on March 20. They were greeted by three bands combined into one, and a crowd estimated at 3,000. A procession accompanied the team to the hotel. This was the third year the Pirates were training in Hot Springs, and the first two had led to championship seasons. "The people," observed one correspondent, "seem to think they have a living interest in the pennant." And the upcoming season promised to be the finest of them all.

GAME FOUR, TUESDAY, OCTOBER 6

THE JUBILANT PIRATES left Boston Saturday evening, after their victory in the third game, for the twenty-three-hour train ride back home. They were a raucous, rowdy bunch. The players had a special car, all their own, attached to the Washington Express. Whether in Providence, New Haven, New York, or Philadelphia, wherever it stopped, congratulatory telegrams were brought on board. The players "made Rome howl. The double beating given Boston on her own grounds made the big athletes delirious with joy and there was but little rest for anyone on the car." They played tricks on one another, and dumped a bucket of ice on a teammate who had the audacity to go to sleep before midnight. The players were up by 6:30 for breakfast in Philadelphia, but departure for home was delayed four hours. The Pirates arrived at Union depot in Pittsburgh just after 7:00 p.m., and several thousand fans were there to greet them. The players jumped off the train to the applause and cheers of the crowd. Phillippe was not present, as management had helped him sneak off the train a station earlier so that the enthusiastic crowd would not mob him.

Some players lingered to soak up the adulation, but Wagner hurried to catch a commuter train home to Carnegie. He waved goodbye and screamed that he would see everyone at the game Monday afternoon.

Clarke, for one, was happy the long trip was over. The team had logged thousands of miles in travel since March, when they had left for spring training, and he figured that the last trip he would have to take was the one back to his home in Kansas once the series was over. "We do not expect to be compelled to return to Boston to finish the series," he said.

The Boston players traveled on Sunday morning, leaving South Station at 10:45. While more somber than the Pirates, the fans who accompanied the team to Pittsburgh certainly livened up the trip. About 125 Royal Rooters, who also referred to themselves as the "Invaders," boarded three special cars. The Boston players had their own car to themselves. Their excursion had been organized by a committee that included the team business manager, Joseph Smart, who took some blame for not having arranged for enough police at the grounds the day before, and Michael "Nuf Ced" McGreevey, the leader of the Royal Rooters.

The Rooters arrived at Pittsburgh's station with instruments, megaphones, and bright red silk badges. One newspaper called them "pilgrims on their way to Pittsburgh." The train took a western route, through Albany and Buffalo, and arrived at 9:00 on Monday morning. Players settled at the Monongahela House, the most famous hotel in town, where Lincoln had stayed on the way to his inauguration in 1861. Some fans found rooms there as well. Drenching rains had fallen during the night, and all waited to see whether the game would be postponed.

Pittsburgh in 1903 was a muscular, bellowing city of rough edges, a city whose name, for the time being, ended in "g." The city had a population of 350,000 and Allegheny County totaled over 775,000. It was a city of industry, the "smoky city" of flames and furnaces. It was a city of steel and coal and railroads, one of the centers of the industrial revolution that transformed the

United States between the Civil War and World War I. Pittsburgh was moving both upward and outward. New twenty-story buildings were popping up, and the area surrounding the city was annexed into a "greater Pittsburg." Immigrants flooded in and gathered into distinctly ethnic neighborhoods, as they did all across urban America; Germans constituted the largest group. Municipal leaders labored to develop a cultural life, and the library, the orchestra, and the theater all showed a more refined side to the metropolis. But Pittsburgh was hardly a model of harmony. The rifts between elites and workers ran deep, and the terrible labor violence of the Homestead steel strike in 1892 was but a decade removed. Lincoln Steffens, the muckraking journalist who published a series of exposés about corruption in American cities in *McClure's Magazine* in 1903, repeated James Parton's infamous remark that Pittsburgh was "hell with the lid off," a city, Steffens said, "that has tried to be free and failed."

As the Boston players journeyed from the train station to their hotel, electric lights were still burning, even though it was Monday morning. The "smoke enveloped city" was dark and soaking wet from the heavy rain. Exposition Park, where the Pirates played, stood on the north shore beside the Allegheny River close to where it joined the Ohio and Monongahela. Located near the water, across from downtown Pittsburgh, it did not dry out quickly after a downpour. The outfield looked like a frog pond and the infield a mud bath. By noon, Pittsburgh manager Fred Clarke called off the game. He was eager to do so in order to skip Bill Kennedy's turn in the rotation. Kennedy had started 15 games for the Pirates during the season, but the manager did not want to use him in the first home game if he could help it. On Tuesday, Clarke would go back to Phillippe, who would pitch for the third time in six days. Boston's Jimmy Collins could not really complain, as his players, having arrived only a few hours earlier, could also use the extra rest. In this way, the chances were that the two teams would play their best ball, and the World's Championship Series deserved nothing less.

Exposition Park

Fans who traveled from towns across western Pennsylvania were disappointed by the postponement, and many of them sought out accommodations in the city. "The importance of these games in the eyes of baseball lovers is shown by the fact that there are men here from all over the country to witness them," reported the *Gazette*. Boston's Royal Rooters spent the day rehearsing their songs and cheers, hiring a band to join in the procession to the park, and reminiscing about games and days past. One old-timer, Major J. J. McNamara, a veteran of "the war of '61," recalled a game in which he had helped save an umpire's life. Hugh Duffy had also made the trip. Duffy had played for and captained the Boston Nationals between 1892 and 1900; in 1894, he had hit an astonishing .440 and blasted 18 home runs. The former major-league outfielder, and current player-manager of Milwaukee's Western League franchise, spent part of the afternoon with his old teammate Jimmy Collins, and he predicted that the series would return to Boston. Two decades later, he would find himself the manager of the Boston Americans, who by then were known as the Red Sox.

The Royal Rooters also passed the time looking to wager on the remaining games of the series. They arrived in Pittsburgh with a bankroll large enough to burn a "wet elephant," but even though the city had a reputation as the "undisputed Monte Carlo" of baseball, they were disappointed by the action that was available. The Boston fans could not get the odds they wanted, and considered the Pittsburgh fans unfair in their unwillingness to offer them. In Boston, fans "fell over each other" to bet 10 to 8 in favor of Cy Young in the first game, and they lost a fortune. The Pittsburgh gamblers lay low in the second game, knowing that Leever's arm was not right. In the third game, again Boston fans offered odds of 2 to 1 and 5 to 3 in favor of the Americans, and again those betting on Pittsburgh made thousands. Now Boston Rooters expected the odds to go in their favor, but the Pittsburgh fans refused to offer anything other than even money. So desperate were some Rooters for action that one Boston man gave odds against his team and one Pittsburgh fan took them. The bet was $500 to $400 that Boston would lose. "Sentiment is one thing, business another," said the Royal Rooter. "I expect to have money to loan those who follow sentiment in betting."

As the evening grew late, umpires Hank O'Day and Tommy Connolly discussed whether the skies would clear. "It's going to be a fine day tomorrow," proclaimed O'Day. "I have been in this section many times and know something about the weather here."

Ten minutes later, rain pelted against the windows. "Yes," said Connolly, "you know how to guess Pittsburgh weather."

Tuesday morning dawned drizzly, but the forecast was for clearing skies. The groundskeeper said that he could have the field ready for play two hours after the rain stopped. He had covered the pitcher's mound, bases, and home plate with canvas and, in between showers on Monday, he mopped the water on the base paths. Unfortunately, the rain washed out much of the work he had done while the Pirates were in Boston: neatly cut grass, newly planted flower beds, freshly painted fences.

The day "was virtually a holiday" in Pittsburgh. By early afternoon, a procession had formed at the Monongahela House to escort the visiting players to the park. Pittsburgh fans were awed by the sight of "15 open carriages, two busses, and a score of footsoldiers [that] formed an imposing cavalcade as it moved from the hotel through the principal streets of the city to the grounds." The Royal Rooters entered the park, singing and cheering, and took their seats in Section J, directly behind the Boston bench.

The Pirates' organization had added 2,000 seats that had been rented from the circus and placed on the field in front of the grandstand for the game, but a crowd of less than 8,000 came out. The postponement may have confused some fans who did not realize that their Monday tickets were good for Tuesday's affair. And the weather did not help; rain was still falling at noon. Exposition Park, located on the north side of the Allegheny River across from

Game Four set to begin

downtown, had opened in 1882. The Pirates had first played there in 1891. Typical of the single-level wooden facilities of the era, the ballpark featured a covered grandstand that stretched from first to third base and open bleacher seats extended along each baseline. The Park could seat nearly 16,000 fans. Standing room ran along the fence in right and right-center field, which stretched 450 feet from home plate.

Phillippe came out to the mound and received an uproarious ovation in tribute to his work in Boston. After a few warm-up tosses, he delivered the first pitch at 2:56 p.m., four minutes earlier than the scheduled start time. Everyone was anxious to play ball and, with the skies threatening, to avoid another postponement.

Dougherty swung at Phillippe's offering and grounded out to Ritchey at second. Collins then popped up to Ritchey, who made the catch even though the footing on the wet infield was treacherous. Stahl lofted one to Leach at third, and once again Phillippe had shown his ability to put the Boston hitters down. The Royal Rooters band struck up a chorus of "Ain't It a Shame," and Dinneen walked to the mound to see if he could duplicate his performance of the second game.

Center fielder Ginger Beaumont was ready to lead off. He much preferred his nickname, given to him by Barney Dreyfuss because of his aggressive play, to his given name Clarence. When he first broke in, ballplayers on other teams would tease him, "Clarence, Clarence, don't dirty the seat of your pants." But Beaumont could mix it up with any of them. Only five foot eight inches, he weighed 190 pounds. It was said he looked like a bowling ball with legs, yet he had surprising quickness and was second on the team in stolen bases behind Wagner. That season, he had led the National League in runs scored. But he couldn't score if he didn't get on base, and so far Beaumont had been hitless in the series.

Dinneen delivered, and Beaumont promptly bounced a ball up the middle for a leadoff single. Clarke hit a routine ball to Parent at shortstop, who got the force at second with a flip to Ferris, but the ball was not hit sharply enough for Boston to turn a double play. After Leach lined out to Stahl in center, Wagner strode to the plate and hit one that fell into center field for a single. Men on first and second with two out. It was not a good sign that Dinneen was being hit right up the middle, and Collins watched anxiously from third base. Kitty Bransfield duplicated Wagner's hit, and Clarke, who with two out was running on contact, trotted home with the first run. Wagner, thinking Stahl was going to throw home, tried for third. But he could not get any traction on the muddy field, and when Stahl threw to Collins, Wagner was tagged out easily for the final out.

For the next three innings, Phillippe and Dinneen engaged in a pitchers' duel. Boston managed only a single by Parent to left field in the second. But the Boston players and fans still exuded confidence. Phillippe was not as sharp as he had been previously; he had struck out only one man through four innings. And a couple of Boston hits had traveled deep to center field before Beaumont hauled them in. If Dinneen could keep Pittsburgh to one run, Boston's chances to prevail seemed favorable.

The Royal Rooters kept everyone amused with their songs after Boston made three outs at bat. "Won't You Come Home, Bill Bailey?," "What a Difference a Few Hours Make," and "I've Got Mine, Boys; I've Got Mine," were among the selections crooned by the Rooters.

In the top of the fifth, Boston rallied. After Parent was retired by Leach on a long throw across the diamond, LaChance singled to left. Ferris also grounded out to third, while LaChance moved on to second. Criger stepped in. The catcher had contributed nothing offensively so far in the series, but now he came through with a two-out base hit to right. LaChance scored to tie the game at one run apiece, and Criger took second on the throw home. The Royal Rooters went wild. "Nuf Ced" McGreevey climbed on the roof over the Boston bench and danced "a hornpipe and a jig and a breakdown." The Rooters "jumped up in the air and waved handkerchiefs and hats and screeched until their red faces

became purple and their horns curled up in envy." Even the Pittsburgh fans applauded.

Dinneen came to bat and provided Leach with his third fielding chance of the inning. Criger, though not forced, ran to third
and was easily tagged for the final out. For the first time in the series a game was tied beyond the early innings. The band broke
into a rendition of "In the Good Old Summer Time," though the
gray skies and damp, chill air signaled a different season. Every
Boston fan "waved his horn as though it was a baton and sang and
sang with all the vim his lungs would allow." Some fans thought
that the Royal Rooters were putting up a better show than the
Boston players.

Phillippe led off the bottom of the fifth and did what pitchers
frequently do: he struck out. But Beaumont smashed a liner over
Stahl's head in center and ended up with a triple. The center
fielder had misjudged the ball, first breaking in and then scram-
bling back too late. The soggy ground slowed down both ball and
runner; otherwise the shot might have gone for an inside-the-
park home run. Clarke fouled out and stormed back to the
bench, angry with himself for failing to come through with a
runner on third and less than two down. Leach then smashed the
ball to LaChance. The first baseman knocked it down, tried to recover, but he slipped and fell in the mud. The sawdust sprinkled
over the infield before the game had done little for the footing.
Beaumont scored, and just that quickly, Pittsburgh had reclaimed
the lead, 2–1. Wagner stepped in, but he was called out on strikes.
The shortstop shook his head. With his bat he drew a line several
inches outside the plate, showing umpire O'Day where he
thought the ball had crossed.

O'Day was a patient man. Once Brooklyn's Bill Dahlen had
come to the plate and called the umpire Henry, instead of Hank.
He asked O'Day if he would throw him out of the game if he
called him "a big beer-soaked, fat-headed loafer and thief?" "I
should say I will," answered O'Day. "I'll call you that and you
chase me. I want to get to Harlem in time to bet on the fourth

race," said Dahlen. O'Day would have none of it. "You couldn't get out of this game if you called me everything in the world," he told the hitter. O'Day looked away as Wagner returned to the bench.

The sixth inning passed uneventfully. In the seventh, Boston caught a break when Parent hit a routine ground ball to Leach and Bransfield dropped the throw for an error. But just as quickly LaChance, who "made a mess of trying to sacrifice," popped a feeble fly to Ritchey, who charged in and threw on the run to double up Parent. The inning ended with Ferris grounding out. The Rooters' band mourned with the tune "Hiawatha, My Indian Maid."

Up to this point, neither Dinneen nor Phillippe had been as dominating as in previous games. Pittsburgh led by only one run when Phillippe led off the bottom of the seventh and singled. Dougherty fumbled the ball in left, and Phillippe, with the play in front of him, ran safely to second. Beaumont bunted. The Pirates were playing for one run here and counting on Phillippe to preserve the lead for two more innings. The bunt rolled toward first and LaChance charged the ball. He turned to throw, but Dinneen was not there. The pitcher had neglected to cover the vacated bag and the Pirates had runners on the corners with no one out.

Fred Clarke stepped in and lifted the ball to shallow left field. Phillippe tagged up, but he bluffed going home. The throw came to the plate, which allowed Beaumont to advance to second. Dougherty had made a mental error, because Phillippe's chance of "going home was not one in a hundred." Two runners were now in scoring position with one out. Collins decided to play the infield in so that the runner on third could not score on a routine ground ball. Tommy Leach was up. The spunky third baseman, whom Pittsburgh reporters lovingly called the Wee because of his size, smashed the ball down the right-field line for a triple. The ball was fair by less than six inches. Phillippe and Beaumont scored, and Pittsburgh had stretched its lead to 4–1.

Another run might prove insurmountable. Wagner was up. It

was impossible to know how to pitch to him. "His only weakness," said one opponent, "is a fast ball straight over the plate waist high. He doesn't think any pitcher has nerve enough to put one there." "Hans the Hitter" promptly singled to center; Leach walked home from third. Bransfield struck out and the speedy Wagner was thrown out trying to steal second. Pittsburgh's lead was 5–1. Boston was running out of innings.

The Americans' manager wasn't pleased with his left fielder. When the team returned to the bench, Collins and Dougherty got into an argument and called one another "ugly names." Dougherty, who no doubt was also frustrated by being hitless in his last seven at-bats, blamed Collins for not directing him where to throw the ball. One spectator heard Collins say, "If we lose this series you will suffer for it, I tell you."

Both teams played the eighth inning as if in a hurry to leave the park. For Boston, Criger struck out, Dinneen popped to second, and Leach popped to first. The Royal Rooters' band played "We Love You in the Same Old Way." Ritchey, Dinneen, and Phelps all grounded out for the Pirates.

The Pittsburgh fans gave Phillippe a rousing ovation as he walked to the mound for the ninth inning. Although he appeared to labor throughout, he had relinquished only four hits and had walked none. Collins led off for Boston. The Royal Rooters screamed for the manager to spark his team, and he obliged by sending the ball into center field for a single. Stahl then singled sharply to left, Collins took third, and for Boston fans, "hope began to crowd out oppression." Freeman stepped in and promptly singled to right. Collins scored and Stahl went to third. A nervous silence descended on the Pittsburgh crowd. Phillippe, it seemed, had little left. His fastball had slowed and his curve was flat. Another batter or two and he would be facing the bottom of the batting order, but could he hold the score until then?

Parent hit a ground ball to Wagner, and Freeman was forced at second. Stahl scored, however, and suddenly the Pirate lead had been shaved to two runs, 5–3.

The hits kept coming. LaChance bounced a ball over Phillippe's head, which the pitcher just managed to knock down, but the runner was safe with an infield single. With only one out, Hobe Ferris came up with runners on first and second. His wife looked pale sitting in the grandstand. Collins could be heard pleading for a hit. By this point, the Royal Rooters had transformed themselves into "howling maniacs." Ferris delivered a soft single to right, but the coach held Parent at third rather than sending him home. Had there been a throw home, LaChance could have advanced to third. But Boston played it safe. The bases were loaded with one out; a base hit could tie the game.

Collins decided to pinch-hit for Criger, who had looked overmatched when striking out in the eighth. The band members "were blowing and tooting their instruments like fiends and the Boston Rooters had simply lost control of themselves, war dances, cheers, yells and songs resounding clear across the Allegheny river." By comparison, the home-team crowd sat in "sphinx-like silence."

Charles Farrell dug in on the right side of the plate. The veteran catcher's best season was long in the past, when in 1891 he blasted 12 home runs and knocked in 110 runs for Boston in the American Association. Although he had lost much of his power, he could still make contact. Even in a handful of at-bats at the start of the season, before he broke his leg, Farrell showed that he could hit for average.

He took the first pitch for a ball. He checked his swing on the second pitch, which cut the plate in two for a strike. Phillippe peeked at the runners, stared toward home, and delivered his third pitch. The ball flew off Farrell's bat with a "sharp ring" toward the gap in left-center field. The flight of a ball takes only seconds, but for those in the stands it provides enough time to wonder. There was the ball, floating toward open ground. But there was Clarke, racing "with the speed of a greyhound" to make the catch. Parent tagged and scored easily. Boston had reduced Pittsburgh's lead to a single run, 5–4. There were now two outs.

Collins sent Jack O'Brien up to bat for Dinneen. The fans didn't know what to do with their hands. They applauded, they made fists, they squeezed everything and everyone near them. The pinch hitter quickly fell behind in the count, 0–2. Both Pittsburgh and Boston fans whispered silent prayers. O'Brien swung at the next pitch and lifted a high pop toward second base. Both base runners were racing around the diamond, mud and water slopping onto their pants.

Wagner looked up from short and yelled, "Squeeze 'er, Ritch!"

O'Brien lumbered toward first, his eye on the ball. Some fans could not bear to look and turned their faces away.

"Squeeze 'er, Ritch!" Wagner cried again, and his best friend on the team complied.

The game was over. The Pirates had held on for a 5–4 victory. The ninth inning felt as if it had lasted all afternoon, but the entire game was played in ninety minutes. "Another finish like that," quipped M'Quiston, "and there will be a wholesale canceling of life insurance policies in Pittsburg. Heart disease got an awful boom in that ninth inning."

As the brass band played "Good Night, Gentle Folks, Good Night," fans drifted out of the gates and into the late afternoon. The Boston players took time to pose for a souvenir picture with the Royal Rooters. None of them looked happy. Pirate fans lifted Phillippe on their shoulders and carried him to the clubhouse where, for half an hour after the game, he shook hands with his admirers. This was what Pirates fans craved. Reading accounts of the games played in Boston was not the same as seeing "the players in the flesh performing." The fans "want to join in the shouts over some clever bit of work, and applaud the home team when it wins."

For frustrated Boston fans, the game seemed a lot like the other losses where "Pittsburg had the luck and was always quick to take advantage of openings." At the same time, teams make their own luck, and it seemed clear to all that "the Boston men

The Boston Americans pose with the Royal Rooters following the game.
Mike McGreevey is seated in the first row on the right behind the players

MCGREEVEY COLLECTION, BOSTON PUBLIC LIBRARY

are not putting up the kind of ball that won the American race."
Four of the Pirates' five runs might have been prevented, they
thought. How could Dinneen have failed to cover first on a bunt,
a play that had cost a run? What was Dougherty doing throwing
home in the seventh? And Boston's cautious play in the ninth was
especially irksome. When Parent was held at third because of "the
lack of a little courage and heady coaching," even though the
chances were "ten to one that he would have scored from second," the Americans failed to pressure the opposition. By contrast, in the first inning, Pittsburgh scored from second on a base
hit, and in the seventh its players ran aggressively and advanced
runners the extra base. "It was the refusal to take a reasonable
chance that beat Boston," argued Tim Murnane in the *Boston
Globe*, "and the taking of a similar chance which won for Pittsburgh."

The slippery conditions offered no excuse. They were the same for both teams, yet the Pittsburgh infield managed to skate delicately around and keep their feet. The Boston infield, by comparison, "slipped, sprawled and lost plays and the game by reckless work when cooler heads would have made the plays easy." The more one thought about it, the more the defeat could be chalked up to mental, rather than physical, errors.

In the ninth inning Boston had showed what it could do at bat, and Pittsburgh fans and players took note: "The only time when it is a cinch that Boston is beat is when the other team is 1,000,000 runs ahead and such people as Collins, Dougherty, Stahl, Freeman, Dinneen, Young, Criger, and some others are locked up." Dinneen again had good stuff. The darkness of the day made his pitches look like "peas as they whirled over the plate." And Boston's infield was aggressive. At second base, Ferris, "who is about the size of a cake of soap after a hard day washing," got to balls no one else could reach, and at first base, LaChance did a belly flop in the mud in an attempt to stop Leach's RBI single in the fifth.

Phillippe, however, had once again been up to the task. For the third time in six days, he had defeated Boston. No one could blame him for faltering in the final frame. He got through it on sheer determination. "If any small boy from Maine to California were asked this morning to name the greatest pitcher in the world," the *Dispatch* reported, "he would most likely say Phillippe, though he could not spell the name." Pirate fans jammed the streetcars that took them home and gave thanks both to Phillippe and to the person "who decreed that a baseball game shall be of only nine innings duration."

Clarke's team was now ahead three games to one. "Pirates Have Almost Cinched Championship," spouted the headlines. If the Nationals were to win two of the three remaining contests scheduled for Exposition Park, they would become the world champions without having to return to Boston. How quickly judgments had changed. A week earlier, American League fans thought Boston would trample the hurting Pirates. Now, the "same people were loud in their statements that the Boston team was 'easy meat' for Pittsburg." Jimmy Sebring was outplaying Buck Freeman, and Tommy Leach was outhitting Jimmy Collins, two developments no one would have predicted prior to the series. And defensively, while Boston showed good work, the team's seven errors so far had been costly. By contrast, the Pirates had made all the routine plays, and some spectacular ones, when they were needed. They did not beat themselves.

As Boston fans replayed the games over in their minds, something did not seem quite right. Statistics showed the teams to be so close, and the margin of difference so small, that some wondered whether the Boston players were throwing games on purpose. Knowledgeable baseball fans discounted the rumors as "fictions from the dizzy brains of Boston gamblers who have bet 'not wisely but too well.' " "The salvation, the life of baseball, is its honesty," declared John Morrill, who had played in Boston between 1876 and 1888. Collins reacted indignantly to the charge of losing intentionally. "If I tried to answer any person making the crack, I would be as crazy as he is," Collins said. "We must get back to Boston, there is no may about it. We will win two games, if it takes an arm," he predicted. "Phillippe can't do all the pitching. Things broke well for the Pirates again. Will it ever stop?"

THE FOURTH GAME

PITTSBURG.	AB.	R.	B	P.	A.	E.
Beaumont, cf......	4	2	3	3	0	0
Clarke, lf.........	4	1	1	1	0	0
Leach, 3b.........	4	1	2	2	5	0
Wagner, ss........	4	0	3	1	1	0
Bransfield, 1b	4	0	1	9	1	1
Ritchey, 2b.......	3	0	0	5	5	0
Sebring, rf.......	4	0	0	1	0	0
Phelps, c.........	4	0	1	4	0	0
Phillippe, p.......	3	1	1	1	1	0
Total..........	34	5	12	27	13	1

BOSTON.	AB.	R.	B	P.	A.	E.
Dougherty, lf.....	4	0	0	3	0	1
Collins, 3b........	4	1	1	1	2	0
Stahl, cf..........	4	1	2	3	1	0
Freeman, rf.......	4	0	1	0	0	0
Parent, ss....	4	1	1	1	3	0
La Chance, 1b.....	4	1	2	6	0	0
Ferris, 2b.........	4	0	1	2	0	0
Criger, c..........	3	0	1	8	1	0
*Farrell	1	0	0	0	0	0
Dineen, p.........	3	0	0	0	1	0
†O'Brien	1	0	0	0	0	0
Total..........	36	4	9	24	8	1

*Batted for Criger in ninth.   †Batted for Dineen in ninth.

Pittsburg................	1	0	0	0	1	0	3	0	x—	5
Boston..	0	0	0	0	1	0	0	0	3—	4

Earned runs—Pittsburg 5, Boston 2.   Three-base hits—Beaumont, Leach.   Stolen base—Wagner.   Double plays—Ritchey. Bransfield; Criger, Parent.   First on balls—Off Dineen 1. Struck out—By Phillippe 1, Dineen 7.   Time—1.30.   Umpires— O'Day and Connolly.   Attendance, 7,600.

EVERY SPRING, FANS GREW EXCITED about the upcoming season, but never more so than in 1903, when they predicted competitive pennant races and awaited interleague games. After so many turbulent years, it looked as if professional baseball had righted itself and would reaffirm its position as the national pastime.

As their favorite teams prepared for the season, baseball fans followed along in the newspapers. The rituals of spring training varied little from camp to camp. The first games were intrasquad affairs that pitted the regulars against the Yanigans, a slang term for rookies. Then the major-league teams would play local colleges or minor-league teams. James Hart, owner of the Chicago Cubs, proclaimed that the point of spring training was for the players to get into condition. The Boston Americans worked out twice a day, at 10 a.m. and at 2 p.m., and then found their way to the local bowling alley. The Cincinnati Reds ran from their quarters to the playing grounds every morning and afternoon, putting in five miles of road work each day. The Detroit Tigers (who talked of changing their name to the Wolverines) thought they had their best squad since 1887. The players not only said the climate in Baton Rouge was ideal for training, but also fell "in love with the city and especially its beautiful women." John McGraw of the Giants used spring training to test various innovations, including using multiple pitchers in a game. This was the first spring that the Giants headed south, and the results showed. One New York writer commented that "the condition of the New York Nationals this spring after a turn in Georgia, compared with the condition of the local club of last year, which ran around the Polo Grounds in an endeavor to keep from freezing last spring, is a practical demonstration in favor of Southern training trips."

Not everyone agreed on the salubrious effects of the southern trips. One writer thought it a "waste of good dollars to take a bunch of players on an extensive spring training trip." Players should be expected, he thought, to keep themselves in shape. Rather than spend thousands of dollars each year to move the team south, every club should "build and equip a good baseball 'cage' [where] players could be assembled any old time and given their conditioning indoors." It seemed dangerous to take players from the warmth of spring training and then thrust them back into the freezing conditions of April games in the North, where a "Chicago spring has the thermometer at 26 degrees in the fog."

The writer may have had a point, but spring training was as much about team unity as conditioning. The encouraging reports issued by the various camps reinforced the value of the trips while simultaneously whetting the appetites, and fantasies, of northern fans hungry for the season to begin. To be sure, here and there news filtered through of injury or inability, but even then the spin was usually positive. Even the White Sox, which as a team appeared "weaker at the bat, weaker in the field, slower on the bases, and inferior in the pitching staff," would be whipped into "winning form or I am a crocodile," declared one writer. (The White Sox would finish the season a miserable 60–77; the sportswriter, by all accounts, retained his human form.)

Touting unknowns and minor leaguers as future stars was part of the script. One player on the Cubs, who displayed "the size, the reach, the physique, and the proper spirit" to become a star, ended up playing only eight games that season. Another, with the Brooklyn Superbas, "has been hitting the ball so hard during the practice at Columbia that residents of the next county have been picking up his home runs and bringing them in to [manager] Hanlon, who offers a reward of ten cents for every ball that is returned." He would appear in a total of 12 games and bat .209. Such was spring training, a time meant as much for the fans in the frigid North and Midwest as for the players rounding into shape in the South. "Just now every wind that blows from the South," commented the *Sporting News*, "is laden with hot air about new phenom, old arms and legs rejuvenated, pennant claims and other kinds of base ball dope, which the average fan devours with the eager hunger born of a winter's starvation."

One sportswriter went so far as to mock his colleagues. "The correspondents," he averred, "do anything but keep the public posted on the real condition of the team. Did you ever read the dispatches of any correspondent who did not say that the team was in great shape and working hard? Did ever a scribe with a team in spring practice tell of anything except pleasing and delightful doings, calculated to make every reader believe that the club was made up wholly of A-1 stars? . . . As pipe smokers and polite polishers the men who go south with the teams in spring are unequaled, but as plain narrators of the unvarnished truth there never was one of them yet."

The writers gossiped among themselves and read one another's accounts in such papers as the *Sporting News* and *Sporting Life*. When not filing reports on the exceptional doings of players, they offered predictions for the upcoming season. All agreed that the year would be "one of the best in the history of the national game," a season marked by unusual parity among the sixteen teams in the two leagues. "This coming contest in both the National and American League pennant races," declared the veteran scribe Henry Chadwick, "bids fair to be the most uncertain from start to finish that we have had for years past."

Still, certain teams looked better suited than others to compete for league championships. In the National League, almost everyone favored Joe Kelley's Cincinnati Reds. His pitching staff showed good form from the start of spring training, and he had at least nine candidates from which to choose. One reporter trumpeted Noodles Hahn, Ed Poole, Bill Phillips, and Jack Harper, who had returned to the National League from a season with the St. Louis Browns, whereas another flagged Jack Sutthoff and Bob Ewing. Harper was trying to repeat the star season he had had in the National League in 1901, when he had gone 23–13. While there were questions about the arm strength of Ewing and Poole, the young lefty Hahn had already won 20 games three times. The outfield also looked strong. Mike Donlin, who played in only 34 games in 1902, was back, and Cy Seymour and manager Kelley rounded out a trio that could cover ground and steal more than a few bases. Clark Griffith, the manager of the New York Highlanders, proclaimed the Reds' outfield as "the greatest . . . that ever stepped on a ball field." Kelley intended to make speed the touchstone of his team. "Speed is everything," he said. "More games are won through speed than through batting." Kelley was only in his second year of managing, but he had the players' support. He was willing "to correct any man, no matter who it is," and he kept a careful eye on every activity on the field. If in practice a player ran from home to first flat-footed, he would stop him, show him how to run on his toes, and have him do it again. Speed, he thought, would lead the team to a championship.

Early predictions also favored the Pirates, who in both 1901 and 1902 had decimated the competition. "This is going to be a banner year for base ball in Pittsburg," declared owner Barney Dreyfuss. The team had lost its two star pitchers from the previous season—Jack Chesbro (28–6) and Jesse Tannehill (20–6)—and yet the team still figured in everyone's mind to compete for a third successive championship. The Pirates had Deacon Phillippe, Sam Leever, and Ed Doheny on the mound. And returning to the field were a group of veterans entering the peaks of their careers—player-manager Fred Clarke, third baseman Tommy Leach, out-fielder Ginger Beaumont, and Honus Wagner. Reports from Hot Springs indicated that the National League champs were working hard to get into condition. Clarke reminded the bunch that they opened their season at Cincinnati and that gamblers had made the Reds the favorites. Even on rainy days, the Pirates practiced.

The Giants also looked as if they might contend for the pennant. It was John McGraw's team now, and McGraw knew how to win. There wasn't a manager in baseball who did not covet Christy Mathewson and Joe McGinnity for their pitching rotation. Finally, Frank Selee's Cubs had Jack Taylor back from a season in which he had won 23 of his 34 decisions, posting a 1.29 ERA, and he had an infield with Joe Tinker at shortstop, Frank Chance at first, and a rookie named Johnny Evers, who was "knocking the tar out of the ball," at second. None of the other teams seemed likely to succeed, though no manager would admit as much. The effects of the baseball wars had hit the St. Louis Cardinals, Brooklyn Superbas, Philadelphia Phillies, and Boston Braves especially hard, with each team losing one-third to one-half of its roster to the American League. Though adherents tried to place the best spin on matters ("in spite of the fact that it was looted of so many players, [the National League] was never so weak as its enemies painted it"), National League owners and fans entered the season resentful of the upstart American League.

Nearly everyone agreed that Cleveland was the team to beat in the American League, provided second baseman Nap Lajoie was healthy. So admired was Lajoie that his team became known as the Naps this season. But he had suffered terribly all winter from what doctors thought was pneumonia but turned out to be pleurisy. Three weeks in New Orleans did the slugger some good, and he looked to be slowly rounding into form, though he was still 8 pounds below his playing weight of 185 pounds. He had been hitless in several intrasquad games, before breaking out with a double and a single in three at-bats. In addition to Lajoie, the infield featured first baseman Charley Hickman, who led the league in hits and total bases in 1902. The outfield of Elmer Flick, Harry Bay, and Jack McCarthy was healthy. The pitching staff featured Addie Joss, entering only his second season but already a star, as well as Earl Moore and Bill Bernhard. Manager Bill Armour declared that "if ever a team had a good chance to win a pennant, it was Cleveland."

Jimmy Collins thought the same of his team, and he scoffed at the midwestern writers who made Cleveland the favorite. "Our team will be just about the same as last year and will play better for having been together so long," he said. Indeed, Boston made so few moves from the previous season that some thought the team should be called the "Standpats." Cy Young and Bill Dinneen anchored the pitching staff. And Collins liked the looks of rookie Norwood Gibson, who had pitched in the Western League the previous year. From the start of spring training, outfielder Patsy Dougherty was smashing the ball. Buck Freeman, who had 121 RBIs in 1902, and Chick Stahl, who batted .323, filled the other outfield positions. Collins had some questions yet to be resolved. He thought first baseman Candy LaChance needed to improve his defense and, at one point in the spring, was looking for a replacement before deciding to stick with the ten-year major-league veteran. LaChance would end up leading the league in games played with 141. The manager also knew he needed a catcher to replace Jack Warner, who had done a competent job behind the plate but was "not a good man for a team, as he dearly loves to belong to a clique." The issue facing Boston was whether a group of veterans could win. Some thought "it takes youngsters with lots of spirits to make a championship team." Others argued that experience and leadership outweighed youth. In the first team scrimmage, Cy Young pitched for Mercer College against his professional mates and went the full nine innings. "How many pitchers," wondered one writer, "could go in and pitch the limit at so early a stage in the proceedings?" The thirty-six-year-old ace was worth a complete staff of youngsters.

Another team of veterans was the Highlanders. Ban Johnson knew it was important that the American League franchise in New York put a good product on the field, and the wealthy owners did not skimp on a payroll that approached $50,000. The team featured one of the strongest pitching staffs on any roster: Chesbro, Tannehill, and manager Clark Griffith, who had won at least 20 games in seven of the nine previous seasons. The team also had "Wee" Willie Keeler in the outfield. In a career going back to 1892, he had never hit under .312, and he would end his career in 1910 with a lifetime batting average of .341. Starting in 1894, he accumulated more than 200 hits in eight consecutive seasons. The diminutive Keeler (five feet four inches and 140 pounds), when asked what accounted for his success, said it was simple: he "hit 'em where they ain't." Keeler earned the highest salary in baseball: $10,000. That was more money than entire teams had earned just twenty years earlier. The question faced by the Highlanders, thought the sportswriters, was whether Griffith could control "his own bad temper to govern a team" that had "an array of pitchers and outfielders fit to stagger any opposition." It was also unclear whether this group of stars would care about competing or would "neither enthuse at winning nor weep at losing, nor take great interest in anything provided the semi-monthly checks are received regularly."

In Philadelphia, Connie Mack's A's were coming back from a season in which they had won 83 games and the pennant. The team featured Rube Waddell and Eddie Plank, two of the best left-handed pitchers in the game. They were joined by an eighteen-year-old who was poised to make his professional debut—Chief Bender, a Chippewa Indian who was born in Minnesota and pitched at Dickinson College. Detroit was also the focus of some attention, in large part because of a press agent who accompanied the team and issued reports that had the Tigers playing in midsummer form with the batters regularly "knocking the ball away over the fence and some distance into Texas." As a result of the peace settlement, the team had acquired outfielder Sam Crawford, only twenty-three years old and already a star. "Wild" Bill Donovan, coming over from Brooklyn, promised to fill the hole created by the suicide of pitcher Win Mercer. And Kid Elberfeld, starting his third year with Detroit, was a sleek young shortstop.

The Tigers were the only American League team not to have lost a game in March. But no one really attached much importance to the outcomes of spring contests. When the Pirates lost 2–1 to the Little Rock Southern League team, in part because the players decided to swing for the fences rather than work together to manufacture runs, supporters thought "the defeat coming as it did was the best thing that could have happened." One writer put it this way: "no correct line of a ball player's ability can be secured by watching him at practice or in exhibition games. It is not until the player is up against the real thing that his strong and weak points come to the surface." No one could know for sure what the teams and players would do until the games counted for something. During the first week of April, teams headed home from training camp. A few more exhibition series and the season would start for real.

The baseball buzz of early April was the planned interleague exhibition games to be held in St. Louis between the Cardinals and the Browns and in Philadelphia between the Phillies and the A's. The two Chicago teams had also intended to play one another, but the owners called off the series when they could not agree on a schedule. They did, however, promise to play a fifteen-game local championship series at the end of the season, a plan that seemed to indicate that "the cruel war was really over." Rivalries, of course, last longer than wars, and when Connie Mack's Athletics challenged the Pirates to a preseason series of games, Dreyfuss said he would do it only for $5,000 and the entire gate receipts.

In St. Louis, despite a snowstorm and conditions described as "pneumonia weather," 16,000 fans packed the Browns' Sportsman's Park on Saturday, April 4; the next day, nearly 20,000 would crowd the Cardinals' field. The players entered the series "more intent on winning these games than the regular championship events in their respective races." More money, an estimated $75,000, was bet on the four-game series than on all the games combined during the previous season. And novelty vendors flooded the town with buttons featuring the respective managers against cardinal and brown backgrounds. Public sentiment was with the National League Cardinals, a St. Louis institution, who were considered an underdog against the rival Browns.

Ed Siever dominated the first affair. The Browns' lefty starter had come over from the Detroit Tigers, where he had compiled a league-leading ERA of 1.91 but had a losing record on the mound. He was thrilled to be playing in St. Louis because he was looking forward to the Exposition in 1904. Siever opposed rookie Mordecai Brown. Because of a childhood accident that had cost Brown part of his index finger and deformed his thumb and pinky, he was known as Three Finger Brown. Brown put the handicap to his advantage, gripping the ball so that he could make it spin in unusual ways. (Ty Cobb, who batted against him in the 1907 World Series, called Brown's specialty "the most devastating pitch I ever faced.") After his rookie year, the Cardinals would trade Brown to the Cubs, where he would eventually win 20 or more games in six consecutive seasons.

Although the Browns dominated the first game, the Cardinals also showed some resolve, especially once their young pitchers relaxed and realized that they did not have to strike out everyone. Mike and Jack O'Neill, brothers and battery mates, kept the Browns in check in Game Two. At one critical point in the game, manager Patsy Donovan made a leaping catch in the outfield, grabbing the ball with his bare hand and then falling to the ground. The following weekend, on April 11 and 12, the teams played again, and again they split the two contests. Both clubs looked to be in good form, and although neither nine would have a satisfying season, the spring series got both players and fans thinking about a championship run.

Unlike the successful St. Louis contests, the Philadelphia series almost collapsed before it began. The Phillies and Athletics were scheduled to play four games at Philadelphia Park and three at the Athletics' Columbia Park. The anticipation was great, and clearly attendance would be high. But prior to the initial game on Saturday, April 4, the Athletics players went on strike. They refused to play unless they received 20 percent of the gate receipts. Veteran third baseman Lave Cross spoke for the players. He pointed out that in the 1880s, when there were local championship series, player contracts started earlier and that the games were not mere exhibitions but full-fledged affairs in which players would work as hard as they would during a league championship race. They deserved to share in the profits. The Athletics' disappointment over their take from several benefit contests played the previous fall, as well as the rumor that the Phillies would receive some of the receipts, further emboldened the athletes.

The striking players were roundly condemned. "It is unfortunate," wrote the *Sporting News*, "that the players should cheapen themselves by wishing to be rewarded for doing their duty." The move was "foolhardy" and "ill-timed." The players had just returned from an extended outing in Florida, paid for by management, a trip that the average person could not dream of taking. Didn't the owners deserve a chance to earn back their expenses? Although some patrons were willing to support the players' cause, "the base ball fan is a peculiar animal and is not quick to overlook being deprived of what he thinks his dues. The fans wanted to see that game and the striking players gained no friends among the rooters by their action." Public sentiment would "not approve the subordination of sportsmanship to mercenary considerations in magnates or players." The whole sordid affair, concluded one writer, provided a "strong argument both against expensive training trips and against spring exhibition games between the two big leagues."

After meeting with the owners, the players settled by agreeing to forgo any claim on the receipts for the local series. In return, they would receive a share of the money brought in by any exhibition games played during the season. The series was also shortened to five games. The first interleague contest was played on April 6 at Columbia Park, where 5,600 shivering fans admired the improvements made at the stadium. The baseball diamond had been torn up and resodded and, with the addition of a grandstand, seating capacity was expanded. The champion Athletics were expecting to play to large crowds; defeating their rivals would make a fine prelude to the regular season.

In the opening game, Athletics ace Rube Waddell faced the Phillies' Fred Mitchell, who had played for Connie Mack's squad the previous year; each threw shutout ball through nine innings. Waddell struck out ten, while Mitchell kept the Athletics off balance. Batters on both teams fought the cold as much as they fought the curve. In the top of the tenth, Waddell walked leadoff hitter Shad Barry. Bill Keister then bunted back to Waddell, who failed to make a play at any base. Unnerved, he hit lefty Klondike Douglass, loading the bases with none out. Roy Brashear's fly ball to right field scored Barry, and Rudy Hulswitt's single to right-center field drove Keister home. Two runs were all that Mitchell needed to close out his former teammates. Mitchell, discarded by both the Athletics and Boston in the American League, looked as if he might become a star pitcher "under the sheltering shade" of the foul-strike rule.

The story was little different in the remaining games. The scene shifted to Philadelphia Park on April 9, and 6,640 fans witnessed another ten-inning victory by the Phillies. Monte Cross, the Athletics shortstop, got thrown out of the game. Chief Bender came in to play short, and he immediately booted a ball and made a wild throw leading to two Phillies runs. The National League won the game, 6–5. Before even greater crowds, the Phillies went on to win Games Three and Five as well, both in ten innings. The Athletics managed only one victory, a 7–1 triumph in the fourth game, filled with Phillies errors. Though four of the games were extra-inning affairs, the triumph of the National League over the American League champions from 1902 surprised most observers and won the Phillies "a place in the fans' affections."

In the only other spring interleague games that were played, Washington defeated the Phillies twice and divided two games with the Superbas. In all, the preseason games resulted in a near-even split between the two leagues: the American League had won seven games, while the National League triumphed in six contests. The outcome, remarked the writers, "has not been such a signal walkaway for the American League as some would have had people believe before the teams actually met in combat." In the end, many felt that games between the leagues should not take place in the spring. Players were not anywhere near season form, and the cold weather skewed results. Owners feared that by losing spring interleague city games, their teams would suffer in popularity and attendance. Games between the two leagues, concluded most observers, were "the tidbits of the base ball year, and they should be like a good dinner's dessert reserved to the last, just before the fans light their cigars for the winter's hot air sessions." It was time for the separate championship seasons to begin. Battles between the leagues could wait until October.

GAME FIVE, WEDNESDAY, OCTOBER 7

THE WEATHER BROKE clear and mild for what was regarded as "the crucial game of the series," the fifth game of the World's Championship. With Pittsburgh ahead three games to one, Boston had to win to have any chance of turning the series around. As avid as the Royal Rooters had been, they made plans to leave Pittsburgh that evening should the Americans, with the inimitable Cy Young on the mound, go down in defeat. For now, the Rooters prepared for another afternoon of wild and enthusiastic cheering. To change Boston's luck, they hired a German band to accompany them to Exposition Park. The evening before, the Rooters and an Italian band had assembled before the Monongahela Hotel and sang songs and played music until 11 p.m. The players on both teams had attended a performance of *Notre Dame* at the Grand Opera House; as they entered the theater, the orchestra played "See the Conquering Hero Comes." And gamblers on both sides had scurried around town Tuesday night looking for action on the fifth game but had had difficulty finding favorable odds. One Boston zealot bet $130 to $500 that the Americans would still win the series. "The gamest crowd of rooters I have ever known," marveled a Pittsburgh sporting man.

Between 12,000 and 15,000 fans turned out for the contest. Every seat was taken, as was every foot of standing room. The crowd overflowed onto the outfield, where they massed behind ropes; balls hit into the crowd would be ground-rule triples, as they had been in the first and second games in Boston. Fred Clarke sent Roaring Bill Kennedy to the mound and hoped that the veteran would succeed. Maybe the Pittsburgh hitters would get to Cy Young, as they had in the first game. More likely, Young would be as tough as he had been in his seven innings of relief in the third game. Ahead three games to one, the Pirates could absorb a loss in the fifth game, but a win would almost certainly clinch the series. For Boston, losing was not an option. Their ace was on the mound, and the day before, their bats had shown late signs of life. If they did not win this game, they might as well take the train home with the Royal Rooters that night.

Kennedy jogged to the mound and received a rousing ovation. "Pittsburg! Pittsburg! Hooray!" shouted the fans, eager to show that the hometown wasn't going to be outrooted by several scores of visitors. Kennedy himself exuded confidence. He had begged Clarke for a chance to pitch, joking that he would commit suicide if the manager did not let him. The right-hander from Bellaire, Ohio, who this day turned thirty-six, certainly had plenty of experience behind him. His career began in 1892, and he pitched ten years for Brooklyn. Four times he won 20 games, and he regularly threw over 300 innings per season. Yet he was not a strikeout pitcher, and he hadn't thrown 300 innings in the last three years combined. But maybe, just maybe, he would get the job done today against his fellow Ohioan.

Patsy Dougherty stepped in to start the game. Boston needed its leadoff man to do well to have a chance to win. In Boston's one win, he had gotten three hits in four times at bat, but he was hitless in his twelve at-bats in their three losses. Kennedy understood the significance of retiring the first batter of the game.

Dougherty popped up to the catcher, and Pirates supporters exhaled with relief. The first out relaxed the Pirates and their fans, but their easy breathing did not last long. Jimmy Collins came to bat and tripled into the crowd in right. Chick Stahl then bounced a grounder to Wagner. Collins dashed for home on contact, but Wagner threw him out at the plate. Stahl then stole second. Two were out with a runner in scoring position for Buck Freeman. There was no way Kennedy was going to pitch to the lefty cleanup hitter when the righty Freddy Parent was due up next. Freeman was given a free pass to first. It looked as if the strategy would pay off when Parent hit a weak grounder to third, but Leach could not make a play at any base. Suddenly, the bases were loaded, and once again a first-inning score seemed imminent.

Candy LaChance settled into the batter's box. Boston fans hoped that his two hits the day before signaled the end of his slump. But Kennedy got LaChance to pop up to third. The threat was ended, and Boston's hopes of dictating the early tone of the game were erased.

Young entered the game. He received appreciative applause from all the fans, exuberant cheers from the Royal Rooters, and enthusiastic greetings from a group of about a hundred Ohio Rooters who had come especially to support their local hero. His wife, Robba Miller Young, sat with other Boston players' wives behind the Americans' bench. Ginger Beaumont led off the bottom of the first by flying out to left. LaChance then made a lovely defensive play at first base when he snared Collins's errant throw on Fred Clarke's ground ball. Perhaps today the Boston fielders would show their true ability. With two out, Tommy Leach came to bat. There are some hitters who always seem to have good at-bats against certain pitchers, and Leach loved hitting against Young. The Wee promptly singled for his fifth hit in eight at-bats against Young in the series. Wagner strode to the plate. Having gotten three hits the day before, it looked as if the batting champion was finding his stroke. But Young induced a ground ball to second that ended the inning.

Kennedy worked quickly through the next few innings. He retired the side in order in the second, and fans rejoiced that the veteran looked good. In the third, Collins singled to center and stole second, but with two out, Kennedy struck out Freeman. Again in the fourth inning, Boston went down in order. With one out in the fifth inning, Young reached second on an error by Leach, whose throw across the diamond sailed over Kitty Bransfield's head. One out later, with the pitcher on third, Collins flied to left, and another runner was left stranded. Boston had five base runners in the first five innings, but none of them had scored. Collins squirmed, knowing that in a pitcher's duel, the first team to score has a tremendous advantage.

Young had also managed to hold off the Pirates, but not without some consternation for the Boston fans. In the bottom of the second, Claude Ritchey singled and advanced to second with two outs, but Ed Phelps grounded out to end the threat. In the third, Kennedy lashed a double beyond Stahl's reach to open the frame, but could not advance, as Beaumont fouled out, Clarke grounded out, and Leach hit the ball solidly, but right at Dougherty in left. The Pirates had squandered an ideal scoring opportunity. In the fourth inning, they went down in order as Wagner struck out, Bransfield flied out, and Ritchey grounded out.

Jimmy Sebring led off the fifth with a routine ground ball to the shortstop, but LaChance mishandled Fred Parent's throw and the batter advanced to second while the first baseman chased after the ball. Phelps sacrificed Sebring to third. A routine fly ball or a well-placed ground ball would score the run and put the home team in the lead. Kennedy came up for the second time. He had already knocked one ball over the center fielder's head. The pitcher now swung hard and pulled the ball on a line. But Parent snared the ball at shortstop and almost caught Sebring dangling too far off third. Beaumont grounded out to the reliable Collins, and another scoring threat had evaporated. "Three times in the first five innings," reported the *Post*, "the Boston Rooters began to despair and to examine their timetables for trains running out of Pittsburg, and three times Cy Young staved off the scoring efforts of the Pirates."

In a tense, scoreless game, Boston came to bat in the top of the sixth. Chick Stahl lifted a routine fly to Clarke in short left field, but Wagner, going out on the play, did not hear the manager call for it. The two nearly collided, Clarke dropped the ball, and Stahl stood safely at first. For once "luck favored the Collins team." Freeman singled to left-center field and Stahl cruised into second. Runners stood on first and second. Everyone in Exposition Park knew that Parent would be called on to sacrifice. He bunted toward third. Leach raced in, turned, and threw to Wagner, who was covering third base for the force to get the lead runner. But the most sure-handed fielder in baseball dropped the ball, and Boston had the bases loaded and no one out.

In the stands, Mike McGreevey again leaped atop the Boston bench and repeated his "Irish reel" from the day before. The band was "puffing and blowing like 'red devils,' " and it felt as if the stands in section J, where the Royal Rooters assembled, would splinter and crash to the ground.

Candy LaChance walked to the plate. He showed great patience and worked the count full. Phelps tried to reassure his pitcher, but Kennedy, perhaps unnerved by the errors in the field, walked LaChance to force in a run. Boston had broken through first and still had the bases loaded with no one out. Hobe Ferris stepped in. His wife, sitting near the players' bench, screamed encouragement. The second baseman hit the ball directly at Wagner. It was a routine double-play ball, and the Pirate infield had already shown in the series that it was adept at turning two. Wagner spun and threw to third, but the ball sailed ten feet over the third baseman's head. Both Freeman and Parent scored. It was Wagner's second error in the inning. "Even the king of ballplayers is not infallible," commented a reporter. Boston was ahead 3–0, runners were on first and second, and still there was no one out.

In the stands, "Boston's loyal rooters acted more like escaped patients from an insane asylum. Pittsburg rooters fumed and raged.

A Royal Rooter leads the cheers in Game Five

MCGREEVEY COLLECTION, BOSTON PUBLIC LIBRARY

Barney Dreyfuss began to bite his mustache and Harry Pulliam savagely twirled his cane."

Lou Criger came to bat and sacrificed the runners over. Cy Young was due up. He had to feel confident that he could hold the lead. Although he had pitched out of trouble, Young had scattered only three hits through five innings. Young felt comfortable coming to the plate. Look for something and drive it, he told himself.

Kennedy delivered to his counterpart, and Young sent the ball sailing toward the ropes in left field. Clarke had no chance. Two more runs scored and Young stood at third base. Patsy Dougherty, who was remembered fondly by the fans from his minor-league playing days in nearby Homestead, then duplicated Young's blast to make it 6–0. The game had been broken open.

Clarke knew Kennedy had to come out, but why waste another pitcher in what now surely was a mop-up effort? Scoring six runs off Young was a lot to ask. Then again, Boston had rallied in the ninth the day before, and the Pirates still had four times at bat. Kennedy retired Collins and Stahl to end the error-plagued inning, and Pittsburgh set out to get back in the game.

Young realized the importance of shutting the Pirates out in the sixth. The game revolved as much around psychology as around skill. If the Pirates cut into the lead in the bottom of the inning, they would believe they had a chance to come back and win. Young went to work. Clarke popped up to second; Leach made good contact yet again, but drove the ball straight at Dougherty in left. Wagner, still in disbelief over his performance in the field, grounded out to short. The heart of the Pirate lineup had gone down meekly.

Kennedy came out to start the seventh, but the man known as Roaring Bill had little strength left. Freeman and Parent started the inning with back-to-back singles. LaChance forced Parent at second, as Ritchey made a diving stop of another hard-hit ball. Ferris then singled to center, scoring Freeman. Criger walked, and the bases were loaded for Young. This time the pitcher grounded out, but a run scored and the base runners advanced. Dougherty put an end to all dreams of a miracle comeback by the home team when, for the second time, he tripled deep to left field. When the inning finally ended, Boston had tacked on four more runs and led by ten.

It was hard to blame Kennedy. He had pitched well enough to have won "in nine games out of ten." He had "curves and speed, but he lost his game through the errors which his teammates made behind him," concluded one assessment. Kennedy walked somberly off the field and cried when he reached the clubhouse. His playing days were over.

Fans, who had begun leaving after the sixth, now streamed out of the park by the thousands. The emptying stands made the Royal Rooters, whose "half-crazy antics" had the crowd watching them as much as the game, even more visible and voluble.

Clarke brought Gus Thompson in to pitch the eighth. The reliever had appeared sporadically during the season, winning 2 and losing 2 in 43 innings of work. Stahl greeted him with a triple, Boston's fifth of the game, and scored the team's final run on a groundout. Ahead 11–0, Cy Young looked to speed the game to its conclusion.

The Royal Rooters wanted a shutout, a "whitewash." When Phelps was called out on strikes and Thompson popped out, Young quickly had two outs in the eighth inning. Ginger Beaumont hit a slow roller to second and was called safe on a questionable call by Hank O'Day. Clarke then reached on an error by Parent. That brought Leach up to bat, and again the pesky hitter got the best of the winningest pitcher in baseball by smashing a two-run triple to right that broke up the shutout. Wagner, who had one of his worst games ever, grounded out, which quashed whatever rally the remaining hometown fans might have imagined was in the making.

In the ninth, the teams simply played out the inevitable. Criger hit a ground ball and Young a fly ball for two outs. Dougherty, still hungry for hits, got a two-out single, but Collins popped up to end Boston's day at bat. In the bottom of the inning, Young induced two quick outs as Bransfield hit a routine fly ball to right field and Ritchey struck out. Jimmy Sebring managed his first base hit, but Young closed out the contest by inducing Phelps to ground out to second. The game ended 11–2.

"Pittsburg Meets Her Waterloo," screamed the *Post*'s headline. "Hard Hitting Does It," celebrated the *Globe*. The Pittsburg *Dispatch* summarized the game with a simple statement: "Boston Batters Have Big Picnic at Our Expense."

Young had been "masterly. . . . The way he whizzed the ball over the plate made the Pirate batters dizzy." Boston played sensational defense and displayed its potent offense. By contrast, Pittsburgh fumbled and flailed. The team "went into the air . . . and before they came down Boston had the game clinched beyond a shadow of a doubt." Outfield errors might have been expected as a gusting, paper-filled wind blew across the field, but it was the Pirate infield that had disintegrated. "It is Wagner who must bear the brunt of the defeat," thought the *Gazette*. At the theater in Boston a week earlier, the players had heard a song with the lines "Ain't it funny what a difference / a few hours make?" M'Quiston joked that Barney Dreyfuss could be heard mournfully humming the tune as he undressed that night. Collins was singing a different song. "The teams will not only go back to Boston to finish the series, but the Boston Americans will win out," he crooned. "Tonight the good citizens of Pittsburg went to bed," announced the *Globe* correspondent Tim Murnane, "with a firm conviction that Boston has a ball team able to beat the National League champions when luck breaks even."

Following the game, the Rooters formed a procession to march back to the hotel. Boston fans sported a red badge and carried red, white, and blue canes and parasols. They marched four across, and among them was a seven-year-old black boy named Hiram, whom one of the Rooters had earlier swept off the streets and brought to Exposition Park for the game. "I knew that if we could get the real thing in a pickininny the Pirates could not hit Young," explained the Boston fan. The rooter tied a horseshoe around the mascot's neck and claimed that "each player of our team on going to bat rubbed his hand on the kinks of that black head and drew forth skill, strength, and certainty."

On their return from the ballpark, the Royal Rooters presented an evening concert. Their musical engagements, however, did not come without a price. In the morning, McGreevey and Charley Lavis, the leaders of the Rooters, had been served with breach of contract papers by the band they had hired the day before. The plaintiffs, the Greater Pittsburg Band, claimed that the Rooters had hired them for four days at $80 per day. Lavis denounced the charges and claimed that the Rooters had intended all along to hire a different band each day. McGreevey and Lavis might have to go to court to fight the charges, a prospect that did not faze them, unless it interfered with their attending the next day's game.

THE FIFTH GAME

PITTSBURG.	AB	R	B.	P.	A.	E		BOSTON.	AB	R.	B.	P.	A.	E.
Beaumont, cf	4	1	1	0	0	0		Dougherty, lf	6	0	3	3	0	0
Clarke, lf	4	1	0	3	0	1		Collins, 3b	6	0	2	0	4	0
Leach, 3b	4	0	2	2	1	1		Stahl, cf	5	2	1	2	0	0
Wagner, ss	4	0	0	1	3	2		Freeman, rf	4	2	2	2	0	0
Bransfield, 1b	4	0	0	9	1	0		Parent, ss	5	1	2	1	4	1
Ritchey, 2b	4	0	1	1	4	0		La Chance, 1b	4	2	1	13	0	1
Sebring, rf	4	0	1	2	0	0		Ferris, 2b	5	2	1	1	3	0
Phelps, c	3	0	0	9	0	0		Criger, c	3	1	0	5	0	0
Kennedy, p	2	0	1	0	1	0		Young, p	5	1	2	0	2	0
Thompson, p	1	0	0	0	1	0								
Total	34	2	6	27	11	4		Total	43	11	14	27	13	2

```
Pittsburg...............   0   0   0   0   0   0   0   2   0—— 2
Boston .................   0   0   0   0   0   6   4   1   0——11
```

Earned runs—Boston 4. Two-base hit—Kennedy. Three-base hits—Leach, Dougherty 2, Collins, Stahl, Young. Sacrifice hits —Phelps, Criger. Stolen bases—Collins, Stahl. First on balls— Off Kennedy 3. Struck out—By Kennedy 3, Thompson 1, Young 4. Time—2h. Umpires—Connolly and O'Day. Attendance— 12,322.

PITTSBURGH'S SEASON

ONE OF THE ADVANTAGES of playing so many games during the regular season was that it allowed a team to discover something about itself. The Pirates knew that a single drastic defeat meant very little. Earlier in the year, they had lost at home by a score of 10–2 to their nemesis, the Giants, but they had rebounded to take the final two games of the series. Had he thought about it, Clarke's recollection of the Pirates' regular-season performance would have given him confidence that his team would prevail in the postseason as well.

The Pirates had opened their pennant defense in Cincinnati, in a series that sportswriters viewed as an early indication of who would compete for the National League championship in 1903. The Reds were the spring training favorites, and the Cincinnati players returned from Georgia eager to see the refurbished park in which they would play. In less than two weeks, workers had added concrete wings and new bleachers to a stadium known as the Palace of the Fans. The clubhouse featured skylights and high ceilings, modern plumbing, and a reading and smoking den.

Manager Joe Kelley declared the diamond as green as Ireland's flag, and on Thursday, April 16, his team took to the field.

The Pirates arrived in Cincinnati with sportswriters wondering about the team's outlook. The *Pittsburg Dispatch* reported that the squad was a disappointment and simply was not as strong, especially in the pitching department, as previous teams. After leaving Hot Springs, they had played several exhibition games against minor-league clubs in Little Rock and Louisville and had won only one of those affairs, needing ten innings to do so. Against Louisville, the Pirates were "outbatted and outfielded." And the champions had tried their hardest. By comparison, Kelley's "Red Legs" were playing well and working together as a team. "The prospects for bringing the pennant again to Pittsburg," confessed sportswriter Frank M'Quiston, "are dim."

The night before the opening game, the Pirates gathered together at the Burnett House in Cincinnati and sang songs, just "as did the old Romans on the eve of Battle." They crooned "Mr. Dooley," "My Old Kentucky Home," and "It's the Custom in Ireland." Fred Clarke named Deacon Phillippe his opening-day starting pitcher. As the players received their new uniforms, Tommy Leach was heard cursing and screaming. Although the team had sent in his correct measurements, his uniform hung on him like a sheet over a chair. Leach spent the evening trying to secure the services of a tailor so as to be ready for the next afternoon. The weather outside was windy and raw, and the prospects for a sizable opening-day crowd seemed dreary. The local weather man, joked one writer, had received so many calls inquiring about the conditions for the game that he had taken to drink.

Despite the weather, 12,000 fans turned out for baseball. They watched as helplessly as the Cincinnati players while Deacon Phillippe dominated. In nine innings, he pitched to only 30 Reds and yielded only two hits as the Pirates won easily by a score of 7–1. Fred Clarke and Tommy Leach each tripled, and Honus Wagner had two hits. He also made a defensive play in the fourth inning that made headlines. Joe Kelley smashed a line drive to

Wagner's right at shortstop. Honus leaped, got his glove on the ball, but was off balance and couldn't hold on to it. The ball fell to one side, but Wagner lunged and grabbed it with his bare hand before it touched the ground. After the game, Kelley was both disgusted and astounded. Wagner's catch was "little short of a crime," and he had never seen such dominance so early in the season as displayed by Phillippe. "It was surely championship ball on the part of Pittsburg," he said.

The Pirates repeated the feat in the next game, as Ed Doheny beat the Reds, 9–2, and Clarke and Wagner starred. In the third game, the Reds carried a lead into the eighth, but the Pirates scored three times in the top of the inning and won the contest 5–4. The season was several games old and already Cincinnati was in a panic. Some fans in Porktown, as the city was known because of its role as the pork-packing center of the Midwest, "feel almost ready to bet that Cincinnati will not win a game this year." In the fourth game, on April 19, the Reds sent their ace, Noodles Hahn, to the mound. The twenty-four-year-old lefty had won 20 games or more in three of his first four years in professional ball. He pitched well in his season debut, but two throwing errors led to four unearned runs and Pittsburgh swept the four-game series. Dismayed with his team's effort, Kelley held a three-hour practice the next day and predicted that the results would be different when the teams met again.

As for the Pirates, dire predictions just days earlier now turned to a rosy forecast. "Pittsburg is strong all down the line," said one manager. "Sherlock Holmes himself couldn't find a weak spot in the team." "A team, like an individual," mused M'Quiston, "is helped or retarded by the start made." The Pirates' start showed that the players "fit together like the parts of a clock." "The whole base ball world was surprised at the wonderful showing made by the Pirates at Cincinnati," reported the *Sporting News*.

The way the Pirates started thrilled Pittsburgh fans, and more than 20,000 turned out for the home opener against St. Louis on Tuesday, April 21. The streets surrounding Exposition Park "resembled nothing so much as a gigantic pair of ant hills." The fans, who included hundreds of women and girls who were "dyed-in-the-wool" supporters, crowded into the stands and stood ten deep on the field. A band led the way as the team rode through in carriages. The official song of the National League, "In the Good Old Summer Time," was played, and Harry Pulliam, the National League president, stepped forward to present the 1902 pennant to proud owner Barney Dreyfuss. His remarks placed winning a baseball championship in the context of all the triumphs that mattered most to men of his class:

> In all walks of life and in every vocation there are goals which ambitious men strive for. In commerce it is the accumulation of wealth and the founding of mercantile names that reach around the globe; in war it is the winning of immortal victories; in art it is the creation of masterpieces that will live forever; in literature, it is the authorship of books that molds the thoughts of men. . . . The striving for the best in all things holds true in athletics as well as it does in any other occupation. In base ball the zenith of a ball player's desire from the time he first learns the rudiments of the game on the lots until he becomes a member of a uniformed team is to be a member of a team holding the championship.

The day's game, which the Pirates lost, seemed an afterthought to the ceremony in which Pittsburgh's second pennant was lifted into the breeze. The next day marked the emergence of Jimmy Sebring as a star. The twenty-one-year-old rookie from Bucknell College smashed two home runs and made a throw from right field that helped save the game. Most of the Pirates had nicknames, but Sebring was so unknown that the players simply called him Jimmy. Phillippe was the Deacon, Fred Clarke was Cap, catcher Harry Smith was Smithy, Eddie Phelps was Smilie, Sam Leever was Schoolmaster or Professor, Ed Doheny was called Irish, Bucky Veil was Shadow, Bransfield was Kitty, Ritchey was Little All Right or Heine, Leach was the Wee, Beaumont was Red or Ginger, and Wagner was the Carnegie Dutchman or Honus or simply Hans. Nicknames were like individual tattoos and they seldom faded over time. One former player, Jimmy Holliday, who was now umpiring, squirmed every time a player greeted him as Bug.

The Pirates played well in April, winning 9 out of 13 games for the month, but found themselves in second place behind the New York Giants. John McGraw's team had two of the finest pitchers in the game: Christy Mathewson and Joe McGinnity. The two would combine to appear in 94 out of the 139 games played in 1903. The Pirates would travel to New York in mid-May, but first they had to play multiple games against Chicago, St. Louis, Cincinnati, and Philadelphia.

Great teams can survive accidents and slumps; good teams can not. It was unclear still whether the 1903 Pirates were truly great or merely good. Jimmy Sebring fell ill with a high fever toward the end of April, and Wagner moved to right field to fill in. While his outfield play was "on the sensational order," he slipped into a batting slump. Having hit over .400 for the first two weeks, Wagner scratched out only five hits over the next fortnight, and his average dropped over 100 points. Frustration mounted as Chicago's Jack Taylor beat the Pirates three times in nine days, including a game in which Phillippe yielded nine runs on nine hits in the ninth inning. The infield play was far from championship caliber. In one game against St. Louis, Doheny and Bransfield watched one another as a bunted ball rolled untouched and remained fair. "That there is something wrong with the twice champions can be seen without glasses," observed M'Quiston. "That something must be done to get them working together is also patent."

Cincinnati came into Pittsburgh on May 7, looking for revenge from the opening series. The Pirates lost in extra innings despite the extraordinary play of Fred Clarke, who came to bat six times and hit for the cycle, sacrificed, walked, and stole a base. In the fifth inning, Wagner tried to steal and came into the bag with spikes high. Second baseman Jack Morrissey took exception, and the two players bumped one another. Morrissey later claimed that Wagner threw a punch. Players rushed into the fray, and when it was over, umpire Holliday ejected Wagner (maybe Honus had called him something worse than Bug). The next day, Harry Pulliam suspended him for three games for deliberately trying to spike another player. "Wagner is a whole team in himself, and whenever he is not playing there is an enormous hole in that Smoketown crew," wrote the *Sporting News*.

The Pirates lost three out of five to the Reds and fell into third place behind New York and Chicago. Wagner returned to the lineup for the fifth game of the Cincinnati series, but he managed only one hit, and the Pirates lost 3–1. The team was playing lackluster ball: "they did not hit the ball hard enough to win a game of ping pong." After a team meeting, Clarke announced that the players had voted to "cut out all kicking" with the umpires. They wanted to focus on a run at the pennant and did not want to risk any further suspensions. The team prepared to leave for a critical trip east to Philadelphia, New York, Brooklyn, and Boston, a trip that could influence the outcome of the season.

The Pirates took three of four from the Phillies. Sebring returned to the lineup, and Wagner again found his batting eye as he stroked eight hits in fifteen at-bats. The team had regained some confidence as it came into New York, but the sight of the crowd at the Polo Grounds on Saturday, May 16, must have given the players some pause. In what was considered the largest crowd ever to witness a game in the city, more than 30,000 fans turned out. For the first time in the history of the Polo Grounds, all balls hit into the crowd assembled in the cavernous outfield would be ground-rule doubles. Twenty-two-year-old right-hander Christy Mathewson took to the slab for the Giants. In only his third full season of professional ball, Mathewson would eventually establish himself as the dominant pitcher of the era. Starting in 1903, he would win 20 or more games in twelve consecutive seasons.

Mathewson was admired not only for his pitching, but also for his clean-cut, gentlemanly demeanor, which stood in stark contrast to the gruff appearance of other players, most notably his manager John McGraw. Matty's mother had never wanted her son to be a professional baseball player. "Sometimes I find consolation," she said, "in the thought that perhaps he *is* a preacher. His work has brought him before the multitude in a kindly manner; his example is a cleanly one. He reaches the masses of the people in his own way and he must give them something through his character."

With Matty matched against the less formidable Bill Kennedy, oddsmakers made the Pirates an underdog for the first time in two years. Pittsburgh fans bet heavily on their team, and lost heavily as well. Mathewson tamed the Pirates and coasted to a 7–3 victory. Roger Bresnahan, who would hit .350 for the season and play four different positions, led the Giants with a double and a triple.

The Pirates won the next game on May 18, managing to beat McGinnity, 3–2. The game was marred by several incidents that involved Giants catcher Frank Bowerman. The Pirates brought out the worst in Bowerman, who had not forgotten how Fred Clarke had unceremoniously dumped him from Pittsburgh's roster before the season started in 1900. On one play, Clarke interfered with the catcher; on another, pitcher Ed Doheny threw his bat as Bowerman tried to settle under his pop-up. The umpire had already called him out on the infield fly rule, but the fans thought the pitcher was trying intentionally to interfere. As the crowd booed, Doheny turned and bowed, further inciting them. After the game, a mob followed Doheny to the clubhouse and threatened "to knock his block off." The crowd started to throw stones at the Pirates, and the police had to escort the team to the clubhouse. Because of his antics, Doheny was suspended for three days without pay.

In the third game, Mathewson came in to pitch the final two innings, struck out four, and earned the win when the Giants scored in the bottom of the eighth. He came back the next day to

John McGraw, Christy Mathewson, and Frank Bowerman

defeat the Pirates 2–0, earning all three Giants' victories in the series. It was the first time all season that Pittsburgh had been shut
out. The Giants had won three out of four from their rivals.

The Pirates were more than happy to cross the bridge to
Brooklyn, where they found success in the first two games against
the Superbas (Leach hit two home runs in one of the contests),
but disaster in the final two (Phillippe again lost concentration in
the ninth inning and gave up three runs to lose the game).

The champions were losing not only games but also star players. Fred Clarke had been battling back pain and exhaustion for
ten days. "The trouble with me," he said, "is a bad case of lum-
bago, the kind that makes a fellow feel as if he were ossified and
about to break into 40 pieces every time he makes a move." Dreyfuss ordered Clarke to rest and sent him to Cambridge Springs in
Pennsylvania to recuperate. In his absence, Wagner took over as
acting manager. Tommy Leach also left the team. His only son
was gravely ill with pneumonia, and he returned home to be with
his family. Other players complained of minor injuries. Harry
Smith, the catcher, had a split finger and could not play. Claude
Ritchey's arm was so sore he could barely make the throw from
second. More seriously, in a game against Boston, backup outfielder George Merritt slid into second and fractured his ankle.

The Pirates thrived on the adversity. They took two out of
three games from Boston, and then returned home on May 30
and swept a morning/afternoon doubleheader against the Reds,
who felt as if a spell had been placed on them when they met
Pittsburgh. Leach played in the second game, though an attendant
stood by the clubhouse phone, ready to relay any news of Leach's
son, and the team arranged for a carriage to carry him home immediately if he were to be summoned by the doctor. Despite all
their difficulties, the Pirates managed to win 16 and lose only 12
in the month of May. They stood in third place, five games in
back of the Cubs, who led by a few percentage points over the
Giants.

On June 1, New York arrived at Exposition Park and sent

Mathewson to the mound to open the three-game series. Once again the easygoing college graduate dominated, this time by a score of 10–2 over Ed Doheny. The Pirates "were apparently beaten before they put on their uniforms, for someone had whispered that the really and truly 'Bogie Man' Matty was to appear and do things to them in the afternoon at the ball park." The defeat placed Pittsburgh six games behind the Giants in the loss column.

But suddenly and inexplicably, fortunes turned around. Maybe it was as simple as the advice Honus Wagner gave his charges before the next day's game: "spit on your bat and hit the ball." Whatever it was, Phillippe shut out the Giants 7–0. The losing pitcher was Luther Haden Taylor, known as Dummy because he was deaf and mute. (Another deaf player, Dummy Hoy, who was active between 1888 and 1902, was said to be the reason umpires adopted hand signals on the field.) Beaumont, Sebring, and Wagner each had more than one hit; Frank Bowerman was tossed from the game after arguing with the umpire while Tommy Leach was at bat. Tensions between Bowerman and the Pirates were worsening, and the two teams still had many games to play against each other.

The following day, the Pirates did it again, blanking the Giants 5–0 and defeating McGinnity. The New York players were so jarred by their inability to hit Sam Leever that even placid Christy Mathewson, coaching third base, got thrown from the game for arguing with the umpire. The Pirates had taken two out of three from New York, were now playing good baseball, and were only four games behind the Giants and five behind the Cubs.

The Boston Nationals came into town and, in the first game, were also shut out, this time by Kaiser Wilhelm, a reliever getting a spot start. Fred Clarke returned to the lineup and smashed two hits and stole a base. That made three consecutive shutout victories. Headlines told the story of the second game against Boston: "Pittsburgs Continue Their Whitewash Crusade Making it Four Straight." This time Doheny blanked Boston 9–0. Clarke had five hits and Beaumont four, including a home run. Fans started to wonder whether anyone would ever score against the Pirates.

The final game of the series against Boston, on June 6, began in a rain that grew harder as the innings progressed. The field turned sloppy and players sought shelter in the dugouts. Finally, after six innings, Al Buckenberger, the Boston manager, requested that the game be called: the score was 4–0 Pittsburgh. That made five consecutive shutout games, forty-two innings with zeros on the scoreboard. And the Pirates had blanked their opponents for three innings prior to the start of the shutout streak. Forty-five innings of whitewash was a record as far as any of the reporters could discover. Phillippe again was the winner and Wagner, who was now batting over .350, the hitting star.

Two days later, Wagner was the fielding star. The in-state rival Phillies were in town, and the Pirates held a 2–0 lead going into the ninth. The scoreless innings streak now stood at fifty-three. With Kid Gleason and Shad Barry on second and third for the Phillies, and two out, Klondike Douglass stepped in to face Sam Leever. He hit a scorching, rising line drive between third and short. Wagner lunged to his right, leaped, and stopped the ball in its flight. "Little children in the coming years," mused Frank M'Quiston, "may forget the year Columbus discovered America . . . but they will never—no, never—forget the day that Hans Wagner made that catch!" The game was over, and the Pirates had posted their sixth consecutive shutout.

The next day, June 9, Pittsburgh held a 4–0 lead going into the fourth inning when a leadoff bunt, a base hit, and a sacrifice fly yielded a run for Philadelphia. The Pirates would win the game by a score of 7–3, but the streak was over. For fifty-six consecutive innings the Pirates had blanked the opposition. It was a record, thought one sportswriter, "that will probably stand as a league record as long as this earth manages to keep away from Mars or whatever planet is to break the one we live on to pieces."

The Pirates were winning—seven in a row, nine out of ten— but so were the first-place Giants. All that success, and still

Clarke's crew found itself four games behind McGraw's bunch. The two teams would meet in the Polo Grounds at the end of June, but the Pirates could not afford to let down and look past the dozen games to be played before then.

The team continued its winning ways. It completed the sweep of Philadelphia. On June 11, the Pirates won the first game of a scheduled three-game series with Brooklyn. They lost the next two to rain, not runs. Chicago arrived next, and the one-time league leader fell two days in a row. That made eleven consecutive victories, a Pirates record. Everyone was satisfied, except perhaps Wagner, who, although batting over .300, had gone without a hit over several games. In the second game of the series, the Pirates faced the Cubs' Jack Taylor, who, like Christy Mathewson, seemed to win every time he faced Pittsburgh. Wagner came to bat in the eighth, and after being hitless in three at-bats, decided to turn around and bat lefty. He later recalled that "there was a murmur of surprise from the fans. Even the umpire looked as if he thought me crazy. . . . I'll be doggoned if I didn't hit that ball right on the nose and whipped it down the right foul line for two bases. Everybody, including the players, roared with laughter."

On June 16, the Pirates left home for their swing across the East. They had lost only one game at home during the month. "The great record of the two-time champions is now the talk of the country," proclaimed the *Sporting News*. And they kept it up. They took three straight games from Boston and one from Philadelphia, which made fifteen consecutive victories. Wagner, after his lefty experiment, rediscovered his stroke and had ten hits, including two home runs, in eighteen at-bats. Their victory on June 19 against the Braves inched the Pirates ahead of the Giants into the National League lead.

As they arrived for a three-game series at the Polo Grounds starting on June 26, Fred Clarke found Frank Bowerman, the Giants catcher, waiting for him. Bowerman, who was built like a steel safe, asked Clarke to step into the club's office, where he confronted the Pirates manager. Earlier in the month, after Bowerman had been ejected from the game, he sat in the stands and criticized his replacement, Jack Warner. Clarke had overheard the remarks and passed them on to Warner, who then bickered with Bowerman. Now the conversation between the Giants catcher and the Pirates manager suddenly turned violent and, in what was later described as a "premeditated and malignant" attack, Bowerman assaulted Clarke. He knocked the manager on his back and pummeled his face. Clarke's cheek was swollen and his eye blackened, but still he played in the game and even managed to scratch out a hit. The Giants had Mathewson on the mound and again Matty won, this time 8–2.

The Giants had someone else that day as well: McGraw played George Davis at short. The action violated the peace agreement that had awarded Davis back to the White Sox in the American League, and it threatened to unleash another war both between the leagues and within the National League, where the owners in Cincinnati, Chicago, and St. Louis declared that they would refuse to play the Giants if Davis was in the lineup. John Brush, owner of the Giants, used the trade of Kid Elberfeld from Detroit to the New York Highlanders as the excuse to break the peace treaty. Brush despised the presence of a competing American League team in New York, and he argued that the personnel on that team had been set by the terms of the peace agreement. But the Giants owner was merely looking for an excuse to play Davis, especially now that the pennant race with the Pirates was so tight. He petitioned Harry Pulliam for permission, and the National League president granted it. Baseball fans, pleased with how the season was going, denounced Brush and Pulliam for hatching a "selfish and unscrupulous scheme to abrogate the peace agreement and renew the major league war."

In the wake of Bowerman's attack and Pulliam's ruling, Pirates owner Barney Dreyfuss rushed to New York to meet with the National League president. Dreyfuss called for the expulsion of the Giants' catcher, but he declined comment on the Davis matter. The first matter would be resolved on the field when the Gi-

ants came to Pittsburgh in July. The courts would resolve the
other. Ban Johnson denounced Pulliam's actions as "unwarranted
and absurd." "By your decision," he wrote, "you condone dis-
honesty and have placed a premium on contract jumping." Johnson took to the courts, and at the request of the American
League, a federal judge issued an injunction that enjoined Davis
from playing in any more games. Davis's season came to an end. It
had consisted of 4 games, 15 at-bats in all. The next year he would
play for the White Sox in the American League, and would remain there until he retired in 1909.

The Pirates won a remarkable 17 out of 20 games in June, and
they started July just as hot. Despite fearful thunderstorms, 19,000
Pittsburgh fans turned out for a July 4 doubleheader in which
Leever and Phillippe swept both games from the last-place
Phillies. But the day had its price. Late in the second game, Clarke
dove for a ball and landed on his right shoulder after making the
catch. He came up with his arm hanging at his side, the ligaments
in his shoulder badly strained. He would be out for nearly a
month. Again, Wagner would lead the club.

Even without Clarke, the team kept winning at Exposition
Park. "The word ball game seems a misnomer," declared the *Dispatch*. "There are supposed to be two sides to every decent game,
but there is but one side in this daily affair over at the park."

By mid-July the Pirates led the standings by two games in the
loss column, and the second-place Giants were coming to town
for a four-game series. Perhaps in an attempt to thwart trouble,
Pulliam announced on July 15, just prior to the first game of the
series, that Bowerman was fined $100 for his assault on Clarke.
The Giants arrived with two New York City detectives to protect
the players from any reprisal from the fans. But other than being
booed lustily whenever he appeared, Bowerman came away un-
scathed. The same could not be said about the Pirates. Although
they had jumped out to a 2–0 lead against their nemesis Mathewson, they could not hold it. Doheny weakened in the ninth inning
and allowed the Giants to go ahead 3–2 on a two-run single by

none other than Frank Bowerman. The Pirates tied it in the bottom of the ninth when Tommy Leach singled to score Bransfield. The teams went back and forth until finally, in the fourteenth inning, the Giants broke through and won the game. Mathewson and Doheny both stayed in until game's end.

The Pirates exacted revenge the next day, as they scored sixteen runs and knocked McGinnity out of the game in the fifth inning. Sebring led the attack with two home runs, a triple, and a single. Kitty Bransfield contributed four hits, and Sam Leever earned his thirteenth victory of the season. The next day the Pirates won in twelve innings. The fourth game of the series would prove critical. A Pittsburgh victory would stretch their lead in the pennant race to four games; a loss would return it to two. Recognizing the importance of the contest, McGraw asked Mathewson to pitch. But the star refused. He felt overworked and was still angry over being forced to go fourteen innings three days earlier. Little-used Roscoe Miller got the emergency start and took a game tied at two into the ninth inning. With two outs and a man on second, Beaumont was down to his last strike when he lined a double that drove home the winning run.

A disgruntled, disheartened Giants team left town. There were two months of ball left to play, but McGraw knew that if the Pirates kept playing the way they had been since June, the contest in the National League would be for second place. The Pirates went on the road and promptly lost four out of their next five; but the Giants lost five in a row.

Given the depth of the Pirates' pitching staff, everyone believed Pittsburgh would win going away. Barney Dreyfuss certainly felt confident. On July 27, he issued a challenge to the American League for a postseason championship series between the two leagues to settle "the question of baseball supremacy." He would end up waiting until September for a response.

The day after the announcement, Ed Doheny deserted the team. He was in Cincinnati, playing billiards with Ginger Beaumont when he yelled out, "There's one of them, Beau." Doheny had become delusional and believed he was being followed by detectives; the twelve-game winner suddenly packed his bags and returned home to Andover, Massachusetts. No one quite knew what to make of the situation. Some said he had been drinking. Others noted his erratic throws on the field and his despair over losing the fourteen-inning affair to Mathewson. Quietly, the players acknowledged that they had grown nervous with Doheny on the mound. Others insisted that the desertion of the left-handed pitcher badly weakened the team.

The growing list of injuries was as problematic as Doheny's behavior. "Big Hospital List," read the headlines as several starters suffered from nagging injuries: swollen hand (Wagner), sprained ankle (Bransfield), sore back (Phillippe), and even dizzy spells (Ritchey). The Giants stood seven and a half games behind the Pirates in the standings. Desperate to get his team back in the race, McGraw gave himself a rare start at third on August 1 and watched as Joe McGinnity pitched complete-game victories in both ends of a doubleheader in Boston. McGinnity would accomplish the feat twice more in August. The pitcher, who would throw 434 innings in 1903, certainly lived up to his nickname, "Iron Man."

But it did not matter how well the Giants did. The Pirates followed their record of 17 wins and 9 losses in July with an even better record of 18 wins and 9 losses in August. Although the Giants won 21 out of 30 games in August, their record of 16 losses to only 11 wins in July had doomed them. The Pirates got Clarke back, and Doheny returned in mid-August, though he pitched unevenly. After splitting four games with the Giants in mid-August (Mathewson won the two games, making it eight times that he had defeated Pittsburgh during the season), the Pirates reeled off fourteen consecutive victories.

Opposing teams were so taken with the Pirates that some players offered to wager on them in a postseason championship series against Boston, who looked as if they would capture the American League pennant. Jock Menefee, who pitched both ends of a doubleheader for the Cubs against the Pirates on September 7, was willing to bet $2,500. "Pittsburg outclasses the Boston American League players at every turn," he said. But even as he spoke, in one of the Labor Day games against the Cubs, Wagner hurt himself and was feared lost for the season. He couldn't put his foot on the ground without feeling pain in his left leg. Without Wagner, there would be no postseason championship series. "The Pittsburg team without Wagner is not the Pittsburg team. It would be like Romeo and Juliet without Romeo," lamented Frank M'Quiston.

A week later, Wagner returned to the lineup, but he still wasn't feeling right. Between games of a doubleheader on September 18, Wagner met with Bonesetter Reese, an oil driller, not a physician, who had a reputation across baseball for knowing "a lot about twisted ligaments . . . and can get them back into place without the aid of instruments." Wagner recalled that "he tried to work my left leg up around my neck like a contortionist. I was afraid he'd cripple me." But the treatment seemed to help; Wagner said the leg felt fifty pounds lighter than before Bonesetter worked on it.

Pittsburgh's victory in the second game clinched the team's third consecutive pennant. Clarke rewarded his players. He allowed Phillippe and Leever to go on a fishing trip, and he rested Wagner. But still all was not well. Doheny again left the team, this time for good. And both Leach and Ritchey were suffering from injuries. Their play, however, belied the complaints. The season ended in Pittsburgh with a series against New York, and in the first game the Pirates lashed twenty-two hits for a total of thirty-eight bases in a 15–7 victory over McGraw's club. Wagner was batting over .350 for the season. So was Clarke, though in nearly thirty fewer games. Beaumont was at .340. Both Leach and Ritchey raised their averages near .300. The Pirates had great hitting going into the series with Boston. The question to be answered was whether or not their pitching would hold up.

Barney Dreyfuss, for one, was confident that it would. And

even if it did not, the series would promise to be a financial boon. Dreyfuss had spent more than $125,000 on the team in 1903. He figured that it required half a million admissions to earn back his investment, but that season the Pirates drew only 326,000 fans. The owner devoted his energies to knowing who all the young players in the country were, and he spent freely to acquire them. "The baseball business," he said, "is largely a game of chance." It was an "expensive luxury," but one that he relished. No one believed that Dreyfuss was not making a fortune on the team. He "wears a continual smile," reported the *Sporting News*, "and occasionally touches his coin-pocket with a complacent gesture."

But the series with Boston involved much more than making money. Arthur Soden, the owner of the Boston Braves, from whom Dreyfuss had to get permission to play because the series would infringe on the chance for Boston's National League franchise to earn postseason money, expressed his hope that "the result of said games may establish more firmly the supremacy of the National League." With great anticipation, Dreyfuss prepared for the World's Championship Series. He couldn't help but agree with one sportswriter's prediction: the Americans "will get the beating of a lifetime."

FINAL NATIONAL LEAGUE STANDINGS

TEAM	W	L	WL%	GB
Pittsburgh	91	49	.650	—
New York	84	55	.604	6.5
Chicago	82	56	.594	8.0
Cincinnati	74	65	.532	16.5
Brooklyn	70	66	.515	19.0
Boston	58	80	.420	32.0
Philadelphia	49	86	.363	39.5
St. Louis	43	94	.314	46.5

GAME SIX, THURSDAY, OCTOBER 8

BARNEY DREYFUSS AROSE EARLY. His team had been ahead three games to one. Now Boston was one game away from tying the series. And Dinneen was pitching again. Dreyfuss wasn't even certain whom Clarke was going to start. Perhaps it would be Bucky Veil, the twenty-two-year-old rookie who had started only six games all season. Although hurting, Leever had told his manager that he was able to pitch. Dreyfuss certainly hoped so. If Leever could perform well, then Phillippe would only have to win one more game. Whatever happened in the sixth game, Dreyfuss felt the team could use a rest. Four games in four days in the most intensely watched series anyone could remember would have everyone a little on edge. A day's rest after the third game in Pittsburgh would be good for the players, and it would be good for business. Postpone Friday's game to Saturday and the gate would increase by at least 6,000 people. Good baseball, good business.

Dreyfuss dressed and scrambled over to the Monongahela House to call on Collins and business manager Joseph Smart. He proposed postponing Friday's game to Saturday, and mentioned that the steelworks around Pittsburgh would close for the afternoon so fans could take in the game.

Collins's face grew red. He saw through Dreyfuss's request as an attempt to buy Phillippe an extra day's rest. Postponing "might mean more money," he exclaimed, "but money does not alone actuate us. . . . We are conceding nothing."

Dreyfuss left for Exposition Park hoping for a good effort that afternoon and rain the following day. Nearly 12,000 people found their way to the ballpark. The Royal Rooters, having spent the morning looking to bet on the game, assembled at 1:30 p.m. for a procession to the park. For the third day, a different band led the way, followed by the Boston players in ten open barouches and the fans. They arrived at the park waving their red parasols and preparing for another afternoon of raucous singing and rooting. That day, however, the Pirate fans refused to be outdone by the small but visible contingent of Boston Rooters. They tore paper and scorecards into little pieces and watched them blow like a "fake snow storm" across the field. They too cheered and sang. Old-time baseball fans sitting in the stands declared it was "the loudest and most effective rooting in the annals of the American national game."

When the Pittsburgh battery of Leever and Phelps was announced, a roar went through the crowd. The *Boston Post* reported that Leever "was saved for today's game under cover of an alleged sore arm," and that the pitcher bet $200 of his own money at even odds that he would win. But anyone who saw the righty grimace every time he threw the ball knew the injury was not phony, and that Leever showed pluck and determination in taking the ball for the sixth game. No one would blame him if he faltered. Just his presence on the mound gave the Boston players pause. After all, Leever had led the National League in ERA and shutouts in 1903.

The first inning of the game gave the Americans little reason to think anything was wrong with the ace. Dougherty grounded out to Ritchey to open the game, and Collins flied out to Sebring in right field. When Stahl fouled out to Leach, Leever strode to the bench and received a wild, standing ovation from the crowd.

Dinneen came out for the bottom of the first and heard three cheers from the Boston Rooters. He had pitched well two days earlier, but had lost to Phillippe. Although Dinneen had struck out 7 batters in the fourth game, he had surrendered 12 hits. He would have to keep the Pirates off base, or at least have better luck, if he was going to prevail today.

Beaumont grounded out to Ferris to begin the Pirates' turn at bat in the first inning. Clarke then showed his speed when he beat out an infield hit. Leach hit into a fielder's choice and forced Clarke at second. Leach, who had good speed, stole second and continued on to third when Criger's throw scooted past the bag. Wagner was up. A run would boost the struggling Pirates, but Honus popped up to short to end the threat.

In the second inning, both teams went down easily. The Pirates turned a double play to end Boston's turn at bat. They then squandered a two-out hit by Sebring when Phelps struck out. So far Leever was holding up and Dinneen was working effectively.

In the top of the third inning, Ferris bounced back to the pitcher. Leever made a nice one-handed stop, and recorded the out. Criger fouled out to his counterpart behind the plate. There were two quick outs with only the opposing pitcher left to retire. Dinneen hit the ball up the middle. It would have been a routine play for Wagner, but Leever deflected the ball away from the shortstop and Dinneen was credited with an infield single. Dougherty then walked. With runners on first and second, Collins stepped in and delivered a base hit to center field. Dinneen rounded third and scored the first run of the game; Dougherty stopped at second. On the first pitch of the next at-bat, Chick Stahl singled and Dougherty scored. Collins took third on the play. With runners on the corners, Buck Freeman settled in at the plate. He took the first pitch in order to give Stahl a chance to steal second. Stahl, who had had 10 stolen bases all season, succeeded, and two men were now in scoring position. Freeman hit a slow roller to third, but Leach mishandled the chance, and Collins came home. The inning ended when Parent bounced back to Leever. Boston had scored three runs with two outs and with a bit of luck.

The Pirates managed to place a runner in scoring position in the bottom of the third with one down, but left him stranded there when Clarke struck out and Leach popped out. In the top of the fourth inning, the Americans loaded the bases on singles by Ferris and Criger, and Dougherty reached on yet another error by Wagner, his third in two games. Fortunately for the home team, with two outs, Collins grounded out to end the threat. Boston was not hitting Leever hard, but they were making him work. Pittsburgh also had its chances. They put two men on in the bottom of the fourth, after Wagner grounded back to the pitcher, but still were unable to cut into Boston's three-run lead.

To lead off the fifth inning, Stahl tripled into the crowd in left. Some viewed it as the longest shot of the series so far, a sure inside-the-park home run but for the outfield fans that necessitated the ground rule. Freeman did his job by hitting a deep fly ball to the center fielder. The out allowed Stahl to tag up and score. Leever then hit Parent with a pitch. That brought LaChance to the plate, but the first baseman could only hit a routine fly for the second out. Hobe Ferris had better luck and lined the ball into center field for a single. Parent was running hard on contact and scored from first when the relay throw was mishandled and reached home off line. The inning ended when Criger grounded out, but Boston had tacked on two more runs, to lead 5–0.

The Pittsburgh fans sat in stunned silence. The game was half over, and their Pirates looked flat at the bat and sluggish in the field. Ever since their rally in the ninth inning of the fourth game, Boston's luck had changed. The Pirates needed to find a way to turn it back again in their favor. The Royal Rooters, meanwhile, sang and cheered incessantly. During one of Boston's rallies the day before, they had crooned the popular hit "Tessie," and now they wouldn't stop:

Tessie, you make me feel so badly,
Why don't you turn around?
Tessie, you know I love you madly;
Babe, my heart weighs about a pound.

Worse yet, the Royal Rooters adapted the lyrics to tease the opposing players:

Honus why do you hit so badly
Take a back seat and sit down.
Honus, at bat you look so sadly
Hey, why don't you get out of town.

The competition between the teams extended into a competition between the fans. The Pittsburgh fans continued to fill the air with paper that settled on the caps and shoulders of the Boston

Rooter's Souvenir
BOSTON - PITTSBURG
Oct., 1903.   M. T. McGreevy

No. 1.
    Boston, Pittsburg,
    Who are we?
    We are the rooters for 19–3.
    We will win,
    Go tell your pa,
    We Beaneaters, Beaneaters,
    Rah! Rah! Rah!

No. 2.
    Five games, Five games,
    We want five,
    We are here and all alive;
    Biff! Bang! Bang, Bang, Bang!
    Zim! Zam! Zam, Zam, Zam!

No. 3.
    In the good old summer time,
    Our Boston Base Ball Nine
    Beat the teams—east and west,
    Now they're first in line.
    The Pittsburgs they are after us,
    O me! O me! O my!
    We'll do them as we did the rest
    In the good old summer time.

3rd Base.   Nuffsaid.

players in the field. And they "roared like Niagara Falls," just as the pitcher started his motion. Tim Murnane of the *Globe* took offense at the fans' actions: "The Boston rooters are educated in the fine points of their art," he observed, "and never root to bother an opposing pitcher. Not so with the local enthusiasts, who never lost a chance to ruffle the feelings of the Boston men."

In the bottom of the fifth, Beaumont singled and stole second with one out, but again the Pirates failed to deliver, as Clarke struck out and Leach flied out to Stahl in center. In the sixth, Boston could not muster a threat, and the Pirates followed by going down in order. The game was growing short. Leever had scattered only eight hits, but Boston had five runs to show. In the top of the seventh inning, Boston added another run when Parent smashed a triple to left and LaChance followed with a double. The score stood 6–0 heading into the bottom of the seventh. Although Dinneen had struck out only three, he seemed to be pitching effortlessly.

Jimmy Sebring led off the bottom of the seventh with a single to right, and Ed Phelps followed with a poke past second. The fans awakened and hoped that, at last, the lethargic Pirate bats had done the same. Leever was due up, and Clarke must have thought about pinch-hitting for him, but he had no reliable reliever to bring into the game. Leever did his job by grounding to first and advancing the runners into scoring position.

Beaumont stepped in. The center fielder had already singled twice in the game; after going hitless in twelve at-bats in Boston, he had amassed six hits in Pittsburgh. Beaumont promptly lined a single over second base and knocked in the first two Pirate runs of the game. The crowd pleaded for the home team to keep the rally going and crawl back into the game.

Fred Clarke came up and did not disappoint. He doubled over Dougherty's head in left. Beaumont probably could have scored, but he remained at third, realizing that if he was thrown out at home the rally would receive a blow from which it would not recover. Collins walked over to Dinneen to try and settle him down and then jogged back to his position at third base. Leach came to bat and hit the ball deep to center, but Stahl brought it in. Beaumont scored easily from third, and the Boston lead had been cut in half, 6–3.

With two out, Clarke stole third in "a daring and beautiful bit of running." Maybe a wild pitch would bring in yet another run. Wagner was up. He had been hitless in his last seven times at bat. But the fans' memory was long term, not short. Time and again he had delivered, and there was every hope that he would do so again. Perhaps Dinneen felt the same way. He gave the batting champion nothing good to swing at, and Wagner took first with a walk. The problem with working around a batter is that it can disturb a pitcher's rhythm. Sure enough, Dinneen also walked Kitty Bransfield. The Pirates had the bases loaded with two out.

The fans could not contain themselves. They prayed. They pleaded. They screamed. Frank M'Quiston observed that "men who could write their checks in six figures stood on chairs along side of the day laborer and yelled until black in the face." People "were slapping one another on the backs, jumping up and down, and carrying on like a lot of maniacs, and such yelling was enough to put any twirler up in the air." The situation thrust everyone into a "prolonged siege of yelling and rooting," into a "state of almost drunken ecstasy." Everyone but the Royal Rooters, that is, who "watched with death-like silence."

Claude Ritchey came up to bat. A shot beyond the ropes would tie the game. Having not done much during the series offensively, the second baseman was due to produce a big hit. Dinneen delivered and Ritchey made sharp contact. But Parent gobbled it up at short and tossed to Ferris at second for the force to end the inning.

Pittsburgh's three-run outburst had renewed the confidence of their fans. The rally, they believed, had turned the game around. Dinneen had slowed considerably. There were still two innings to play. When Leever retired Boston in order in the top of the eighth, the fans rose as one to greet the Pirates as they jogged off the field.

Collins had Norwood Gibson warming up after the seventh, and was ready to change pitchers. But Dinneen pleaded with his manager to leave him in, and Collins relented. The decision appeared sound when the bottom of the Pittsburgh order put up no struggle in the home half of the eighth. The game turned to its final inning.

In the ninth, Leever again put the Americans down in order. With a sore shoulder, he had pitched gamely. He had yielded ten hits, only one more than Dinneen, who still had an inning to pitch. Leever had walked only two; Dinneen had walked three. Neither had the stuff to strike batters out. A timely hit or two, and better defense, could well have had the Pirates ahead. Up to this point, Dinneen "did not pitch a better game, but he had far superior support." Such was baseball, and the top of the Pirates' order came to bat determined to knock Dinneen out of the box.

Beaumont led off and singled sharply for his fourth hit of the game. Delirium filled the park as "11,000 now thoroughly mad people set up a howling that would do credit to any army of Indians."

Fred Clarke walked to the plate. He wanted badly to win this game and secure a chance to end the series in Pittsburgh. The idea of another day-long train ride to Boston filled him with despair. Clarke "swung viciously," and the fans shrieked as he made contact. His line drive was headed up the middle. From shortstop, Fred Parent raced toward second, picked the ball clean while it was an inch off the ground, and in one motion fired to first to double up Beaumont, who didn't realize that the ball had never touched the ground. Two outs. Fans dropped to their seats in disbelief.

Tommy Leach was the Pirates' last hope. "Peace and Leach," they had declared was all the National League had gained from the baseball war. Well, he had proven he was a valuable asset.

Coming into the game, he had more hits than anyone in the series. He took a pitch for a ball, then one for a strike. He wouldn't be hurried or anxious. A full game was 27 outs, not 26. Dinneen came right in with a fastball over the plate and Leach swung, but he got under the ball. It sailed straight back and Criger took off after it. The ball floated down toward the extra seats that had been added on the field. The catcher reached out and snared it to end the game. Boston had won 6–3. The series was tied, three games apiece.

Dinneen left the field on the shoulders of the Royal Roosters. He had pitched his third complete game of the series, and had won two of them. Credit for the day's victory went to his determined pitching and the outstanding defense played by the Americans. Collins had twice made one-handed plays on bunts. Ferris covered the entire right side of the infield. LaChance, whom Collins had considered trading in the spring, played the best defense that had been seen all season at first base. And the play of Parent, some Boston partisans felt, "made the great Wagner look cheap."

Collins also gave credit to the Boston fans. "I do not know what I would have done without them," he said. "Their encouraging us to victory has meant lots to us in these games. They share in the victory with us."

After the game, the Boston players couldn't have been more confident. Fred Parent proclaimed, "Boston will win. These fellows stop when you once get a lead on them and they have nothing on us at any time." And Collins made it clear to any who had doubted that the team was "out to win the series. Pittsburg had all the luck at the start and our boys failed to hit. They are hitting now, and Phillippe or any other player cannot stop us."

It had been "a nerve-racking, thrilling game," filled with "anxiety and suspense." But Boston had prevailed and the Pirates looked nervous, much as the Americans had in the first game. The losers returned to the clubhouse, sat quietly, and began to change out of their uniforms.

Barney Dreyfuss walked in. No one hated to lose more than Dreyfuss, whose entire "heart and soul" was wrapped up in winning the World's Championship. The players expected to receive a verbal thrashing from the owner, but what they got was encouragement: "Boys you're doing well and you'll win yet. I am proud of the way you are fighting for none save you and myself know under what adverse conditions we entered this fight. We are going to keep right at them and we'll beat them yet. We will beat them to-morrow and then finish them in sight of their friends in Boston. If we don't beat them tomorrow, we'll beat them two in Boston. Cheer up."

The players went home eager to win the next day, not only for themselves and their fans, but also for an owner who still believed in them.

THE SIXTH GAME

PITTSBURG.	AB.	R.	B.	P.	A.	E.		BOSTON.	AB.	R.	B.	P.	A.	E.
Beaumont, cf.....	5	1	4	5	0	0		Dougherty, lf.....	3	1	1	1	0	0
Clarke, lf.........	5	0	2	2	0	0		Collins, 3b........	5	1	1	1	2	0
Leach, 3b.........	5	0	0	1	2	2		Stahl, cf.........	5	1	2	2	0	0
Wagner, ss........	3	0	0	2	5	1		Freeman, rf.......	5	0	0	1	0	0
Bransfield, 1b.....	3	0	1	11	0	0		Parent, ss.........	4	2	1	5	2	0
Ritchey, 2b.......	3	0	0	1	3	0		La Chance, 1b.....	4	0	1	9	2	0
Sebring, rf........	4	1	2	2	0	0		Ferris, 2b.........	4	0	2	1	3	0
Phelps, c..	4	1	1	3	0	0		Criger, c.........	4	0	1	6	0	1
Leever, p.........	4	0	0	0	2	0		Dineen, p.........	4	1	1	1	2	0
Total	36	3	10	27	12	3		Total...........	38	6	10	27	11	1

Pittsburg.................	0	0	0	0	0	0	3	0	0— 3
Boston............	0	0	3	0	2	0	1	0	0— 6

Earned runs—Pittsburg 2, Boston 3. Two-base hits—Clarke LaChance. Three-base hits—Stahl, Parent. Stolen bases—Beaumont 2, Clark, Leach, Stahl. Double plays—Ritchey. Wagner, Bransfield; Parent, LaChance. First on balls—Off Leever 2, Dineen 3. Hit by pitcher—Parent. Struck out—By Leever 2, Dineen 3. Time—2.02. Umpires—O'Day and Connolly. Attendance—11,556.

BOSTON'S SEASON

BOSTON HAD STARTED POORLY in the World's Championship, but now it seemed that the players were clicking. Collins knew his team well, and at the beginning of the season it had worried him how the Americans would always seem to lose the first game of a series, but would then rally back. Even at the end of the season, playing at home with the pennant secured, they had surrendered the opening game of the final series before winning three straight. They were slow starters, but strong finishers. The question was whether that pattern would continue.

The Americans had begun their season with a morning/after-noon doubleheader on Monday, April 20, to celebrate Patriots' Day, observed each year throughout Massachusetts in celebration of the Battles of Lexington and Concord. More than 27,000 fans attended the two games—the largest paid attendance ever for a single day. The day was perfect for baseball: "a warm sun shone from a clear blue sky from start to finish." "There are many sports and pastimes," offered one editorial, "but base ball is the only real game." The caption beneath a *Boston Globe* drawing of joyous fans stated the meaning of opening day: "Ah-h-h-h-h . . . Life is again worth living."

Jimmy Collins's crew began against Connie Mack's champion Athletics, who sent the formidable Rube Waddell to the mound. Waddell threw hard and lived hard. Starting in 1902, he would lead the league in strikeouts for six consecutive seasons. Sometimes, in exhibition games, he would call the outfielders off the field and then strike out the side. He also led the league in barroom brawls and erratic behavior. In July, he not only deserted the team but, upon his return, jumped into the stands and throttled a fan who criticized his pitching. The courtly Mr. Mack, as he was known, bailed Waddell out, but the tempestuous relationship between the stern Mack and the sinner Waddell would not last. In February 1908, Mack would sell the pitcher to the Browns for $5,000.

Waddell struck out the first four men that he faced, but in the top of the fifth, Boston exploded for five runs and went on to win, 9–4. George Winter started for Boston. Only twenty-three years old, Winter had joined the Americans in 1901 after playing for four years at Gettysburg College. He was trying to show that he was fully recovered from the typhoid fever that had nearly killed him in 1902. Collins pulled him after six innings, and Bill Dinneen came in to finish the game. Observing the effects of the foul-strike rule for the first time, the fans hissed every time it worked against their team.

But the fans had plenty to cheer about. They gave a rousing ovation to Charley Farrell, the Boston catcher, when he came to bat. Farrell had just jumped to the Americans from Brooklyn, where he had played for four seasons. Farrell broke into baseball in 1888, at age twenty-one, playing for Chicago in the National League. Boston fans fondly remembered his one season with Boston in the now defunct American Association: in 1891 he connected for 12 home runs and knocked in 110 runs. Farrell was now back in Boston, and in the first game he stroked a single and threw out five runners trying to steal; "his salary wing was in apple pie order," noted one journalist. Before the second game, the team and the Royal Rooters presented Farrell with a diamond ring to welcome him back.

In the afternoon contest, two thirty-six-year-olds comprised the Boston battery: Cy Young on the mound and Charley Farrell behind the plate. For six innings, Young allowed only one Athletic to reach base. In the seventh, however, he gave up several hits, including an otherwise routine fly ball that was ruled a triple when it landed in the overflowing crowd massed against the left-field wall. By the time the inning came to a close, Young had yielded six runs, and when the game ended, the Boston Americans had lost, 10–7. Prior to the games, no one would have predicted that both Waddell and Young would lose. "The result of the two games," reported the *Sporting News*, "illustrates the uncertainty of base ball."

April proved cruel to the team. Collins's men went on the road and lost five of their next eight games. Although they failed in their first starts, Young and Dinneen could normally be relied upon. After that, who knew? George Winter, who had showed some success in his first two years, was hit hard. And rookie Norwood Gibson, who had pitched for Notre Dame, walked nine men in his first start. To compound their troubles, the team was listless at bat. Only Patsy Dougherty and Charley Farrell were hitting over .300.

In a game against the Washington Senators on April 27, catastrophe struck. In the second inning, Farrell singled to right field. He then stole second, but his spikes stuck in the dirt and his foot turned under his body. Teammates carried him off the field with what turned out to be a broken right leg. Lou Criger, known for his defense, took over the catching duties. While in Georgia, Collins had proclaimed, "Barring accident we have no club in the American League to fear." Now he had to wonder. By the end of the month, the team found itself in sixth place with a record of four wins and six losses.

Even the newly established New York Highlanders had a better record than the Americans. All of baseball had noted the drama of the home opener for New York's American League entry. Workers raced to have the field ready for the Highlanders' first home game on April 30. Just two days before, workers still had to sod the outfield, complete the third-base bleachers, and finish installing seats throughout the park. The roof over the grandstand would not be completed and a hole in right field would not be filled until the season was under way. On opening day, more than 15,000 fans entered the grounds, and each patron was handed a small flag to wave. Ban Johnson paraded around the field, puffing on a cigar. He had promised to deliver an American League franchise to New York, and he had done so. To make the day complete, the Highlanders defeated the Senators, 6–2, behind the pitching of Jack Chesbro and the hitting of Wee Willie Keeler. Boston fans took note and began "making up parties to attend the first New York game." The rivalry between Boston and New York began long before the Red Sox sold Babe Ruth to the Yankees in 1920.

The Highlanders would be in Boston on May 7, but the Americans needed to start winning before then. The nadir came when the Athletics took two out of three at Huntington Avenue, including a 3–0 shutout in which a strong pitching effort from Cy Young was squandered. Americans "Fail to Hit," declared the headlines.

The Washington Senators arrived on May 4 with Ed Delahanty in their lineup, now that his contract status had been resolved. In the opening game, played on a cold, wet day before only 700 fans, Delahanty, perhaps the most feared batsman in baseball, went hitless in four at-bats, while Hobe Ferris, Boston's light-hitting second baseman, smashed two home runs to lead his team to victory. The next day, Boston fell behind 3–0 in the first inning, but got lucky when heavy rains came and washed the contest away. Cy Young went to the mound on May 6. In the second inning, he came to bat and swung at a fastball "like a man stung by a yellow hornet." The ball sailed over the center fielder's head and kept on rolling. The portly Young rounded the bases and touched the plate standing up for his first and only home run of the year. It gave his team a lead they would not surrender, and Young won for the third time in five starts.

The Highlanders arrived the next day and could not alter Boston's winning ways. In the first game of the three-game series, Dinneen won easily. Like Young, he seemed to be rounding into form. But both Collins and New York manager Clark Griffith argued repeatedly with the umpire. The next day, both were suspended by the league for three games. Ban Johnson had promised a pastime free of rowdyism, and he intended to deliver. In the third game of the series, Highlander pitcher Jesse Tannehill was ejected for disputing a call. Cy Young won the game, 12–5; suddenly Boston was hitting, pitching, and winning.

After playing only .500 ball on a midwestern road trip through Cleveland, Detroit, St. Louis, and Chicago, the Americans returned home at the end of the month and swept four games from the last-place Senators. In the final game of the series, Ed Delahanty, who had scored four hits and a home run in the previous two games, faced Cy Young. The veteran pitcher had a shutout going when Delahanty, hitless in two at-bats, stepped to the plate. The two had faced each other since 1890, when Young broke in. They knew one another well. Young got ahead on the count and then fired a fastball. Delahanty swung with all his might, but the ball swept into Criger's glove. It was the last time that the two stars would face each other.

In all, Boston won 15 and lost 9 games in May. The Americans' success left them in a tie with Chicago for first place. Both teams had 19 wins, as did the Athletics. Three teams had 17 wins. The pennant race was so close that the results of one week of play could have moved teams near the bottom of the standings to the top and vice versa.

June began with the Americans' first trip to New York. They admired the new grounds and then promptly took three games from the Highlanders: "Griffith's men simply couldn't hit a lick,

while the Collinsites flattened the ball into a shapeless mass."
Boston inched into first place, percentage points ahead of the
Athletics. The quirky schedule in which Boston and Philadelphia
met in nine out of the first twelve games of the season dictated
that they would not go head to head again until August.

Boston returned home for a stretch of games against the midwestern clubs. The team's potent offense muted its fans' rabid opposition to the foul-strike rule. Indeed, those in the American
League who had been against it, especially Philadelphia and
Boston, now seemed to favor the rule. Connie Mack became a
temporary convert and stated, "I like its effect very much." By
June, there was little talk of opposing a rule that simply "forced
the batters to attend to their knitting and play ball instead of fouling off the good ones sent up and wearing down the twirlers."

When the Americans swept the White Sox at Huntington Avenue Grounds, and then beat Detroit with Cy Young entering the
game in relief, Boston had earned its eleventh consecutive victory.
The games "had the true ring of championship ball," but fans
were cautious in their expectations. After all, Boston had competed for the pennant in 1901 and 1902, only to fall back a handful of games by season's end.

The St. Louis Browns came east in third place, but in two
successive games on June 11 and June 13 they were held scoreless
by Tom Hughes and Cy Young. It was Young's third shutout of
the year. The two best hitters on the Browns, Jesse Burkett and
Bobby Wallace, were hitless against "Old Reliable." Dougherty,
Collins, and Parent each doubled, and Freeman had two triples.
No one noted it at the time, but Young's victory, the 361st of his
career, made him the winningest pitcher in baseball history. He
had surpassed Pud Galvin, who in the 1880s had pitched for Buffalo in the National League. At the close of his career in 1911,
forty-four-year-old Cy Young would have amassed 511 victories.

Young left the team to return to Ohio to attend the funeral
of his mother-in-law and, as a result, was not available for the
following home-and-away series against Cleveland. The team,

known variously as the Blues, the Bronchos, or the Naps, had played well recently and stood only a game behind Boston in the loss column. Their second baseman was Napoleon Lajoie, considered by many the best hitter in the American League. The upcoming seven games, reported the *Sporting News*, were "expected to do much toward determining the championship of the American League." Dinneen pitched the opening game in Boston, but lost 7–0, as Lajoie went two for four with two RBIs. 19,000 fans turned out on June 17 for a mid-week morning/afternoon doubleheader. The teams split the two games and left together in the afternoon for the trip to Cleveland, where the teams would meet again.

Boston had slipped into second place behind the A's. Cleveland, St. Louis, Chicago, and even New York were still in the running. Boston lost the first game in Cleveland, but then recovered its equilibrium and won three straight, including a Sunday contest that had to be played in Canton, Ohio, because of the enforcement of the blue laws in Cleveland.

Young rejoined the team in Detroit's Bennett Park. In one of the best pitching duels of the season, he faced Wild Bill Donovan, who had jumped to the American League from Brooklyn, where he had won 25 games in 1901. Donovan would play in three consecutive World Series between 1907 and 1909, but each year Detroit would lose to the National League challenger.

On a field soaked from rain, and with baselines caked in mud, Donovan and Young kept the game scoreless through seven innings. As usual, Young had impeccable control, walking only one batter, and that one intentionally (during the season he averaged less than one walk per nine innings pitched). In the eighth, Dougherty hit a slow roller that stuck to the infield, and he was safe at first. Collins flied out to right. Then Donovan issued one of his four walks, advancing Dougherty to scoring position. Freeman smacked a clean single up the middle, and Boston went ahead 1–0. But Detroit threatened in the bottom of the frame. With one out, Donovan helped his own cause with a single.

Jimmy Barrett bunted, and Collins slipped fielding the ball. Billy Lush then cracked a shot to third that Collins uncharacteristically misplayed, and the bases were loaded with one out. Sam Crawford came to bat. The twenty-three-year-old lefty batter, who had jumped to Detroit from Cincinnati, was a dangerous hitter who led the league in triples and would finish second in batting average for the season. He smashed the ball at Young, who plucked it on a hop and threw to Criger for the force at home plate. The catcher then threw to first to complete the inning-ending double play. Young held on to win 1–0. With the victory, Boston again took over first place.

Five days later, Young took the mound in St. Louis before a crowd of 20,000, the largest of the season. Again he squared off in a pitchers' duel, this time against journeyman Red Donahue, who gave up only one run. But Young did better than that. For the second consecutive start, he threw a 1–0 shutout.

Young's next start came in Chicago on July 1. The warm summer weather helped the pitchers get a little extra hop on their fastballs and a little more break in their curves. Patsy Flaherty, a young lefty trying to come back from arm troubles that had kept him out of baseball for three years, held Boston in check and scattered seven hits through nine innings. He had a shutout going. But so did Cy Young, who scattered only five hits. The game went into extra innings. In the tenth, Young came to bat with Ferris on second. All season he hit as he never had before and never would again. He drove a pitch just fair along the foul line into left field and knocked in the go-ahead run. In the bottom of the tenth, with a runner on first, player-manager Nixey Callahan grounded into a double play to end the game. By season's end, Flaherty would lose an American League record 25 games, but if there is a good loss, this was it, and as the losses mounted, the Chicago pitcher could take solace in having matched Cy Young inning after inning. For Young, it was his fourth consecutive shutout; the last three had been by a score of 1–0. "Like good wine, he seems to get better as he gets older," reported *Sporting*

Life. The Americans came home for July 4 with a three-game lead over the second-place Athletics.

As Boston continued its winning ways, the baseball world paused in dismay when news of Ed Delahanty's disappearance on July 2 filled the papers over the holiday weekend. Delahanty was in Detroit with his Senators, and he was miserable. His team languished in the cellar of the American League and was concluding a road trip in which they had lost twelve out of fourteen games. The news that George Davis, who had also been awarded to the American League by the terms of the peace conference in January, was now playing with the New York Giants deepened Delahanty's despair at being forced to play for Washington rather than for McGraw's team. Delahanty's attempt to stop drinking exacerbated his mood. His teammates noted dramatic shifts in his behavior. He would stay sober for a few days, then show up at the hotel drunk. Through it all, he still could hit a baseball: he was batting .333 at the time of his disappearance.

The mystery of Big Ed's whereabouts was solved on July 9, when one of the Senators' owners traveled to Buffalo and identified the mangled body of the ballplayer. He had been found in the river below Niagara Falls, a leg torn off, apparently by a propeller of the *Maid of the Mist.* Delahanty had boarded an express train destined for New York, but he had grown drunk and rowdy, and the conductor evicted him on the Canadian side of the crossing. The burly outfielder started to walk across the bridge, and a night watchman tried to stop him because the bridge had been opened for a boat to pass. Big Ed pushed on and "plunged into the dark waters of the Niagara."

Some thought his death a suicide. Moralists placed the blame on Delahanty's addiction to drinking and gambling. Others faulted John Brush for raising the player's hopes of playing in New York. His relatives suspected foul play. The tragedy of Delahanty's death, thought one writer, was that it showed what could happen when "a player gets too popular for his own good," and then is no longer the most talked-about man in baseball. The one-time

Nap Lajoie, Ed Delahanty, and Rube Waddell

greatest player in the game had "become so dissipated that if he did not take his own life he wandered onto a bridge in a helpless condition and fell into the swirling Niagara."

The day after the news of Delahanty's death reached the papers, Cy Young took to the mound against Chicago. A sweltering heat wave had engulfed Boston for days, and many more fans opted for the beach than the ballpark that Saturday afternoon. Prior to the game, Young stood outside the gates and handed out free passes to children. If his thoughts turned to Delahanty, he must have recalled the day in July 1896, in Cleveland, also a hot one, when he carried a no-hitter into the ninth inning and, with two out, Delahanty lined a single to break it up. Now Young struggled in the heat, yielding four walks and "laboring like a waterlogged ship in a storm." But Jimmy Collins hit safely in each of his five at-bats and the Americans won, to take three out of the four games from the White Sox.

The heat finally broke when summer storms passed through Boston. Fans flooded back to the Huntington Avenue Grounds. A four-game series against Cleveland in mid-July drew nearly 40,000 people: "on every street corner there was talk of the games and the Bostons were praised and lauded to the skies." They split the series with Cleveland, but took two of three from Detroit and three of four from New York. Much of the credit went to Lou Criger, who had emerged as a star after Farrell had broken his leg in the first week of the season. Criger was not only hitting well, but also setting a new standard for defense behind the plate. Fans had not before seen a catcher, on an attempted sacrifice bunt, consistently get the runner at second base, yet Criger had accomplished the feat three times. He was quickly earning a reputation as the best defensive catcher in baseball. To be sure, there were days when the Boston Americans played anything but championship ball. On July 29, with New York in town, Cy Young faced Jack Chesbro and neither, it seemed, could get an out. The Boston fielders made eight errors behind Young, four by Fred

Parent alone. Collins left Young in for the full nine innings and the game ended with New York winning, 15–14.

By the end of July, it was a two-team race: Boston led Philadelphia by two and a half games. Each team had lost only nine games the entire month. Cleveland had fallen to nine games out of first, New York was twelve games behind the leader, and Chicago stood fifteen games out. But Collins faced a difficult schedule in August, having to play all but three games on the road. A three-game series beginning August 5 in Philadelphia, followed immediately by three more games in Boston, would do much to clarify the championship race.

The opening game pitted Waddell against Dinneen. Waddell was masterful, striking out eleven, but Dinneen had the benefit of several superb defensive plays behind him. Collins, on edge from the pressure of the series, was ejected from the game for arguing a call at second base. Boston managed to scratch out a 3–0 win over the Athletics.

Cy Young had delivered clutch performances all season long, but could not do so in the second game of the series. Philadelphia hit him hard. The top four in the order—Danny Hoffman, Ollie Pickering, Harry Davis, and Lave Cross—amassed seven hits, and Chief Bender, after yielding a first-inning run, kept Boston scoreless for the next five innings. Down 4–3, Boston batted in the top of the eighth and failed to score. With skies threatening, the umpire decided that it was too dark to continue play and called the contest, depriving the Americans of one last chance to tie or go ahead. In the rubber game on Friday, August 7, Tom Hughes faced Philadelphia lefty Eddie Plank. Boston scored two in the first and kept on hitting. Four runs in the fourth sent Plank to the dressing room, and with Dougherty, Collins, Parent, and Criger combining for twelve hits, Boston cruised to an 11–3 victory.

The scene shifted back to Boston, where nearly 15,000 fans swarmed the grounds on August 8 for a key Saturday afternoon contest against Philadelphia. After taking two out of three in

Philadelphia, Boston now led by three and a half games. One of the largest crowds ever for a non-holiday ball game filled the park. In the second inning, with a man on second and two out, Boston rallied. Ferris singled, Criger tripled into the crowd, Dinneen and Dougherty got base hits, Collins and Stahl walked, Freeman doubled, clearing the bases, and Parent singled, scoring Freeman. The home team had scored six times and went on to win easily, 11–6.

Philadelphia was showing signs of disarray. Waddell didn't travel with the team for the Saturday game, and when he finally appeared on Monday after an off day he sat away from his teammates over by the Boston side. It was ladies' day at the ballpark— every woman escorted by a man entered for free. A crowd of more than 10,000 turned out, including league president Ban Johnson. Cy Young sought to avenge his loss to the Athletics four days earlier, and for three innings the game was scoreless. Boston broke through with three runs in the fourth and added three in the fifth as Young not only dominated on the mound, retiring twenty-one consecutive batters, but also stroked two hits of his own.

Fans and players at the grounds that day had more on their minds than the game. Reports of a terrible tragedy that had occurred two days earlier at Philadelphia Ball Park, home of the National League Phillies, filtered through the stands. More than 10,000 people had been at the park for a doubleheader against Boston's woeful National League team. The left-field bleachers along Fifteenth Street were packed to capacity. The ballpark had a gallery that overhung the street by several feet and was supported by timbers that rested atop a brick wall. During the top of the fourth inning, with Boston's Joe Stanley at bat, a brawl on the street twenty feet below drew the attention of the fans. Some 500 spectators rushed from their seats to view the contretemps. Suddenly a fearful cracking noise pierced the din of the game. The wood supports had splintered, and the gallery gave way. Fans plunged to the street below, bodies piled upon bodies, "a mass of struggling, writhing, groaning humanity." More than a dozen people were killed, and scores were injured. *Sporting Life* called the accident "the greatest tragedy in the history of the national game." Ben Shibe, a stockholder of the Athletics, was so dismayed by the catastrophe that he had Columbia Park inspected while his team was away. In 1909, Shibe Park would open—the first concrete and steel stadium in baseball.

A cautious crowd filled Huntington Avenue Grounds for the third and final game of the series with the Athletics on August 11. The contest held the key to the pennant for Boston. A victory would place them seven games ahead in the loss column, and although the team was headed for an extended trip west, they would have to collapse completely or the Athletics would have to play brilliant ball to place the American League championship in doubt. Mack sent Waddell to the mound against Tom Hughes. Collins knew his team needed to jump out to a lead against Waddell, who often got stronger as the game went on, and they did just that. After Philadelphia failed to score, Dougherty and Collins led off the home half of the first with singles. Waddell was having trouble throwing strikes. He hit one batter and then, with the bases loaded, walked in a run. He escaped the inning by allowing only two runs, but that turned out to be all Hughes needed, as he shut down Philadelphia and went on to win, 5–1. Boston had swept the three-game series, won five of six, and had stretched their lead to six and a half games over the defending American League champion Athletics.

With Boston and Pittsburgh all but assured the American League and National League championships, and with talk emerging of a postseason championship series between them, some owners began to cut expenses, much to the chagrin of players and fans. Charles Comiskey of the White Sox, who was notorious for his stinginess, refused to provide more than two new balls for home games. On one occasion, "when these were gone old balls that had done service in former games were rung in. Some of them were so dead that they would not go out of the diamond no matter how hard hit." Chicago was not alone in its frugality. Detroit's Sam Crawford recalled that "we'd play a whole game with one ball, if it stayed in the park. Lopsided, and black, and full of tobacco juice and licorice stains." In a game between Cleveland and Detroit, Lajoie was so disgusted by the condition of the ball being used that he fired it into the stands, forfeiting the game for his team.

By August's end, the American League pennant race was over, although Boston did not officially clinch until September. The team had returned from a successful western swing with a ten-game lead. People continued to come to the Grounds; the Americans averaged over 5,000 fans per game (their National League counterparts averaged only 2,000). And they kept on winning, taking 19 out of 26 contests in September to dominate the American League by 14½ games over Philadelphia.

Baseball also had a new National Agreement, forged at a meeting in Buffalo on August 26. Harry Pulliam, along with Reds owner Garry Herrmann and Cubs owner James Hart, met with Ban Johnson, Charles Comiskey, and Henry Killilea, as well as representatives of the minor leagues, to place all of baseball on a common footing. The preamble of the agreement stated that it had as its objectives: "the perpetuation of base ball as the national pastime of America by surrounding it with such safeguards as will warrant absolute public confidence in its integrity and methods, and by maintaining a high level of skill and sportsmanship in its players." The agreement sought to protect the business interests of owners while promoting the welfare of ballplayers. The minor leagues yielded some of their autonomy to the two major leagues in return for protection against their rosters being raided or their territories being invaded. The agreement also established a National Commission to run baseball. No one knew it if would last. After all "history always repeats itself, and base ball moves in cycles just as do all other things on this mundane sphere." "But, for a time, at least," wrote the editor of *Sporting Life*, "we shall have rest from war and rumors of war."

Throughout September, all conversation revolved around the

upcoming series for the world's championship. Collins's team had played sharp baseball for much of the year, and there was no reason to think that its performance would drop off. Pittsburgh and Boston both could hit (each led their respective leagues in team batting), and both could field. But Boston seemed to have the edge on the mound, and, as one commentator observed, "everything depends on pitching these days."

FINAL AMERICAN LEAGUE STANDINGS				
TEAM	W	L	WL%	GB
Boston	91	47	.659	—
Philadelphia	75	60	.556	14.5
Cleveland	77	63	.550	15.0
New York	72	62	.537	17.0
Detroit	65	71	.478	25.0
St. Louis	65	74	.468	26.5
Chicago	60	77	.438	30.5
Washington	43	94	.314	47.5

GAME SEVEN, SATURDAY, OCTOBER 10

"BASEBALL IS THE SOLE TOPIC OF CONVERSATION in this city tonight," reported one correspondent from Pittsburgh, after the Americans, on Thursday, October 8, had tied the series at three games each. Pittsburgh was a National League city, and everything fans had heard prior to the series had persuaded them that the American League could not compete against the Pirates. But with two consecutive victories, Boston had "dispelled . . . the illusion," and fans realized that, regardless of the outcome of the seventh game, "Pittsburg must return to Boston for the toughest proposition of a lifetime."

At midnight, rain splattered the streets. By Friday morning, October 9, the rain had stopped, but a cold wind blew across the city. Before noon, Fred Clarke went to the ballpark and walked the grounds. The temperature was in the fifties, and the wind, "blowing up the river and across the ball park," made the day too uncomfortable for fans or players.

"The wind over there must be blowing 60 miles an hour,"

Clarke said. "A player would run a great risk in playing in such weather. There will be no game today."

Jimmy Collins heard the news from a Boston fan who had read it on a bulletin board, and he raced over to the Pirate offices and confronted Clarke and Dreyfuss.

"What's the matter with you people?" he screamed.

"Nothing, but it's too cold to play today, and tomorrow, being an open day, we called the game off," answered Clarke.

"We're willing to take a chance. What's the use of waiting a day?" Collins asked. "It is likely to be just as bad then, and we want to finish these games and get away. I think it is a shame."

Clarke simply said that the weather reports for Saturday were fine. Collins then vented his fury on Dreyfuss. "What does this mean? You have no right to do this. We are ready to play and you are simply sparring for wind. You think I can't see into this thing, but I can," he thundered.

Collins threatened to leave for Boston, but after reading the agreement for the series, which gave the home team the right to call the game for cold or wet weather, he had no choice but to agree to a day off. Had he thought matters through, he might have realized that the delay would do his team some good as well. Cy Young, who was to go against Phillippe, could also use the extra day. And Dinneen would be that much more rested for an eventual eighth game in Boston. But the everyday players still feared losing their rhythm, especially with no place to practice. Hobe Ferris spoke for all when he claimed that "the layoff we had before the series opened in Boston put us to the bad." "We will go to the grounds early . . . and take all the time we want in warming up" before Saturday's game, announced Collins.

The Royal Rooters, who had planned to leave on the Friday night train, altered their reservations so that they could stay over to Saturday. Charley Lavis thought that Dreyfuss had schemed all along to play a Saturday game. A group called on the Pittsburgh owner and asked that the game start at 2:30 instead of 3:00 p.m. so that they could make the 6 p.m. train, but the request was denied.

Pittsburgh fans were pleased with the change. They knew that an extra day's rest could only help Phillippe. And now with the game shifted to the weekend, thousands more could attend the game in person or spend a leisurely afternoon following the bulletins outside the newspaper offices. Determined not to allow the Boston fans to dictate the tenor of the rooting, Pirate fans hired a forty-piece band of their own for Saturday's contest. The band's one object, fans claimed, would be "to drown the strains of 'Tessie,' " which the Boston band had played throughout the sixth game once the Americans scored their first run. Pittsburgh fans believed that the song was the Pirates' "death knell," and they instructed the band to perform a "program of antidotes" for "Tessie" that included "Hail, Hail, the Gang's All Here," "Down, Down, Down Where the Wurzburger Flows," and "The Smoke Goes up the Chimney Just the Same."

Dreyfuss had the Saturday game he wanted. Now he looked for a way to change the mood of the Pirates and inspire them to victory. He decided to make public an arrangement that only Fred Clarke had known about: "every cent over and above expenses gleaned from the post-season series now on between Pittsburg and Boston for the championship of the world, will be divided among the players of the Pittsburg team if they win." It was a magnanimous gesture made by the owner before the series began and was revealed now as an incentive to spark inspired play. Dreyfuss did not care about the money; he simply wanted the honor of being a world's champion.

Boston players also heard on Friday about an offer being made to motivate them. The *Boston Globe* promised to present a gold medal to each player if the team "brings to Boston the world's championship." The medals "will be worth gaining because of their beauty, but they will be most prized by their possessors in the years to come as souvenirs of the most famous series of baseball games ever played." On behalf of the men, Collins thanked the newspaper, which he praised as an authority on the game of baseball (much to the chagrin of Boston's competing papers), and promised that "the boys will do everything in their power to win the honor for Boston, which has given us the best treatment, even when we were not having the best of luck."

Money was an issue not only for the players, but for the fans as well. The extra day meant an extra day for wagering, and Phillippe was established as a 10–8 favorite to beat Young in the seventh game. "So evenly matched are the teams," observed one gambler, "that the pitcher is the whole thing when it comes to picking the winner." As always, some odd, exotic bets were made. One broker wagered $200 against $600 that Pittsburgh would win the next game and that Boston would win the first game back home, but that Pittsburgh would win the final and deciding game in what had become a best two-out-of-three series. Offered even money to bet simply that Pittsburgh would win the series, he refused.

The Royal Rooters also had to face financial issues on Friday. They appeared in court before an alderman who was going to decide whether the fans had breached a contract with the band they had hired for the first game in Pittsburgh. The band, conducted by a Professor Guenther, claimed that it had been hired for $95 a day for three or four days, depending on how many games were played. But after the first game, it found that it had been replaced. The Boston Rooters appeared without an attorney. Mike McGreevey and Charley Lavis testified that they had expected to march with a band, not walk behind one that was riding in a carriage, as Guenther had insisted on doing. And why, they testified, would they hire a band for four days when the series might be over in three? Band members and Rooters argued back and forth, and the alderman said he would have a decision by evening. But it was not until the next morning that he found the Rooters in breach of contract. The Royal Rooters were unperturbed by the decision. McGreevey and Lavis refused to pay, and several prominent Pittsburgh businessmen, who admired the enthusiasm of the Boston fans, offered to hire a lawyer to defend them. They had a new band all ready to go for the seventh game, and they prepared to march to Exposition Park singing "Tessie" all the way.

The Pittsburgh rooters also marched to the park, in a parade that began downtown at 12:30 p.m. "Armed with badges and horns and megaphones," some 500 Pirate fans rode and marched in a procession to the ballpark. They also hired a band for the day—the very one that had sued the Boston rooters for breach of contract. The marchers wore bits of ribbon that read "Loyal Rooters, Pittsburg, 1903," and they chanted "Phil, Phil, Phillippe, Phil—He can win and you bet he will."

What was described as "the largest crowd in the history of baseball in this city" flooded Exposition Park for the afternoon affair. Pittsburgh fans came from towns and cities as far as fifty miles away to witness the contest. The steelworks at Homestead, McKeesport, and elsewhere made it a half-holiday. The seats were filled an hour before the 3 p.m. starting time. Fans stood in the aisles and jammed themselves into any open space. Some adventurous men climbed into the crosspieces that supported the roof and grandstand, and stood perched, like sharpshooters waiting on prey. Thousands more formed a ring behind the ropes in the outfield and along the right-field foul line. Enterprising boys walked behind the rope line offering "old boxes, buckets, chairs, barrels or saw horses, and anything that would raise a man a couple of feet," for spare change. Officially, attendance was listed at 17,038, but thousands more scrambled for a view of the game; outside the park, the "hill tops and adjacent roofs were black with people unable to gain admission into the park." Despite the congestion, the crowd remained perfectly orderly.

Although the weather resembled Thanksgiving, the park looked like the Fourth of July. Flags and bunting surrounded the field. The Pittsburgh band led hundreds of fans into the park and marched around the diamond, as the Boston band, located in the grandstand, started playing "Auld Lang Syne." Just prior to the game, the Boston band struck up "America," and "every man, woman and child in the grounds stood up and joined in the chorus." Not to be outdone, the Pittsburgh band played "The Star-Spangled Banner." Again, the crowd stood and sang as one.

Collins declared, "if it is in the wind, we will win today." Clarke predicted, "Here is where we take the lead. . . . It is about time for us to give the veteran another drubbing." Young, who had won once and lost once in the series, issued a statement that belied his record. "I'll win if I can. It should not be so hard," he said. By contrast, Phillippe, who had earned all three Pirate victories, sounded somewhat resigned: "It's up to me, I guess. Well, I feel like a winner, but you can never tell until it is over."

The Pirates took the field behind Deacon Phillippe. He was being called upon to win his fourth game in the series. One reporter observed that Phillippe, who had learned to play the game on the prairies of South Dakota, "now owns three-fourths of the city. If he continues the successful practice of his art on Boston . . . he will be sole proprietor." But the Americans were a different team than they had been at the beginning of the week, and they entered the game with a swagger.

Patsy Dougherty walked to the plate to lead off the game. The sky looked spectral, a bright sun burning through clouds of dark smoke that drifted from the steel mills. Dougherty swung at the first pitch and grounded out to Ritchey at second. In stepped Jimmy Collins. The captain smashed a triple into the left-field crowd. The Royal Rooters screamed through their megaphones. Pirate fans retorted, "He's not home yet." But almost before they could finish the chant, Chick Stahl promptly lifted the ball into the crowd in right field for a run-scoring triple. The ground rules put into effect because of the overflowing attendance had immediately become a factor. Pirate partisans thought the two triples "would have been easy outs had it not been that the crowd made it impossible for the Pittsburg outfield to get in their work."

Buck Freeman stepped in and hit a grounder to Ritchey, who tried to get Stahl at home. In the collision at the plate, Phelps dropped the ball, and Boston had its second run. Freeman tried to steal second, but Phelps threw him out. The inning ended when

Fred Parent grounded out to Wagner. Boston had won every game of the series in which they scored first, and now they were ahead 2–0 before the Pirates had even batted.

Ginger Beaumont, trying to pressure the confident Americans, led off against Cy Young with a bunt that caught Collins off guard at third. In 1895, Collins had single-handedly redefined the position at third base by playing away from the bag and charging furiously at all bunted balls. But even the best third baseman in the game could not get to them all. Clarke followed Beaumont with a ground ball that Candy LaChance misplayed, and just as quickly as Boston had scored, the Pirates had runners on first and second and no one out. The fans screeched in anticipation as the dangerous Tommy Leach came up.

As he had almost every time he faced Young in the series, Leach hit the ball hard. But it bounded right at second baseman Hobe Ferris, who tagged Clarke and threw to first for a double play. Beaumont advanced to third, but the twin killing momentarily sapped the energy out of the crowd. A hit would slice the lead in half, and the crowd came back to life as Wagner strode to the plate. The shortstop had been hitless in his last seven at-bats, and that meant he was due. Wagner, however, swung through three pitches. He was now two for ten against Young and it must have seemed like much more than ten days since he had knocked in the first run of the World Series.

Both pitchers threw well in the next two innings, though in the bottom of the third Pittsburgh managed a threat. With one out, Phillippe came to bat. Before he stepped into the box, a presentation was made at home plate. For his three victories in the series, the organization gave him a diamond horseshoe scarf pin. Both teams stood on the field and the fans cheered wildly. Phillippe acknowledged the applause, then took Young's first pitch and singled to left field. Beaumont grounded out, but Phillippe went to second and then advanced to third on a rare throwing error by Collins (his first of the series) on Clarke's grounder. Runners were on first and third, with two out, and

Leach was at bat. But like his teammates, the Wee seemed to have lost his stroke, and he went down swinging on a fastball high and inside. The Pirates had placed men on base, but it had been days since they produced a timely hit.

To lead off the fourth, Buck Freeman tripled over Beaumont's head in center. Clarke brought the corners in, trying to prevent the run from scoring. But Parent grounded out to deep short and Freeman, heading home on contact, scored easily from third. LaChance struck out. With two down, Ferris lashed a triple to left-center, near the flagpole. The wind was blowing out and had clearly carried Ferris's ball with it. Lou Criger, batting an anemic .105 in the series thus far, hit a clutch single to right to bring in the fourth Boston run, manufactured after two were out. Young, focusing more on his pitching than on his hitting, flied out to end the inning.

In the bottom of the fourth, Wagner grounded out to short for the first out. With two strikes on him, Kitty Bransfield placed one fair down the left-field line for a triple into the crowd. With a four-run lead, Collins kept the infield back, playing for the out and willing to concede a run. The first pitch to Ritchey almost beaned the second baseman. He worked the count full and then grounded to Collins, who threw across the diamond for the second out, but the Pirates had their first run. Sebring tested the third baseman again, and Collins made a dashing one-handed grab of the line drive to end the inning. "Perhaps the profession has never seen a third baseman who can play the position better than the scowling-faced man," thought the *Boston Herald*'s correspondent.

Dougherty bunted himself on to lead off the fifth, but Boston left him stranded at third base. In the bottom of the fifth inning, Phelps reached first base when Parent made a low throw to first. Phillippe's ground ball forced Phelps at second, and Beaumont's roller forced Phillippe. Two outs, and Beaumont was on first base. The crowd was ringing cowbells and banging clappers, hoping to inspire a two-out Pirate rally. With Clarke at bat, Beaumont blundered: Young caught him leaning toward second, and the runner bounced back and forth like a "shuttlecock for several seconds" before LaChance tagged him out with a shove to the ribs. "Tessie, Tessie, how I love you," played the Boston band. The Pittsburgh fans were not amused: "the music and singing was a novelty for a while and was hugely enjoyed by the majority of the spectators; but there is such a thing as working a good thing to death, and that was the fate of 'Tessie,' and after it had been played about two dozen times it was greeted with jeers instead of cheers."

With Boston ahead by three, Parent beat out a slow roller to open the sixth inning. Playing for a single run, Collins had LaChance turn to sacrifice. But Phillippe mishandled the ball for an error. Without a solid hit, Boston had runners on first and second with no one out. In their two previous losses, Pittsburgh had committed seven errors. And now the Pirates seemed again to be fumbling away the ball and a chance to win.

The situation called for Hobe Ferris to sacrifice, and the second baseman did his job when he bunted down the first-base side and advanced the runners to second and third, where both could score on a base hit. Criger came to the plate. His last at-bat had produced more than just a run. It made him confident that he could hit Phillippe when it mattered most. The catcher settled in for the right-hander's delivery and lashed a single to right field. Two more runs scored, and Boston had a comfortable five-run lead, 6–1. The Rooters sang out "Boston, Boston, rah, rah, rah!" The Pittsburgh band struck up a tune, but the Pirate fans could only murmur to one another.

Cy Young came out for the bottom of the sixth. He knew that with a big lead his first responsibility was to throw strikes, but his offering to Clarke was right down the middle of the plate, and the manager lined it to left field for a leadoff triple. The shot restored the crowd to life. Tommy Leach came to bat, his slump no doubt weighing on his mind. Young had finally figured out how to pitch to the pesky hitter, and he got Leach to strike out again. Wagner stepped in, but he too failed to deliver, as he bounced Young's fastball right back to the pitcher. Young threw to first for the out and

Clarke, who had started for home and then stopped, now started again. LaChance threw to Criger, who scooped the ball out of the dirt and tagged Clarke just before he reached the plate. But umpire Connolly called him safe. For the most part, the umpiring all series had been superb. There had been a few complaints here and there, but reporters agreed that both Connolly's and O'Day's "work has been remarkably good and absolutely impartial." In this case, Pittsburgh received a gift run despite a base-running blunder, and the Americans had no choice but to accept the decision. They took solace from their 6–2 lead with only three innings to play. Bransfield singled with two outs and it looked perhaps as if the call at home plate had unnerved Young, but Ritchey hit a routine ground ball to force Bransfield at second and end the inning.

Once again, the Pirates found themselves behind late in the game. With one out in the seventh, Young walked Phelps, the only walk the veteran would relinquish. But neither Phillippe at the bottom of the order nor Beaumont at the top could advance the catcher. Phillippe was also pitching well, having walked none and having surrendered only a few more hits than his opponent through seven innings. But the Pirate ace had given up four triples and all four hitters had scored. With one out in the top of the eighth, Phillippe again yielded a shot into the crowd as Parent drove the ball to right field. Trying to do more than his arm would permit, Phillippe then threw a wild pitch that allowed the shortstop to score and extend Boston's lead to 7–2.

The only consolation Pirate fans could take was that their team had the heart of the order due up in the bottom of the eighth. They did not know that in pregame practice, Clarke had been struck in the leg by a bat that had slipped from Kitty Bransfield's hand and had been hobbled throughout the game, and that as he came up to hit, his leg was worsening. He poked Young's pitch directly to LaChance, but the first baseman fumbled the easy chance, and Clarke was on to lead off the inning. Perhaps the Boston error would open a big inning for the home team.

Tommy Leach batted next. Given his slump, he might have

thought about bunting Clarke over. But it made no sense to play for one run with the team down by five late in the game. So Leach swung away and, for the third time in the game, Young struck him out. Wagner stepped in, his slump no doubt beginning to weigh on him. He swung hard at Young's offering, but only managed to tick the bottom part of the ball. He watched helplessly as Criger drifted back and caught it behind the plate. With two down, Bransfield singled. There were two runners on base, but two men were out. Claude Ritchey, hitless in his last nine at-bats, hit the ball hard but lined out to left to end the threat. The Pirates had stranded ten runners through eight innings. Only teams that were very good or very lucky won games in which they did that, and since winning the fourth game of the series the Pirates had been neither.

The fans and bands on both sides perked up as the ninth inning began. This would conclude the baseball year in Pittsburgh. The season had been spectacular, and none of the Pirates supporters wanted it to end this way. Phillippe received a thunderous ovation as he came to the mound. He had pitched thirty-five of the sixty-two innings thrown by the Pirates thus far. Lou Criger, whose two hits and three RBIs helped put his team in the position to win, led off and grounded out to third. Cy Young heard the appreciation of the crowd as he came to bat and tipped his cap in acknowledgment. The "old warhorse" grounded to short, but Wagner threw high to first for his fourth error in three games. This time the miscue did not cost his team anything, as Dougherty struck out and Collins lofted a fly to right. The Pirates would have one last chance to get to Young.

Jimmy Sebring came to bat in the bottom of the ninth hoping to start a rally that would erase the five-run deficit faced by his team. He had been the most consistent Pirate in the series, hitting in every game but one. He succeeded yet again when he stroked the ball over Young's head for a hit. Ed Phelps followed with a single to center, and just like that, the Pirates seemed poised to do some damage. Phillippe was due up. Clarke thought about pinch-hitting for him, but he had no one on the bench who gave him any confidence. Otto Kruger, a utility player, was coming off a beaning in September and hadn't batted in over a month. Clarke wasn't going to pinch-hit for Phillippe with another pitcher, not even Bill Kennedy, who had a much better record as a batsman. So Phillippe batted for himself, emboldened by his third-inning single.

The pitcher rewarded his manager for staying the course; he connected on Young's first pitch and lined a sharp single to center. Sebring scored and the Pirates had runners on first and second with no one out. The Pirates were still four runs behind, but Exposition Park erupted. Pittsburgh fans rang cowbells and band members blew their horns. Confetti floated through the air.

The top of the order was due up. The infielders were guarding the lines to protect against an extra-base hit. Beaumont swung and lifted an easy pop-up to Parent at short. One away.

Clarke stepped in, a determined, serious look on his face. Young got ahead with two strikes and, needing to protect the plate, Clarke then swung and hit an easy fly ball to Dougherty in left. Two down.

Tommy Leach came to bat. For a hitter unaccustomed to failure, it was difficult to forget the strikeouts and just concentrate on the next pitch, the next swing. Young delivered a fastball and Leach, his bat still slow, hit a grounder to the right side of second base. Ferris dove for the ball, smothered it, and threw to Parent for the force on Phillippe and the final out of the game. Boston had won, 7–3.

The Americans had accomplished the unthinkable. Down three games to one, they had taken three consecutive games on Pittsburgh's home field. The fifth game was a rout, but the next two could have gone differently. In the seventh game, Young gave up ten hits and a walk, Phillippe eleven hits and no walks. Both pitched steadily, though not brilliantly. Phillippe "went up against the Bostons once too often," thought the *Sporting News*. "It is natural to suppose that after a team has faced a pitcher three times in less than two weeks, that they should have had time to familiarize

themselves with that man's style of pitching sufficiently to hit him."
Boston batters lashed five triples and scored each time. By contrast,
the Pirates could not bunch any hits together, and the two-three-
four batters in the lineup managed one hit among them. The Pirates "played like a lot of nannies," concluded Frank M'Quiston.
And Wagner batted and fielded "in the home series like a hen."

Most reporters agreed that the game was "the worst of the series." Neither team looked sharp; Boston made four errors and
Pittsburgh made three. But Boston's miscues caused no damage,
whereas Pittsburgh's led to three unearned runs. "Both teams,"
said the *Boston Post*, "were off their feed." Pittsburgh never
seemed "dangerous," and Boston methodically added on runs and
easily won the game.

The Pittsburgh press gave credit to the Royal Rooters for aid-
ing in Boston's victory: "Pittsburg had beaten Boston twice in
sight of her friends, and was bringing them over here to kill them
in a four-game series at Exposition Park. Did the Boston rooters
quit? No! No! They dove for their grips and came over on the
train with the boys from home. If there was to be a funeral,
Boston rooters were going to be in the first carriages. But they
came to see that the boys didn't lose, and their purpose was
served." The Rooters left Pittsburgh with more than just bragging
rights. Friday had been payday and many a mechanic and steel-
worker had lost his wages backing the Pirates. The Royal Rooters
had won back all the money they had lost in Boston, and more.

After the game, they marched to the Monongahela House
to gather their belongings. One of the rooters, Denny McGilli-
cuddy, who weighed near three hundred pounds and had the
lungs to match, led a cheer for the good treatment given by the
Pittsburgh fans, and three cheers for each player. The Rooters
then left for the depot. They formed a double-line procession and
began marching, suitcases in hand. Several hundred Pittsburgh
fans fell in and, at the station, cheered the Boston Rooters for
their good sportsmanship.

The Boston players acted "as happy as school boys out for

their first game of marbles in the spring." Collins said he was "happy beyond expression." The team boarded their own car on the same train as the Rooters, scheduled to depart at 7 p.m. As the train pulled out, the band played a song in tribute to the departing fans: "Tessie."

Pittsburgh players and fans sank into despair. Fred Clarke admitted, "I am much disappointed. I felt all confidence we would win today and that meant, in my opinion, the series." As for the fans, M'Quiston observed, "there were a lot of plates on supper tables last night pushed back. The Pittsburg people did not feel like eating. All they wanted was to get a chance to wind the clock and put the cat out and go to bed. The darkness was kind. The Pittsburg ball team had not been kind."

After the game, the Pirates stayed in their uniforms. "Defeated and crest-fallen," they trudged over the Union Bridge to the station where they boarded their special car and undressed as the train pulled out into the evening. The "sole hope of Pittsburg now," wrote the editor of the *Dispatch*, "is that the luck may reverse again when they get back to Boston."

THE SEVENTH GAME

PITTSBURG.	AB.	R.	B.	P.	A.	E.	BOSTON.	AB.	R.	B.	P.	A.	E.
Beaumont, cf......	5	0	1	2	0	0	Dougherty, lf......	5	0	1	3	0	0
Clarke, lf.........	5	1	1	1	0	0	Collins, 3b.........	5	1	1	0	2	1
Leach, 3b.........	5	0	0	0	1	0	Stahl, cf...........	4	1	2	0	0	0
Wagner, ss.........	3	0	0	2	6	1	Freeman, rf........	4	1	1	0	0	0
Bransfield, 1b......	4	1	3	13	2	0	Parent, ss..........	4	2	2	3	6	1
Richey, 2b.........	4	0	0	5	8	0	LaChance. 1b......	3	1	0	11	0	2
Sebring, rf,........	4	1	2	1	0	0	Ferris, 2b..........	3	1	2	4	4	0
Phelps, c..........	3	0	1	2	3	1	Criger, c...........	4	0	2	6	2	0
Phillippe, p........	4	0	2	1	0	1	Young, p..........	4	0	0	0	2	0
Total..............	37	3	10	27	20	3	Total............	36	7	11	27	16	4

Pittsburg.....................	0	0	0	1	0	1	0	0	1—	3
Boston......................	2	0	0	2	0	2	0	1	0—	7

Earned runs—Pittsburg 2, Boston, 2. Three-base hits—Clarke, Bransfield, Collins, Stahl, Freeman, Parent, Ferris. Sacrifice hits—Wagner, LaChance, Ferris. Double plays—Ritchey, Wagner, Bransfield; Ferris, LaChance. First on balls —Off Young 1. Struck out—By Phillippe 2, Young 6. Wild pitch—Phillippe. Time—1.45. Umpires—Connolly and O'Day. Attendance—17,038.

THE NATIONAL PASTIME

ON OCTOBER 13, a Boston politician sat in the stands at the Huntington Avenue Grounds and contemplated the place of baseball in America: "The national game is the greatest out-door game that was ever invented. There is no pastime like it. Its patrons are found in every town and city of our great country. Its votaries are to be found on every lot big enough to toss a ball or swing a bat on. It is essentially America—vigorous, powerful, strong."

The politician's words echoed those of two other commentators. Mark Twain called baseball "the very symbol, the outward and visible expression of the drive and push and rush and struggle of the raging, tearing, booming nineteenth century." And Walt Whitman declared baseball "America's game: has the snap, go, fling, of the American atmosphere—belongs as much to our institutions, fits into them as significantly, as our constitutions, laws: is just as important in the sum total of our historic life."

It seemed clear that, over the first decades of the nineteenth century, baseball was not so much invented as developed. But the origin of the game was a matter of national pride, and figures such as Albert Spalding, a one-time player, club owner, a: goods manufacturer, wanted to liberate the sport fro: debts it owed to older English games such as crick(ball. In 1905, a commission was charged with determining base-ball's beginnings. The final report gave Abner Doubleday credit for devising the game in Cooperstown in 1839, and an origins myth was born. That myth has persisted, though historians generally credit Alexander Cartwright and New York's Knickerbocker Base Ball Club with first systematizing a set of baseball rules in the 1840s.

In his history *America's National Game*, Spalding summarized why it was that "base ball *is* the American game *par excellence*": "it is the exponent of American Courage, Confidence, Combativeness, American Dash, Discipline, Determination; American Energy, Eagerness, Enthusiasm; American Pluck, Persistence, Performance; American Spirit, Sagacity, Success; American Vim, Vigor, Virility."

Spalding clearly loved alliteration almost as much as baseball, but his efforts neither as a writer nor as a promoter account for the popularity of the sport, which had become the national game at the very moment the country was trying to reconstitute itself from the Civil War. "The sport had its baptism when our country was in the preliminary agonies of a fratricidal conflict," observed Spalding. A year after the Civil War, one writer stated that "the game of Base Ball has now become beyond question the leading feature of the out-door sports of the United States . . . the pastime suits the people, and the people suit the pastime." "A thriving town," observed a commentator, "is now said to have one church, one school-house, and eight base ball clubs." "Our national characteristics develop themselves in amusements," noted an essayist in 1871, who went on to declare baseball the greatest of games because it is "healthy, social, and uncertain."

Fitness. Strength. Competition. Here were athletic pursuits that dovetailed with national ideals. And in 1903 no one embodied these values more than the President—Theodore Roosevelt.

By example and by declaration, Roosevelt implored Americans to partake in "athletic exercise, manly out-door sports, and healthy muscular amusements." Baseball was not Roosevelt's favorite game, mostly because he never played it particularly well. He left to his successor, William Howard Taft, the distinction of being the first President to attend a game. In 1908, the sportswriter Grantland Rice suggested in verse that, upon leaving the White House, the President should become an umpire: "Chasing mountain lions and such, catching grizzlies will seem tame / Lined up with the jolt you'll get in the thick of some close game." Whatever Roosevelt's relationship to the sport, he understood what many citizens felt: baseball was "a most admirable and characteristic American game."

By the opening of the twentieth century, the preoccupation with health had become a national obsession. The emergence of the United States as an industrial power was built upon exhausting workdays in factories for millions of Americans: too little light, too little air. The middle classes endured their own hardships as a growing emphasis on achievement and success brought with it an increase in nervous disorders. Advertisers filled the sports pages of the day with notices that promised to cure "Man's Maladies." One doctor ran a regular ad beside the box scores that asked, "Are You One of the Men who Need Help? Have you Muscular Strength, Mental Activity, and Vital Power?" Baseball served as an antidote to the numbing regularity of day-to-day life in American society. It brought people outdoors, and the excitement of the game revitalized them.

Ballplayers were active men, the kind of men who served as models for others. The physical strength and mental quickness displayed by the athletes embodied those traits Americans believed they would need to triumph in life. Social Darwinism, the idea that all of life was a struggle for survival, and that only those who were fit would succeed, was the label given to the dominant social theory of the day. Darwin himself never talked about "survival of the fittest," but the popularization of his ideas carried with them an emphais on combat. "Base ball is War!" declared Spalding; "more a war of skill than of strength." Baseball players became easily enlisted as representatives of social theory. While every child could play ball, only a few would manage one day to be a professional athlete: "Players come into the big leagues after a long, hard, apprenticeship. All the way from the school boy at the bottom to the expert at the top the process of elimination is going on—the struggle for the survival of the fittest."

The game itself, according to the journalist Hugh Fullerton, was "the most highly developed, scientific and logical form of athletic pastime evolved by man, and the ultimate evolution of the one universal game." The men who played, claimed J. P. Casey in "Our Great American Game," were athletes "from head to toe . . . able to jump like a kangaroo, run like the wind, throw like a cannon, and launch [themselves] through the air like a bombshell." These ballplayers were also professionals "exactly in the sense that a doctor or a lawyer is professional." "Man at his best and highest made baseball," declared Rollin Hartt in "The National Game." The game "gallops gloriously to its sublime culmination, holds a nation spellbound from snow to snow, provides always the clash of player against player, and calls for the combined exercise of muscle, brain, skill, and manly daring."

The game reinforced the importance of preparation and training. "Games are lost and won in fractions of a second," and yet for long stretches they went on methodically, systematically, the "very uneventfulness is in itself an event." The key was total immersion and discipline. "Having played baseball, watched baseball, read baseball, dreamed baseball, and devoted little earnest cogitation to anything but baseball ever since he was able to lift a bat," observed Hartt, "[the player] takes in each new move as swiftly as it occurs, and knows by lifelong experience what it portends." The experience of playing baseball as a child, thought H. Addington Bruce in "Baseball and the National Life," was that it had "the effect in later years of making him think and act a little quicker than the other fellow."

At the turn of the century, at the very moment social leaders became enamored with the concept of scientific management and business efficiency, baseball was heralded as a game governed by scientific principles. Essays appeared on "The Science of Baseball," "The Physics of Baseball," "The Science of Base Running," and even "The Science of Coaching." An article in *Scientific American* in 1904 studied "a baseball's curves," and concluded that the movement was created by rotation and resistance. An essay in *American Magazine* declared that base stealing "is the finest drawn and most clearly calculated play in baseball and the one that, above all others, reveals the mathematical exactitude of the national game." Another writer likened baseball to "observing the interplay of vast and complex machinery . . . carried on by co-operating men and, as a rule, by superb specimens of physical manhood." The thrust of all the emphasis on baseball science was a simple one: through study, players could learn the game and improve their performance. "Baseball, like every other trade or profession," concluded Hugh Fullerton in *Touching Second: The Science of Baseball*, "consists more of experience and hard work than of natural ability, and it is hard work that counts for most. An average boy, with average brain, average legs, arms, and health, can in time become a great baseball player if he will work hard, work long, and work faithfully."

Baseball became the national game because of the belief that it developed in players and fans alike those personal characteristics that were key to both individual and national success: "physical fitness, courage, honesty, patience, the spirit of initiative combined with due respect for lawful authority, soundness and quickness of judgment, self-confidence, self-control, cheeriness, fair-mindedness, and appreciation of the importance of social solidarity, of 'team play.' " In a word, baseball shaped character. Spalding called the game "a man maker." It provided "a growing boy self-poise and self-reliance, confidence, inoffensive and entirely proper aggressiveness, general manliness."

No less a figure than William Randolph Hearst, who built the largest media empire in the world, declared that baseball "develops and forces swift and accurate judgment and the habit of quick thinking." It was as a result of playing baseball in their youth, he believed, that American soldiers were the best in the world—"quickwitted, swift to act, ready of judgment, capable of going into action without officers." "Every American boy ought to play base ball," thought Hearst, "and be proud of it as a great national institution."

Just as Hearst believed that the game made American soldiers better fighters, so too would soldiers take the game with them overseas. Baseball followed the flag. "Wherever Uncle Sam goes there goes with him his favorite and characteristic National Game," wrote the editor of *Sporting Life*, who noted that "Base ball is flourishing in Porto Rico and Cuba, and in the Philippines, too." "Wherever a ship floating the Stars and Stripes finds anchorage today," noted Spalding, "somewhere on nearby shore the American National Game is in progress." Punning on Emmanuel Leutze's famous painting *Westward the Course of Empire Takes Its Way*, which depicted a group of migrants climbing over the Sierra Nevada and gazing toward the Pacific for the first time, one writer joked that "westward, of course, the umpire takes his way."

Baseball was democracy at work, a game open to anyone. The sport carried with it a special vocabulary, an American vernacular in which description became inseparable from the game itself. The college rules of English usage would not apply to baseball. Rather, baseball "had a language of its own," one that appealed to every fan and that allowed every fan, regardless of background, to be part of the initiate. To illustrate the point, a writer in the *Literary Digest* offered two descriptions of a game for comparison:

> The baseball game yesterday between the teams representing the cities of Providence and Rochester, respectively, was one of the most exciting affairs ever seen at Melrose Park. The young men

on both teams played marvelously well and proved themselves adept in every department. As Providence made four runs, while its opponent was making three, it won the game.

The Grays and the Hustlers slam-banged each other in the final game of the series yesterday afternoon, and the Grays ran away with the candy 4–3. Both teams uncorked the ginger bottle at the gateway and danced through the whole performance for the snappiest work of the season.

Baseball slang was part of what made baseball uniquely American and transformed the nation into the "The United States of Baseball." Charles Stewart declared that "base-ball is a government of the people as well as by the people." Democracy blossomed on the field, where "at any moment the responsibility for winning a game may devolve upon any member. This is in accordance with the democratic principle of American life and government." And democracy blossomed in the stands. "Baseball is the melting pot at a boil, the most democratic sport in the world and, in the stands and bleachers all are equal during a hard game," proclaimed Hugh Fullerton in his treatise on "Fans." The game broke down social identity: "The spectator at a ball game is no longer a statesman, lawyer, broker, doctor, merchant, or artisan, but just a plain every-day man." The game also allowed for the release of tension: it "clutches spectators and squeezes them till they yell." Some went so far as to assert that it acted as a safety valve for the dispersal of energies that, directed in other ways, would be harmful to the country: "[A] young, ambitious and growing nation needs to 'let off steam.' Baseball . . . serves the same purpose as a revolution in Central America or a thunderstorm on a hot day."

Baseball served to unify the nation. In doing so, it not only embodied democracy, but also protected it. The game, it seemed, developed "social consciousness—and conscience." In a nation built on the ideal of individualism, baseball taught "the lesson of subordination of self for the common good." Only those who worked together would triumph. And the fans in the stands replicated what the players on the field exhibited. "Is there any other experience in modern life," asked one writer, "in which multitudes of men so completely and intensely lose their individual selves in the larger life which they call their city?"

Despite its virtues as a teacher of self-denial and social good, as an inculcator of moral as well as physical well-being, baseball initially competed against organized religion. Protestant America long abjured commercial and recreational activities on Sunday, and local laws (so-called blue laws) that were intended to enforce this view of the Sabbath made such activities illegal. After 1877, the National League banned Sunday games, but it could not ban the rising demand for Sabbath sports. The laboring classes, in particular, who unlike the professional classes could not attend afternoon games during the week, thirsted for Sunday baseball. And the growing number of Catholic, not to mention Jewish, immigrants to America held none of the pietistic assumptions about Sundays as days devoted to religion. When a competing organization, the American Association, challenged the National League in 1882, they did so, in part, on the basis of allowing Sunday baseball.

Sunday ball started in the Middle West—in Cincinnati, St. Louis, and Chicago—and eventually it migrated eastward, but not without a struggle. At a Sunday game in Chicago, in 1893, several players were arrested. Teams in New York, looking for a way to profit from the interest in the game, played Sunday exhibition games across the river in New Jersey, before crowds of thousands. The struggle over Sunday baseball waxed and waned for decades. Puritan Boston did not permit it until 1929. But if the game truly was the national pastime, and if commercial interests were to be served, then it would have to be played on the national day for worship.

Baseball started out competing against religion, but in time it became a surrogate for it. Even the evangelist Billy Sunday, whose first career was as a professional baseball player for Chicago and Pittsburgh, and who vehemently opposed Sunday baseball, found that baseball metaphors appealed to his audience. By warning sinners against "dying on second base," and by threatening to fire "the fastball at the devil," Sunday made baseball a part of his theology. At the close of World War I, the philosopher Morris Cohen argued, "By all the canons of our modern books on comparative religion, baseball is a religion, and the only one that is not sectarian, but national." Stadiums became cathedrals, the players the clergy, the fans the parishioners, the game itself the liturgy in "the establishment of the true Church Universal in which all men would feel their brotherhood in the Infinite Game."

With baseball as its democratic and religious foundation, America became "a nation of rooters, the loudest and maddest on earth." "Every American has played baseball in his boyhood," observed Rollin Hartt, and, as a result, the child serves as father of the fan who renews his "youth while rooting on the bleachers." Sitting in the stands, the fan learns from baseball the "fullness of life—not sport merely, but . . . hero-worship, moral uplift, and a wellspring of national consciousness." The baseball fan, concluded Hugh Fullerton, "is an unique American species and the most rapid of all enthusiasts. . . . Baseball is the most serious pleasure ever invented." Another analyst agreed: "there are three subjects which are not reducible to reason: politics, religion, and baseball; and the greatest of these is baseball." The game was "the people's pastime," a game, concluded the *Sporting News*, that was not "conceived and perfected for one person, but for a nation."

GAME EIGHT, TUESDAY, OCTOBER 13

RIDING THE TRAIN BACK to Boston, the *Globe*'s Tim Murnane had time to reflect on the seven games of the series, and he waxed poetic about baseball: "this shows that baseball is the greatest outdoor sport that has ever been known and it is thoroughly American, combining everything in the way of athletic skill, nerve, grit, and honesty and all that is best in our national character." Another writer proclaimed that "it is the greatest series of games that has ever been played for the world's championship. Never before has there been such a universal interest in a series of baseball games. No two teams were ever more evenly matched, though Boston has a present advantage in the matter of pitchers, and it is still a tossup as to which team will win out." Before leaving the Smoky City, Jimmy Collins expressed his wonder at "the amount of interest that is being taken in this series. I never thought that it would arouse so much enthusiasm. The people of Boston and Pittsburg are simply crazy over it. Well, that was to be expected, but the interest in scores of outside cities is just as great."

The journey from Pittsburgh dragged for losers and winners

alike. The Pirates had desperately hoped to avoid having to make this trip, but now they were riding through the night to play another game, hopefully two. The Boston players, after a few hours of celebration, finally settled down. The men were eager to get home. "We expect to end the struggle" at the Huntington Grounds on Monday, said Collins, "for we are getting tired."

Both teams livened up a bit when they joined together in Albany. The Pirates' train was held at the station so that the Boston special could catch up. Players on both sides mingled and chatted on the way to Boston. The mutual respect and admiration shown by the competitors distinguished the series. Fred Clarke remarked that the games were "free from any sort of friction" between the athletes. And the good will carried over to the fans who admired the devotion of their counterparts and acted "more like judges than partisans" when it came to action on the field. When the train reached Worcester, the hometown of both Kitty Bransfield and Hobe Ferris, the two players departed to spend the evening with their families. As they walked off, the Boston Rooters gave each man, one a Pirate and one an American, "three rousing cheers."

The train reached Boston's South Station at 3:45 on a cold, rainy Sunday afternoon. The Pirates had gotten off a stop earlier at Back Bay, and took carriages to the Vendome, where they again took up residence. Several hundred Bostonians braved the weather to greet the home team. They were a "good-natured crowd" that swarmed the platform and made it difficult for the players to squeeze through. Fans slapped the backs and shook the hands of their heroes. They especially sought out Cy Young, whose "big bulk and rotund countenance" made it easy to pick him out. When the man emerged, his fans hoisted him on their shoulders and carried him to the gate.

The Royal Rooters were nearly as much in demand as the players. Everyone wanted to hear stories of the week in Pittsburgh. Charley Lavis and Mike McGreevey tried to narrate the tale of their legal troubles, but they had lost their voices from days of cheering. An enthusiast declared that "the rooters would put Boston's best lawyers in the shade when it comes to pleading." Another announced, " 'Tessie' did the trick," and insisted that ever since the boys had started singing that show tune, the Americans had played inspired ball. Most of the Rooters were too tired to celebrate further and were eager to get a good night's sleep in preparation for Monday's game. "I've talked enough baseball this week to last me a year," acknowledged one of the travelers.

In appreciation for their support of the team, the Boston Americans put aside a hundred seats for the Royal Rooters for the eighth game. But regular fans had trouble securing tickets. The demand overwhelmed the box office, as orders arrived by telegraph and fans lined up to purchase seats. The various downtown offices that sold tickets had none left just hours after they went on sale. Even the players had difficulty acquiring seats for family and friends. Cy Young, Lou Criger, Candy LaChance, and Fred Parent could secure no more than two tickets apiece. And yet speculators seemed to have plenty of tickets for sale at $2 and $3 each. The speculators paid boys, "to whom dollars are strangers," to wait in line to purchase seats. One letter-writer expressed his disappointment at being shut out from the grounds. "It looks like a game of bunco," he protested, "as I could find no tickets for sale by anyone except speculators."

At midnight on Sunday, the rain that had settled over the northeast for an entire week continued to pelt down. "It is raining one of those dismal, mean Boston rains," reported Frank M'Quiston, "while it is growing cold and the wind is rising." It seemed unlikely that the game would be played the following day.

Collins had announced that Dinneen would start, and Clarke had said that he would use Leever, with Veil ready to relieve, but an extra day off might change the managers' thinking. Clarke tried to ignite his troops: "The championship is not lost to Pittsburg yet, and it won't be until the last man goes down and out. My boys will fight to the last ditch." The Pirates received a lift Sunday night when National League President Harry Pulliam ar-

rived at the Vendome. He shook hands with the players and assured them that they would win.

The winning, however, would have to wait at least until Tuesday. A torrential rain battered Boston on Monday. Jimmy Collins
came down from his hotel room for breakfast, peered out the
window, and said, "I guess it's off." He telephoned the ballpark
and learned that "the field is in better condition for holding an in-
ternational yacht race than for playing the great national game."
Collins notified the Boston players at the Langham Hotel, and
word was spread that the game had been called off. Hobe Ferris
received a call in Worcester that he need not make the trip in.

But no one informed Fred Clarke and the Pirates that the
game had been officially postponed. As a result, the players waited
on edge. Pittsburgh kept a representative at the Huntington Avenue Grounds just in case Boston had any idea of bringing their
team in and claiming victory by forfeit. The Pirates' team secretary tried to contact Collins and the Americans' business manager,
but without any luck. Apparently, the Americans were exacting
revenge for Clarke's postponement of Friday's game in Pittsburgh.
It was "a well-laid plan to worry and annoy" the Pirates, thought
one writer. Finally, at 1:30 p.m., the groundskeeper notified the
Pirates that the field was "a sea of mud," and that the game was
unplayable.

The "shabby treatment at the hands of the Boston club"
annoyed the Pirates. Far worse was the news that they received
about one of their own. Ed Doheny was one of the names that
surfaced whenever commentators talked about the troubles of the
Pittsburgh pitching staff. A tough lefty who had come over from
the Giants in 1901, Doheny was 16–4 in 1902 and 16–8 in 1903.
He had started his career as a power pitcher, but his wildness
hampered his effectiveness. As a Pirate, he struck out fewer batters, but he also learned to throw the ball over the plate. He had
returned from his leave of absence to pitch effectively in August
and September, but again he became delusional. By the end of

September he had abandoned the team for his home in Andover, just twenty-three miles north of Boston.

The Pirates had hoped Doheny would be well enough to return for the start of the series, but when doctors made it clear that he would not be able to contribute, the team returned his uniform to him. Perhaps the Pirates thought it would somehow make Doheny feel better, but it had the opposite effect. "When he got his suit back, he was heartbroken, thinking all was over," said his wife.

Doheny followed the series closely and agonized over each Pirate loss. He moaned as he read about Leever's injured arm. He wanted to rush to Pittsburgh. On Sunday, when he read that Boston had taken the lead in the series, the news "seemed to numb and daze him." Mrs. Doheny sent for the doctor, but Eddie blamed the man for keeping him from attending the games in Boston, struck at him, and sent him from the house.

Mrs. Doheny calmed her husband and went to look after their four-year-old son. The pitcher was left in the care of his male nurse, Oberlin Howarth. Suddenly Mrs. Doheny heard scuffling and yelling, and she rushed to find her husband standing over Howarth and beating him with a cast-iron stove leg. She screamed, "Eddie! Eddie! Don't do that!" Doheny dropped the weapon, stared with vacant eyes at his wife, and collapsed onto his bed. That night, he was committed to the Danvers insane asylum.

Fred Clarke called the players together and told them that he was going to visit Mrs. Doheny. He asked them if they would agree with whatever he decided to do on behalf of the stricken family, and all said yes. During the evening the Pirate players went out in groups of three or four and tried to absorb the day's news.

That same night the Boston Americans and the Royal Rooters attended the theater. Charley Waldron, one of the Rooters who had made the trip to Pittsburgh, was the proprietor of the Palace Theater, and he invited the team and fans as his guests. The Rooters sat in the orchestra, and the players in the first tier of boxes.

The theater was swathed in red, white, and blue bunting and national shields. The Letter Carriers' Band, who would accompany the Rooters to the game on Tuesday, came on stage and, to everyone's delight, played "Tessie." Prior to the performance of the musical comedy *The Baby Trust*, an actor parodied the teams and the audience erupted at the mention of Young, Collins, and Dinneen. Waldron, who stood to win $1,400 on bets that Boston would win the series, made certain that the evening ended early so that the players could get their rest.

Tuesday morning broke clear enough for baseball, though the air was cold and the skies at times threatening. Anticipating an extraordinary crowd, the Boston management arranged for more than one hundred policemen to be on duty. There would be no repeat of the crowd behavior that had adversely effected the third game. The vast crowd, however, never materialized. Many believed that the field would not be playable and that the game would be held on Wednesday. Others grew disheartened by the rumors that all the available tickets were in the hands of speculators. Still others stayed away because they believed that the game was fixed to ensure a ninth and deciding contest. Such rumors made Cy Young indignant: "The story is malicious. Pittsburg may win when we meet, but if they do it will be because they have the ablest team and the luck as well, for the Boston team is going out to play ball to win." Whatever the reasons for the limited attendance, the police would not have to worry. The smallest crowd of the series, 7,500 people, "braved the threats of pneumonia and rheumatism at the ball park" in the hope of witnessing history.

There were seats available in the grandstand and bleachers. The game, it seemed, would be played "under conditions where every ball hit would go for just what it is worth." But for some reason, a sparse outfield crowd was allowed to stand beyond the ropes in center field and, as a result, the ground-rule triple would be in effect.

The Letter Carriers' Band marched in with the Rooters behind them. For this game, the band and Rooters were placed in a special area on the field in front of the grandstand and behind home plate. They sat in four rows of high-backed chairs specially delivered to the grounds at 1 p.m.: royal treatment for the Royal Rooters.

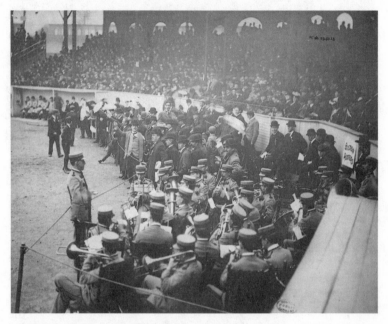

The Royal Rooters and Letter Carriers' Band in their special section

MCGREEVEY COLLECTION, BOSTON PUBLIC LIBRARY

At 2:25 p.m., just before the Pirates went out for practice, the teams posed together for a picture. Managers Clarke and Collins sit beside one another on the left side of the middle row. Dinneen is two players to the right of Collins, and Young is two over from Dinneen. Phillippe is in the back row, the fifth player from the left. Leach is four players to the right of him. Wagner stands at the end, his huge hand resting on his hip. The players look serious, a bit tight. What joy there is emanates from the faces of the rooters and fans. The ubiquitous Mike McGreevey peers over Bill Kennedy's right shoulder. He is all smiles.

The teams pose prior to the game. Top row (left to right): Pirates Claude Ritchey, Harry Smith, Eddie Phelps, Ginger Beaumont, Deacon Phillippe, Sam Leever, Bucky Veil, Gus Thompson, Tommy Leach, Jimmy Sebring, Bill Kennedy, Fred Carisch, and Honus Wagner. Middle row (left to right): Fred Clarke, Jimmy Collins, Chick Stahl, Bill Dinneen, Buck Freeman, Cy Young, Candy LaChance, Patsy Dougherty, George Winter, Charles Farrell, Jack O'Brien, and Tom Hughes. Seated in front (left to right): Fred Parent, Lou Criger, and Hobe Ferris. The ubiquitous Mike McGreevey peers over Bill Kennedy's shoulder

MCGREEVEY COLLECTION, BOSTON PUBLIC LIBRARY

The Pirates loosened up first. They looked sharp in practice, despite the condition of the field, which featured puddles down the baselines. The Pirate outfielders impressed the crowd. They caught everything hit to them, even when the balls that bounced along the grass kicked up "little fountains of spray." And once again, the fans marveled at the way Leach, Wagner, and Ritchey threw the ball around. Little did they know that Ritchey had an infected finger and Wagner, only the day before, could barely lift his arms. In frustration, he had announced that he would not play baseball in 1904. Those around him smiled, knowing that Wagner could no more quit baseball than stop eating. "Dutch is in the dumps now," said Clarke. "He has sore arms and can not throw without pain, beside he has not been having any luck at batting. He will get better breaks soon."

When Boston took the field to warm up, Cy Young grabbed a bat to hit ground balls to the infield. The band played the now famous theme song and the Royal Rooters let loose with their first cheer of the day: "Higgeldy, piggeldy, ainst we nice. The Pittsburg bunch will cut no ice."

The umpires came out of the dressing room. It was nearing three o'clock. The band played "The Star-Spangled Banner." Umpire O'Day brushed off home plate, and the Americans took the field with a well-rested Bill Dinneen on the mound.

Dinneen's first pitch to Beaumont was a called strike. The Royal Rooters chanted. One fan waved a sign that asked, "Are ye There?" And the fans responded. Dinneen's next three pitches were off the plate before Beaumont took another for a strike. With the count full, the lefty leadoff hitter was looking to get on base with a walk, but he took a called third strike and retreated to the Pirate bench.

Fred Clarke, another lefty batter, came to bat. He had had eight hits in thirty at-bats in the series and hadn't had a multi-hit performance since the first game. After fouling off the first two pitches, Clarke smashed a rising line drive over short. But going out toward left field, Parent leaped and brought it down with a "sensational one-handed catch." It was the kind of acrobatic, unexpected play that could have a "mental effect on the game." Leach, now hitless in his previous ten at-bats, lofted a routine fly ball to Chick Stahl in center, and Pittsburgh was retired without a struggle.

The crowd applauded as Deacon Phillippe came to the mound. The extra day's rest allowed Clarke to bring his ace back for his fifth start of the series. Patsy Dougherty led off with a routine fly to Beaumont in center. Jimmy Collins then singled to right. In every game of the series, the team that scored first had won. Here was a chance for the Americans to put that pressure on the Pirates. But Phillippe got Stahl to fly to center and Freeman to fly to Clarke in left. The first inning ended in a standoff.

In the top of the second, the Pirates were retired in order. Dinneen had his best stuff, and the overcast skies made it difficult for the Pittsburgh hitters to pick the ball out of the air. Phillippe seemed equal to the task as well. With two outs, in the bottom of the second, Hobe Ferris hit a shot past Leach that was scooped up by Wagner ranging far to his right, but Wagner's throw to first was not in time. Lou Criger followed with a single to left field. That brought up Dinneen. Throughout the series, the pitchers had done well at the plate, but not this time. Dinneen struck out and left the runners stranded.

In the third inning, both teams went down in order. Dinneen had helped his cause by barehanding a ground ball hit back to him by Sebring. The day was shaping up to be a pitchers' duel. With each recorded out it seemed more likely that the first team to score would win. The longer a championship game goes without any runs scored, the more the tension mounts on players and fans alike. Each pitch becomes more momentous, each swing more fateful. Although baseball is not played against a clock, as zeros are added to the scoreboard the impression is of time running out.

Dinneen had retired the first nine Pirates of the game, and to open the fourth he induced a ground-out from Beaumont and a strikeout by Clarke. The captain threw his bat and cursed loudly as he walked back to the bench. Leach, who had not reached base in his previous eleven at-bats, at last found his way to first when he walked with two out. Wagner, who also had nothing to show for his last eleven plate appearances, came to bat, and the fans applauded for his attempt on Ferris's ball in the second. Leach took off for second, and Wagner hit the ball to the spot vacated by Parent, who was covering the bag. It went as a base hit up the middle, and Leach took third. Clarke had called for a hit and run, and Wagner had executed it perfectly.

The Pirates had their first threat. With speedy runners on the corners and two outs, Kitty Bransfield fell behind with two strikes. Playing aggressively, Wagner took off in an attempt to steal second base. A poor throw by Criger would mean a run. As Wagner sprinted toward second, Leach crept a few steps off third; if Criger tried to throw out Wagner, then Leach would break for home. Criger cocked his arm and violently swung it toward second. Leach started for home. But Criger held on to the ball, recocked, and fired to Collins at third. Leach was caught. He "started bravely for the plate," but he might as well have simply walked to the dugout as Collins threw back to Criger for the easy tag.

The Americans raced off the field. This was the kind of play that inspired one team while it disheartened the other. It brought the Boston fans to a frenzy. Perhaps it also caused Phillippe to lose his concentration. In the bottom of the fourth, he grooved a 1–2 pitch to Buck Freeman, who lashed a leadoff triple to deep center field. Fans stood on their feet, waved their hats, and hollered, "Well, Well, Well." One group along the first-base bleachers released American flags into the wind. Wagner went to the mound to relax Phillippe. Parent came to bat and the fans hollered, "Line her out, Freddie!" He dropped an unexpected bunt; Phelps grabbed for the ball, but fumbled it. Freeman remained at third, and Boston had runners on the corners with no one out.

LaChance, who only had four hits in the series, came to bat and rifled a hard ground ball to first, which Bransfield fielded and threw to Ritchey, covering, for the out. Parent advanced to second, but Freeman held third. The Pirates had one important out with the bottom of the Boston order due up.

Ferris strode to the plate. He had hit the ball well in Pittsburgh, but he was a feeble one for eleven in the first three games played at the Huntington Avenue Grounds. Boston fans hoped that he would at least come through with a fly ball that would allow the runner from third to score.

"Crack! With a report like that of a rifle Ferris's bat met the swift ball squarely, and the leather sailed between right and center fields." Jimmy Sebring recovered the ball and threw it in. Both Freeman and Parent scored, Ferris stood smiling on first, the band blasted "Tessie," and "everyone believed that those two runs meant victory."

Boston fans did not seem to mind that Criger then grounded out and Ferris was thrown out at the plate on a single by Dinneen. The Americans had a 2–0 lead going into the fifth inning, and their fans were happy.

Dinneen struck out Bransfield to open the fifth. Ritchey hit the ball hard to Collins, who fumbled it once, fumbled it again, and then threw to first to get the runner by half a step. Sebring, who had hit the ball well in the first three games in Boston, took an offering from Dinneen and drove it over the outfield ropes for a triple. A two-out run would cut the lead in half and reverse the momentum, but Phelps became Dinneen's fifth strikeout victim.

Boston could not build on its lead in the fifth inning. Dougherty flied out. Collins grounded deep to Leach's right, but the third baseman made a long throw that Bransfield scooped out of the dirt. Stahl hit an easy fly to Clarke. Phillippe was containing Boston's hot bats. The Pirate hitters had four innings left to muster some kind of offensive threat if the team was to have a chance.

Phillippe, leading by example, singled over Parent's head to start the sixth inning. It was his fourth hit of the series. If anyone wanted to know what was wrong with the Pirates, all they had to realize was that Phillippe's World Series batting average of .222 was identical to Wagner's.

Beaumont struck out, and Criger made his second superb defensive play of the game when, in one motion, he caught the ball, fired to first, and caught Phillippe three feet off the bag. If the Pirates lost the game, it would be Criger who defeated them. Leach ended the inning by flying out.

Although Dinneen had relinquished only three hits, Collins

wasn't taking any chances. He had Cy Young warming up behind the stands with catcher Duke Farrell. Farrell would periodically come through the alley to peek at how Dinneen was doing. He predicted to Young that there would be no need for the pitcher's services.

In the bottom of the sixth, Buck Freeman hit a high foul pop that Wagner caught near the grandstand behind third base. Parent then flied out to Beaumont in center. It looked like a quick inning for Phillippe. But LaChance scorched the ball past the right-field ropes for a two-out triple. Ferris, the hero of the fourth inning, stepped in. He singled for the second time, LaChance trotted home, and Boston was ahead 3–0. Criger followed Ferris with a base hit, but Dinneen grounded out to end the inning. The three consecutive hits by the bottom of the Boston order signaled that Phillippe was tiring. After pitching forty-two innings in twelve days, he could not be blamed.

The world's championship was within Boston's grasp, and the players on both sides could feel it. Dinneen was simply overpowering. "Hold them, boys," yelled Collins as the Americans took the field in the seventh, and his pitcher complied. Wagner grounded out, and Bransfield flied out. Ritchey worked a walk, but Sebring grounded back to the mound to end the frame.

Despite exhaustion, Phillippe kept Boston from adding to its lead in the bottom of the seventh inning. Ritchey made a nice backhand catch of Dougherty's pop-up, and Leach threw out Collins trying to bunt. Wagner committed his sixth error of the series when he threw away Stahl's grounder, but no damage was done as Clarke cradled Freeman's fly to left.

Dinneen's eighth inning was even easier than his seventh. He induced a groundout from Phelps and struck out Phillippe. Beaumont, hitless in all the Boston games, tapped a slow roller to first that clipped the bag. Thinking that the ball was foul, he did not run and was put out easily. Clarke argued Beaumont's case, but to no avail. The inning was over. The Pirates would have the two-three-four hitters due up in the ninth.

In the bottom of the eighth, Parent flied to Clarke, LaChance grounded to Wagner, and Ferris, who received an ovation from the crowd for his two clutch hits, popped to Wagner. Once again, Phillippe had pitched well enough to win. He had struck out only two batters, but he had walked none and yielded a mere eight hits. In surrendering only three runs, he had given his team a chance. Now it was up to his teammates.

Dinneen came out for the ninth inning. The index finger on his pitching hand burned from the hard ball hit back to the mound in the third inning by Sebring. The skin had peeled away and his fingertip bled at times during the game. It was "raw as a piece of meat," but this was Dinneen's game to finish.

Fred Clarke led off. He drove the pitch toward left field. In the deepening darkness of an overcast afternoon, Dougherty spotted the ball and pulled it in for the first out.

Tommy Leach came up to bat. He hadn't hit in the sixth and seventh games, and he hadn't hit yet in this one either. He poked a harmless fly ball to Freeman in right for the second out. Without a miracle two-out rally, he would have to wait until 1904 to experience again the joy of a well-hit ball.

That brought Wagner to the plate. The game was not decided as long as the batting champion had life. He had managed only one hit in the last four games, but a blast from him might yet rally the slumbering Pirates. The crowd seemed nervous, unusually quiet because of all that was at stake.

Wagner swung hard at Dinneen's first offering. "Strike One!" yelled O'Day. The crowd released a stifled yell and then fell silent again.

Dinneen threw a wide-out curve, and Wagner swung through it. "Strike Two!" O'Day declared. The fans roared, "Strike him out! Strike him out!" and then again fell hushed.

Wagner fought back and worked the count full. Dinneen, one strike away from his second shutout and his third victory of the series, prepared to throw the most important pitch of his career:

Slowly the big pitcher gathered himself up for the effort, slowly he swung his arms about his head. Then the ball shot away like a flash toward the plate where the great Wagner stood, muscles drawn tense, waiting for it. The big batsman's mighty shoulders heaved, the stands will swear that his very frame creaked, as he swung his bat with every ounce of power in his body, but the dull thud of the ball, as it nestled in Criger's waiting mitt, told the story.

THE EIGHTH GAME

BOSTON.	AB.	R.	B.	P.	A.	E.	PITTSBURG.	AB.	R.	B.	P.	A.	E.
Dougherty, lf......	4	0	0	3	0	0	Beaumont, cf......	4	0	0	5	0	0
Collins, 3b.........	4	0	1	0	2	0	Clarke, lf..........	4	0	1	3	0	0
Stahl, cf...........	4	0	0	2	0	0	Leach, 3b..........	3	0	0	0	3	0
Freeman. rf.......	4	1	1	2	0	0	Wagner, ss.........	4	0	1	3	0	1
Parent, ss.........	4	1	0	1	1	0	Bransfield, 1b	3	0	0	7	1	1
LaChance, 1b......	3	1	1	11	0	0	Ritchey. 2d.........	2	0	0	2	1	0
Ferris, 2b..........	4	0	2	0	3	0	Sebring, rf.........	3	0	1	1	1	0
Criger, c..........	3	0	2	8	3	0	Phelps, c...........	3	0	0	3	0	1
Dineen, p..........	3	0	1	0	3	0	⊢hillippe, p........	3	0	1	0	2	0
Total............	33	3	8	27	12	0	Total............	29	0	4	24	8	3

Boston.....................	0	0	0	2	0	1	0	0	x——3
Pittsburg..................	0	0	0	0	0	0	0	0	0——0

Earned runs—Boston, 2. Three-base hits—Freeman, La-Chance, Sebring. Sacrifice hit—LaChance. Stolen base—Wagner. Double play—Criger, LaChance. First on balls—Off Dineen 2. Struck out—By Dineen 7, Phillippe 2. Time—1.35. Umpires—O'Day and Connolly. Attendance—7,455.

"LIFE ILLUSTRATED BY BASEBALL"

THE CROWD POURED ONTO THE FIELD. Criger tossed the muddy, bloodstained ball into the air, and the players rushed toward one another. Wagner drifted untouched to the Pittsburgh bench. Men threw their hats, strangers smacked one another on the back, people flooded in every direction. "Shouts of triumph" rang forth, drowning out the band, which tried futilely to sound its song.

Fans fell out of the bleachers; they dropped down from the grandstand; they raced in from the outfield. "All individual identity was lost in that wild, swirling mass of humanity," observed the *Herald*. The crowd headed for the players and soon engulfed them. Dinneen, Collins, Parent, Ferris, LaChance, and Criger stood near the mound, reaching for one another in celebration and in fear. Frank M'Quiston of the *Pittsburg Dispatch* described the scene, one worthy, he thought, of Michelangelo:

Around a little island on which stood, almost clutching each other, six ball players clad in white, there rolled and threshed great waves of dark clad humanity. But only for the fraction of a second. Then with a roar like the breaking of the surf there rolled from all sides these waves, blotting out the little mariners in white. The island had been swallowed up by the human sea. Not a glimpse of white could be seen for perhaps ten seconds. Then as if from the center of the storm there shot upward a great white uniform, sent up by willing hands and brawny arms. "Dinneen! Dinneen!" screamed the crowd, and the big pitcher as he came down landed on friendly shoulders and was borne off the field fighting like a demon.

Collins emerged next, his uniform hanging from his body by threads. He was almost split in two when the crowd holding his left leg danced one way, and those holding his right marched off in the opposite direction. The players found themselves riding a sea of shoulders that sailed them across the field toward the clubhouse. It was as if the crowd desired "to secure one of the victorious players as a human souvenir." "Every man was a hero," declared the *Post*; "every man had done his share to bring to Boston the honors supreme in the baseball world."

As the fans celebrated, the Pirates gathered their bags and walked mournfully toward the outfield gates. Tears streamed down Clarke's face. It had been a season awash with injury and tragedy and now it was over. No one spoke or looked up: "With bat bags on their shoulders, without a friend to whisper a word of cheer or sympathy, they passed beyond the gate, turning not once to glance at the scene of revelry and excitement behind them."

A painful reminder of the team's afflictions awaited upon their return to the Vendome Hotel. Claude Ritchey asked for his room key, and the clerk handed him a letter from Mrs. Edward Doheny. He opened it and discovered two $1 bills along with a note: "Eddie said he owed you $2 and asked me to pay you. Here it is." Ritchey began sobbing, and let the money drift to the floor. He offered to give Doheny's family all that was his. He also hoped "that they do not tell him where he is that we've lost the championship."

While the Pirates were on their way to the hotel, the Americans jostled their way to the dressing room, but the fans would not leave the grounds. Led by the band, thousands remained on the field singing, shouting, and marching in a triumphal serpentine procession around the diamond. Eventually, a group of Royal Rooters threaded their way to Mike McGreevey's Third Base emporium, where they jumped on the counter and danced and drank the night away.

Once in the clubhouse, the players celebrated and changed out of their uniforms. For thirty minutes, "mirth and merriment reigned." Friends and dignitaries entered to offer their congratulations. Suddenly the group gathered around Collins, and State Senator Mike Sullivan, who had pitched for several teams in a career that spanned the 1890s, stepped forward. "I have been selected," he said, "to present you with a slight token of esteem from the players whom you have successfully led to victory this year." He pulled a case from his pocket and handed it to the captain. It contained a gold watch and chain, inscribed "To James J. Collins. From the players of the Boston base ball club, American League, Oct. 15, 1903."

Collins was not a man of many words. The player-manager led by example, not verbiage. A reporter once interviewed him and said that "it was like putting questions to an Egyptian mummy." But when Collins spoke, it was simple and sincere. "I don't know what I can say," he muttered. "This is one of the happiest moments of my life, and I want to thank you fellows from the bottom of my heart. I hope that you will all pass a pleasant winter and that we will be together again in 1904."

In the evening, both teams were invited to the theater. No one would have blamed the Pirates had they not attended, but Clarke felt that the Boston people "have been so kind to us that it is our duty to keep our engagement." The Pirates occupied the lower boxes and received warm applause as they entered. They had to endure several barbs cast at them when the performers of *The Bil-lionaire* revised their lines to acknowledge the momentous events of the afternoon:

> There are incidents that happen in the lives of famous men
> There is always something doing that will creep out now and
> then
> When the score is three to nothing, with the Boston no use
> bluffing
> There are incidents that happen in the lives of famous men.

During intermission, several Pittsburgh players slipped away to attend a boxing match at the Criterion Club.

At the Vendome, Barney Dreyfuss gave a midnight banquet for the Pittsburgh players and correspondents. "My confidence in my team remains unshaken," he said. And while he did not want to detract from the Americans' victory, he deplored the situation where "we were so unfortunate as to have only one first-class pitcher in condition to oppose the Boston club."

It was hard for Dreyfuss to stop thinking about the series and about what went wrong. The newspaper verdicts on the final game did not help. The *Dispatch* thought, "Pittsburg was outplayed to-day all the way. She was outpitched, outfielded, and outgeneraled." And the *Post* said that Pittsburgh "came to bat in a listless, half-hearted way that counted them out often before a ball was delivered."

The Pirates tried to be generous in defeat. Kitty Bransfield said, "We were defeated fairly and squarely, and we have no kick to make." But Deacon Phillippe's comment, "My arm is numb and I am tired," reminded everyone of the handicap under which Pirate pitching labored. Fred Clarke probably regretted saying it but, in a moment of exhaustion, bitterness slipped from his throat: "We have lost. I have no complaint to make. I believe that the greatest ball team which ever existed, and which now exists, has been beaten, and by an inferior team. I believe too, that Boston knows this. We could not win with one pitcher when they had two." Bill Kennedy put it more softly: "We have worked hard, but luck was against us. We've lost, that's all there is to be said."

If Clarke's comment riled any of the Boston players, they had the good grace to ignore it. Cy Young said, "I knew we would win." Collins said, "I believed all the way we would win, even when things looked blackest for us." Chick Stahl agreed: "We won, and in my mind there was never doubt of it."

Ban Johnson took special joy in the victory. By force of will he had created the American League and went to war against the National. He had helped fashion a peace that looked as though it would last, and a circuit that attracted fans and played, in the parlance of the times, "a fast game." The results of the four local championship series that overlapped with the World Series had already given Johnson cause for satisfaction. The Philadelphia A's defeated the Phillies, 4 games to 3. The St. Louis Browns defeated the Cardinals, 5 games to 2. The Chicago White Sox and Cubs went back and forth until player contracts ended on October 15, and the series came to a halt tied at 7 games apiece. In Ohio, the Naps triumphed over the Reds, 6 games to 3.

But victory in the first World Series was the sweetest of them all. "Isn't it fine," cooed Johnson, "but it is no surprise to me. I have always contended that Boston was the better club of the two and that when the two leagues would come together the Americans would have the best of the argument." Boston's victory, the Boston *Herald* announced, "meant the supremacy of the American league over the National."

Not everyone agreed with that judgment. The *Sporting News* predicted, "There will always be a difference of opinion among enthusiasts about the relative strength of the American and National Leagues and each organization will retain its partisans, regardless of the results of ante or post-season series." What mattered most was that "the intense interest [in the Series] throughout the country proves conclusively that the game's patrons prefer peace and competition between the major leagues."

The day after the World Series concluded, the Pirates left for Pittsburgh, and the Boston players arrived in the afternoon at the Huntington Avenue Grounds to receive their payment and begin their off season. The men looked worn. Pat Dougherty said that the previous night was the first good sleep he had had in two weeks. Most of the players reported weight loss of six to twelve pounds over the course of the series. Someone must have joked that Cy Young could afford to shed some bulk. "The strain of the series, of the game and of the situation had us all prostrated," recalled Collins.

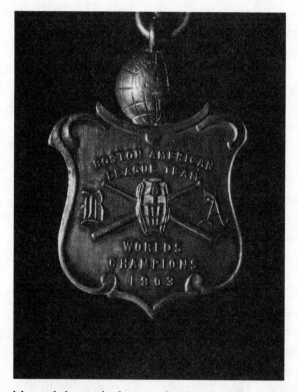

The medal awarded to each player on the victorious Boston Americans by the *Boston Globe* as a souvenir of "the most famous series of baseball games ever played"

BASEBALL HALL OF FAME LIBRARY, COOPERSTOWN, NEW YORK

The team gathered together, and each player received his share of the World Series receipts. More than 100,000 fans attended the eight games and one estimate put the gate receipts at $75,000. Boston's half of $37,500 was divided 75 percent to the players and 25 percent to the owner. Sixteen players and the business manager received full shares of $1,182 each.

Boston politicians tried to organize a banquet for the team, but the players were eager to leave town. They "went through an awful strain," reasoned the *Boston Globe*, and "were heartily glad when the whole thing was over and they were at liberty to return once more to their homes and families."

Financially, the Pirates made out better than the Americans. Dreyfuss announced that, although his team lost, he would still divide all of the money among the players. When implored to recover his gambling debt of $7,000, he declined. As a result of the owner's generosity, each player received a check for $1,316. The team secretary was voted a full share, and a couple of players who had been with the team only a month received a one-sixth share. Money went as well to the groundskeeper and trainer, and a check was sent to Mrs. Edward Doheny. In fact, Dreyfuss had all the checks of married players made out to their wives. "I'm tired of this business of the boys getting money and spending it," he said.

The largesse did not stop there. At the final team meeting back in Pittsburgh, Dreyfuss announced that he would reward Phillippe, the player who "would have pitched all the games for us if we would have let him and would have won them all if he could," with ten shares of railroad stock. In tribute to Dreyfuss's generosity, the team presented him with a gold watch. The players then surprised Fred Clarke by presenting him with a watch chain and an elk's tooth charm. The next day, Clarke announced that he had signed a contract to manage and play for the Pirates "for life—that is, my baseball life."

Clarke's baseball life would one day lead him back to the World Series. In 1909, the Pirates faced the Detroit Tigers, led by

Ty Cobb. Leach and Wagner were the other two position players remaining from 1903, and both distinguished themselves in the series. Leach hit .360 and Wagner made up for his performance six years earlier by hitting .333 and knocking in 6 RBIs. Deacon Phillippe was also with the team, but the star of the first World Series appeared only twice in relief. Still, he managed to pitch six scoreless innings. The Pirates won the World Championship in 1909, but their winners' share was only a few hundred dollars more than their losers' cut in 1903.

The Boston Americans repeated as league champions in 1904, when they beat out the Highlanders by a game and a half to win the pennant. But they would not get a chance to compete in a second consecutive World Series because the winner of the National League pennant, the New York Giants, refused to play. For John Brush and John McGraw, the American League still had no legitimacy, and they betrayed the spirit of the peace agreement signed in January 1903 and the recommendations of a joint schedule committee in 1904 that called for a world championship series again to be played. In 1905, the National Commission regulated the terms of the World Series as an annual event. McGraw's Giants begrudgingly participated, and they triumphed easily over Philadelphia. The feisty McGraw would lead his team to eight more World Series appearances, two of which he would win. Perhaps the Boston players of 1904 took solace from the series in 1912, when a Boston team led by Tris Speaker and Smokey Joe Wood and managed by Jake Stahl, who played with the Americans in 1903 but did not appear in the World Series, defeated McGraw's Giants, 4 games to 3.

The postseason earnings of the players in 1903 paled in comparison to what some gamblers made on the series. Tens of thousands of dollars were wagered. Royal Rooter Charley Lavis made $2,500. And Sport Sullivan cashed out for $4,000, more than the annual salary of most players. It was undoubtedly here, in the first World Series, that Sullivan came to realize that a fortune could be made betting the underdog and then trying to arrange matters so that players on the favored team threw the games. One day he would make $50,000 on a World Series, and he would make headlines as well. Along with eight players and several other gamblers, he was indicted for fixing the 1919 World Series between Chicago and Cincinnati.

Talk of the Boston-Pittsburgh games being fixed lingered throughout the series. In commenting on the concluding game, players and writers argued that the victory by the Americans exposed the absurdity of the rumors. The *Boston Post* reported, "players and men who know how absolutely impossible it is to fix the results without everyone knowing it hailed with delight the fact that the ninth game of the series is not necessary." Jimmy Collins said that "it is impossible for baseball to be played dishonestly, and today's victory showed the public that we wanted the honor of winning, not the money alone." Senator Sullivan also expressed his outrage: "I have seen the four games in this city, and I do not understand how any sane man could even entertain a suspicion about the games. . . . The uncertainty of baseball and the open game makes it honest. It is scandalous that such statements are made—especially in the series which closed today, in which every game was bitterly and stubbornly fought."

It mattered that everyone viewed the series as honest because the response to the eight games between Boston and Pittsburgh ratified baseball's place as the national pastime. Newspapers noted that there was no lack of popularity to baseball before the World Series, "but this final 'playoff' between the victors gives a substantial standing to the championship which it would not have had otherwise."

The series victory had an incalculable effect on the citizens of Boston and became a source of civic pride. It made the city "the centre of the baseball universe" and provided what one editor called "a psychological moment for Boston." Any excuse would do to get to the games: "the office boy's grandmother, like St. Paul, has died daily, though not for the same reason. The aged grandsire has manifested a touching concern for the welfare of 'little Willie' and has attended him to the game to see that he was protected against errant 'fouls.' The riot of the stock exchange has had its afternoon transference to the 'rooters' gallery. Law and gospel, sport and business have been generously represented, all making common cause for or against the players and for or against the umpire. Even the student of psychology has found the diamond and its environment a wondrously profitable field for the pursuit of his investigations, while the professor of mathematics has made fresh observations upon angles, tangents and parabolas."

"If baseball is the national game," reasoned the *Boston Transcript*, "then has Boston attained the climax and coronation of nationality. . . . The successful twirler of the sphere was the hero of the hour; the power of his arm, the art and trick of his method, the quickness of his sight and the infallibility of his judgment have furnished themes of admiring comment in thousands of circles. The Panama Canal, the Alaska boundary question, the troubles in the East have been sidetracked, and sleep has not been thought of until an answer was obtained to this momentous daily question: 'What's the score?' "

It mattered little that the players were not born in Boston and did not live in the city. If anything, it made the victory sweeter. A baseball nine with different histories came together from disparate parts of the country, pulled on the jersey that read Boston, and "under her banner have fought and won the championship of the champions. . . . Here is something for the youth of today to tell the eager grandchild upon his knees on a winter evening before a sea-coal fire in the days to come."

The games of the first World Series crystallized why it was that baseball mattered. "Life Illustrated by Baseball," proclaimed an editorial that appeared in the *Boston Evening News* following the World Series. "A series of baseball games between professionals playing for the money may seem an absurd thing over which to wax enthusiastic," the editor wrote. "And so it would be if the money end were that over which one was waxing enthusiastic. But this is not true. It was the spirit of the sport that bred the enthusiasm. American baseball stands pre-eminently as the American game. That is because it best embodies in the realm of sport the American ideal of life."

Baseball allows individuals to shine, but individual performance alone will not result in success. Teamwork matters. By fusing the individual and the group, the solitary and the communal, baseball illustrates what it means to be an American: "Baseball signifies first of all co-operation. . . . Those nine individuals must be a union of individuals working for the same end. But mark this, each individual must do his own work as nearly perfect as he can and he must let the other fellow's work alone. In no other way can he effectively serve the union. . . . This 'live and let live' principle constitutes what an American means by liberty—liberty for each individual to work out his own salvation but not license for any individual to meddle with another fellow's plan of salvation."

Somewhere between standing alone and joining others lies the balance that makes for an American life. Players and fans alike struggle to satisfy the equation. Baseball provides an escape from everyday routines, not to an ideal place but to a place where certain ideals can be engaged: faith, competition, heroism. Disappointment and failure also dwell there. The World Series is baseball at its apogee, captivating even the most indifferent observers and transforming them into fans. It entertains us, it enthralls us, and, if we are lucky, it renews us. The memory and meaning of the games echo long after stadiums have emptied and seasons have come and gone.

WORLD SERIES COMPOSITE RECORD

HITTING STATISTICS

BOSTON AMERICANS

PLAYER	G	AB	R	H	2B	3B	HR	RBI	BB	SO	BA	OBP	SLG	SB
Jimmy Collins	8	36	5	9	1	2	0	1	1	1	.250	.270	.389	3
Lou Criger	8	26	1	6	0	0	0	4	2	3	.231	.286	.231	0
Bill Dinneen	4	12	1	3	0	0	0	0	2	2	.250	.357	.250	0
Patsy Dougherty	8	34	3	8	0	2	2	5	2	6	.235	.278	.529	0
Charles Farrell	2	2	0	0	0	0	0	1	0	0	.000	.000	.000	0
Hobe Ferris	8	31	3	9	0	1	0	5	0	6	.290	.290	.355	0
Buck Freeman	8	32	6	9	0	3	0	4	2	2	.281	.324	.469	0
Tom Hughes	1	0	0	0	0	0	0	0	0	0	.000	.000	.000	0
Candy LaChance	8	27	5	6	2	1	0	4	3	2	.222	.300	.370	0
Jack O'Brien	2	2	0	0	0	0	0	0	0	1	.000	.000	.000	0
Freddy Parent	8	32	8	9	0	3	0	4	1	1	.281	.303	.469	0
Chick Stahl	8	33	6	10	1	3	0	3	1	2	.303	.324	.515	2
Cy Young	4	15	1	2	0	1	0	3	0	3	.133	.133	.267	0
Total	8	282	39	71	4	16	2	34	14	29	.252	.287	.401	5

PITTSBURGH PIRATES

PLAYER	G	AB	R	H	2B	3B	HR	RBI	BB	SO	BA	OBP	SLG	SB
Ginger Beaumont	8	34	6	9	0	I	0	I	2	4	.265	.306	.324	2
Kitty Bransfield	8	29	3	6	0	2	0	I	I	6	.207	.233	.345	I
Fred Clarke	8	34	3	9	2	I	0	2	I	5	.265	.286	.382	I
Bill Kennedy	I	2	0	I	I	0	0	0	0	0	.500	.500	1.000	0
Tommy Leach	8	33	3	9	0	4	0	7	I	4	.273	.294	.515	I
Sam Leever	2	4	0	0	0	0	0	0	0	0	.000	.000	.000	0
Ed Phelps	8	26	I	6	2	0	0	I	I	6	.231	.259	.308	0
Deacon Phillippe	5	18	I	4	0	0	0	I	0	3	.222	.222	.222	0
Claude Ritchey	8	27	2	3	I	0	0	2	4	7	.111	.226	.148	I
Jimmy Sebring	8	30	3	11	0	I	I	3	I	4	.367	.387	.533	0
Harry Smith	I	3	0	0	0	0	0	0	0	0	.000	.000	.000	0
Gus Thompson	I	I	0	0	0	0	0	0	0	0	.000	.000	.000	0
Bucky Veil	I	2	0	0	0	0	0	0	0	2	.000	.000	.000	0
Honus Wagner	8	27	2	6	I	0	0	3	3	4	.222	.300	.259	3
Total	8	270	24	64	7	9	I	21	14	45	.237	.275	.341	9

PITCHING STATISTICS

BOSTON AMERICANS

PLAYER	G	W–L	GS	CG	IP	H	BB	SO	ER	ERA
Bill Dinneen	4	3–I	4	4	35.0	29	8	28	8	2.06
Cy Young	4	2–I	3	3	34.0	31	4	17	7	1.85
Tom Hughes	I	0–I	I	0	2.0	4	2	0	2	9.00
Total	8	5–3	8	7	71.0	64	14	45	17	2.15

PITTSBURGH PIRATES

PLAYER	G	W–L	GS	CG	IP	H	BB	SO	ER	ERA
Deacon Phillippe	5	3–2	5	5	44.0	38	3	22	14	2.86
Sam Leever	2	0–2	2	I	10.0	13	3	2	6	5.40
Bill Kennedy	I	0–I	I	0	7.0	11	3	3	4	5.14
Bucky Veil	I	0–0	0	0	7.0	6	5	I	I	1.29
Gus Thompson	I	0–0	0	0	2.0	3	0	I	I	4.50
Total	8	3–5	8	6	70.0	71	14	29	26	3.34

BIBLIOGRAPHY

PRIMARY SOURCES

ARCHIVES

Boston Public Library: McGreevey Collection
Carnegie Library of Pittsburgh: clippings files
Massachusetts Historical Society: manuscript diary, Marian Lawrence Peabody Papers. Box 3
National Baseball Hall of Fame Library: player files on World Series participants
New York Public Library: Henry Chadwick Papers

NEWSPAPERS

Boston Evening News
Boston Evening Record
Boston Globe
Boston Herald
Boston Journal
Boston Post
Brooklyn Eagle
Cincinnati Enquirer

Detroit Free Press
New York American
New York Herald
New York Times
Philadelphia Inquirer
Philadelphia North American
Sporting Life
Sporting News
Pittsburgh Chronicle-Telegraph
Pittsburg Disptach
Pittsburg Gazette
Pittsburg Leader
Pittsburg Post
Pittsburg Press
Pittsburg Times
Washington Post

ARTICLES

Ames, Allan P. "How to Keep a Base Ball Score." *St. Nicholas* 31 (June 1904), pp. 694–97.

Bache, Richard Mead. "About Baseball's Curves." *Scientific American* 91 (July 16, 1904), p. 42.

"Baseball Slang Defended." *Literary Digest* 40 (June 25, 1910), p. 1264.

Bloss, Edward B. "The Making of a Baseball Nine." *Outing* 42 (July 1903), pp. 454–61.

Bruce, H. Addington. "Baseball and the National Life." *Outlook* 104 (May 1913), pp. 104–7.

Casey, J. P. "Our Great American Game." *The Independent* 61 (August 16, 1906), pp. 375–79.

Cohen, Morris Raphael. "Baseball as a National Religion." *The Dial* 67 (July 26, 1919), p. 57.

"The Fascination of Baseball." *The Independent* 71 (August 31, 1911), pp. 494–96.

Fleischer, Charles. "Sunday Baseball the Crying Need." *Baseball Magazine* 1 (August 1908), pp. 19–20.

Fullerton, Hugh S. "Fans." *American Magazine* 74 (August 1912), pp. 462–67.

———. "Wagner: The Greatest Baseball Player in the World." *American Magazine* 72 (January 1910), pp. 378–85.

Hartt, Rollin Lynde. "The National Game." *Atlantic Monthly* 102 (July 1908), pp. 220–31.

Jones, Ellis O. "Baseball Fans." *Lippincott's* 85 (June 1910), p. 765.

Kirk, William F. "Shall We Have Sunday Baseball?" *Baseball Magazine* 1 (July 1908), pp. 47–48.

Lane, F. C. "The Greatest Problem in the National Game: The Critical Situation in Sunday Baseball." *Baseball Magazine* 7 (October 1911), pp. 21–28.

Lieb, Frederick G. "Hans Wagner." *Baseball Magazine* 4 (December 1909), pp. 53–56.

Locke, William. "Fred Clarke—Player, Manager, Gentleman." *Baseball Magazine* 1 (October 1908), pp. 16–18.

Morse, Jacob C. "The Story of 'Cy' Young." *Baseball Magazine* 1 (September 1908), pp. 38–45.

Roosevelt, Theodore. " 'Professionalism' in Sports." *North American Review* 151 (August 1890), pp. 187–92.

Stewart, Charles D. "The United States of Baseball." *Century Magazine* 74 (June 1907), pp. 308–19.

Sykes, M. Cready. "The Most Perfect Thing in America." *Everybody's Magazine* 25 (October 1911), pp. 435–46.

Wagner, Honus. "Honus Wagner's Own Baseball Story." *Pittsburgh Gazette Times,* January 16–March 26, 1916.

Young, "Uncle Cy." "How I Learned to Pitch." *Baseball Magazine* 1 (September 1908), pp. 13–15.

BOOKS

Barrow, Edward Grant. *My Fifty Years in Baseball.* New York, 1951.

Evers, John J., and Fullerton, Hugh S. *Touching Second: The Science of Baseball.* Chicago, 1910.

McGraw, John. *My Thirty Years in Baseball.* New York, 1923; Lincoln, 1995.

Mathewson, Christy. *Pitching in a Pinch, or Baseball from the Inside.* New York, 1912; Lincoln, 1994.

Reach's Official American League Base Ball Guide for 1904. Philadelphia, 1904.

Ritter, Lawrence. *The Glory of Their Times.* New York, 1966.

Spalding, Albert. *America's National Game.* New York, 1911.

Spalding's Official Base Ball Guide. New York, 1904.

Spink, Alfred. *The National Game.* St. Louis, 1910.

SECONDARY SOURCES

Browning, Reed. *Cy Young: A Baseball Life.* Amherst, 2000.

Burk, Robert. *Never Just a Game: Players, Owners, and American Baseball to 1920.* Chapel Hill, 1994.

Cohen, Richard M., Neft, David S., and Johnson, Roland T. *The World Series.* New York, 1976.

DeValeria, Dennis, and DeValeria, Jeanne Burke. *Honus Wagner: A Biography.* New York, 1996.

Hittner, Arthur D. *Honus Wagner: The Life of Baseball's 'Flying Dutchman.'* Jefferson, N.C., 1996.

Ivor-Campbell, Frederick, et al., editors. *Baseball's First Stars.* Cleveland, 1996.

James, Bill. *The New Bill James Historical Baseball Abstract.* New York, 2001.

Kanter, Mark, editor. *The Northern Game—and Beyond: Baseball in New England and Eastern Canada.* Boston, 2002.

Lieb, Frederick. *The Pittsburgh Pirates.* New York, 1948.

Okkonen, Marc. *Baseball Memories, 1900–1909.* New York, 1992.

Riess, Steven A. *Touching Base: Professional Baseball and American Culture in the Progressive Era.* rev. ed. Urbana, 1999.

Seymour, Harold. *Baseball: The Early Years.* New York, 1960.

Sowell, Mike. *July 2, 1903: The Mysterious Death of Hall-of-Famer Big Ed Delahanty.* New York, 1992.

Stout, Glenn, and Johnson, Richard A. *Red Sox Century.* Boston, 2000.

Thorn, John; Palmer, Pete; and Gershman, Michael. *Total Baseball.* 7th ed. New York, 2001.

Voigt, David Quentin. *American Baseball. Vol. 1: From Gentleman's Sport to the Commissioner System.* University Park, Pa., 1983.

———. *The League that Failed.* Lanham, Md., 1998.

Ward, Geoffrey C., and Burns, Ken. *Baseball: An Illustrated History.* New York, 1994.

White, G. Edward. *Creating the National Pastime: Baseball Transforms Itself, 1903–1953.* Princeton, 1996.

ACKNOWLEDGMENTS

A FELLOWSHIP from the Simon Rifkind Center for the Humanities & Arts at the City College of New York, and support from the Department of History, gave me time to write when I needed it most. My thanks to James Watts, James de Jongh, Kate Levin, and Frank Grande. I am also grateful to the Gilder Lehrman Institute of American History for a fellowship that supported my research.

I am indebted to the archivists at the Library of Congress, New York Public Library, Boston Public Library, and Carnegie Library of Pittsburgh. Special thanks go to John Dorsey and Aaron Schmidt for their assistance with obtaining photographs from newspapers and the remarkable McGreevey Collection at the Boston Public Library. I am especially grateful to W. C. Burdick, Claudette Burke, Rachael Kepner, and the rest of the staff at the A. Bartlett Giamatti Research Center of the National Baseball Hall of Fame and Museum. My thanks to Liz Jones at the SABR Lending Library for providing reels of microfilm, and to Nicholas Graham of the Massachusetts Historical Society for helping with

diaries. Baseball historian Glenn Stout has been extremely generous in responding to my queries, as has David Kaplan, director
of the Yogi Berra Museum and Learning Center. David Gerle-
man repeatedly demonstrated his resourcefulness as a researcher. I
should also like to thank Jim Trdinich of the Pittsburgh Pirates for
a memorable morning at PNC Park.

Highland Park friends and neighbors have helped sustain me as
have several key establishments in town: Raritan Video, Bagel
Dish Café, the Baseball Warehouse, Highland Printing Center,
and Schwartz and Nagle. My rotisserie baseball league, ably run
by Christian Cardenas and Michael Mai, affords an excuse to
check box scores late into the night. I would like to give a shout
out to my students at the City College of New York.

I appreciate the unstinting support given by Bob Allison,
Kathy Feeley, Ed Galinski, Jim Goodman, Doug Greenberg, Allan Lockspeiser, Peter Mancall, Saul Salkin, Darren Staloff, and
Larry White. I am grateful to Richard Skolnik for sharing lunch
and suggesting the title. Mark Richman, Aaron Sachs, and Tom
Slaughter not only offered inspiration, but they also read and im-
proved the manuscript. I am fortunate to have Elisabeth Sifton as
my editor. Thanks go to everyone at Hill and Wang for their
creativity and professionalism. Thanks as well to my agent, Jay
Mandel.

The book is dedicated to my brother, Dave, and my two
friends from the Bronx with whom I came of age, Mark Richman
and Bruce Rossky. Ra first suggested the topic, Dave, at a critical
moment, encouraged me to pursue it, and Mark interrupted his
vacation for several hours each evening to discuss baseball.

In October 2000, I obtained two tickets to the first game of
the World Series. Sophie displayed her good nature and, with
only the smallest of bribes, she allowed her older brother to go.
Ben plays second base and he continues to teach me the nuances
of the sport. I have so much to thank my children for, not the
least of which is helping me to keep distinct my roles as coach and

father. I've been taking Jani to baseball games for nearly thirty years. Occasionally, when a player crosses home plate, she still calls it a point, and not a run, but she is enough of a fan to have named our dog Yankee. The love of baseball is part of the wild, real love that we share as a family.

L.P.M.
Highland Park, N.J.
September 2002

INDEX

Page numbers in italics refer to illustrations.